THE
FAMILY BREWERS
OF BRITAIN

THE
FAMILY BREWERS
OF BRITAIN

A Celebration of
British Brewing Heritage

ROGER PROTZ

CAMRA
BOOKS

Published by the Campaign for Real Ale Ltd
230 Hatfield Road, St Albans, Hertfordshire AL1 4LW
www.camra.org.uk/books

ISBN 978-1-85249-359-2

A CIP catalogue record for this book is available from the British Library

Printed and bound in the Czech Republic by Latitude Press Ltd.

Managing Editors: Katie Button and Alan Murphy
Project Editor: Julie Hudson
Book design/typography: Dale Tomlinson
Cover: Mulberry Advertising
Sales & Marketing: Toby Langdon

PICTURE CREDITS

The publisher would like to thank all the breweries and others who have kindly
given permission for their photography and artwork to be printed in this publication.
We are especially grateful to the **Brewery History Society** (breweryhistory.com)
for its assistance in sourcing historical images for the book. Specific thanks go to:

(*Key*: t = top, b = bottom, c = centre, l = left, r = right)

Anonymous, 1819 128(l); Simon Barber 189(t); Geoff Brandwood 226(t);
Brewery History Society 7(all), 9(all), 34(t), 35, 40, 42(t,c,b), 43(t), 44, 45(t,c,b), 46,
47, 62(c), 125(t), 141(tr,b), 146(t), 149(t), 171(l), 176(t), 231(r), 236(c), 243, 244(b), 253(bl);
Adam Bruderer/flickr (CC BY 2.0) 123(t); tom_bullock/flickr (CC BY 2.0) 121;
George Cruikshank, 1821 8(t); Anthony Cullen 182, 187(t); Dunk/flickr (CC BY 2.0)
10(bcr: Threlfall's); Robert Foyers 185(br), 189(b); Tim Green/flickr (CC BY 2.0) 31(br),
104(tb); Trevor Hatchett 272; tpholland/flickr (CC BY 2.0) 37(b); Paul Horton 234;
Imperial War Museum 208(b); brett jordan/flickr (CC BY 2.0) 150(t); Alex Liivet/flickr
(CC BY 2.0) 253(cl); Jim Linwood/flickr (CC BY 2.0) 78; Stephen J Mason Photography/
flickr (CC BY-SA 2.0) 238(b); Metro Centric/flickr (CC BY 2.0) 240(t); Mooganic/flickr
(CC BY 2.0) 256(b); Mark Newton Photography (courtesy of Black Sheep Brewery)
222(t), 224(tl,cr,br), 225(tl); Roger Putman 52, 135(t), 148(t), 164(t), 177, 226(b),
228, 240(b), 242(t), 243, 244(t) 247(t); Reading Tom/flickr (CC BY 2.0) 10(br: Wethered);
Robinsons 120, 122, 123(b), 124, 126, 127, 128(br), 129(t,b); Sgobbone/flickr
(CC BY-SA 2.0) 60; Emma Sweet 43(b); tomline43/flickr (CC BY 2.0) 179;
Dale Tomlinson 66, 74, 99; Unknown, May 16 1942 *Billboard* magazine 209;
vagueonthehow/flickr (CC BY 2.0) 27, 136; Willem van de Velde II, 1691 185(bl);
Ed Webster/flickr (CC BY 2.0) 201(l), 202(cl,bl); chris weger/flickr (CC BY-SA 2.0) 168

Contents

Preface

THIS BOOK is a celebration of the remarkable family brewers of Britain. They are the great survivors who have flown the flag for good beer during world wars, recessions and merger mania. Today some thirty are still in production and their main beers are the cask ales that make Britain a unique brewing nation.

The family brewers have not been passive observers of social change over the past 300 years. They have been at the cutting-edge of profound changes in the demand for beer and the way it's produced. Some of the brewers in this book were participants in the great porter revolution of the 18th century that led to the rise of the mass market in beer. A century later, brewers grasped new technologies in malting and beer-making to fashion the world's first pale ales, several decades ahead of golden lager in central Europe. In more recent times, family brewers have withstood attempts to buy them and close them, have seen off the challenge of keg beer and fake lager, and now embrace the exciting new styles of beer sought by drinkers both young and old.

ROGER PROTZ, 2020

This book has been produced with the support of the **Independent Family Brewers of Britain**: most but not all the breweries featured are members of the IFBB. I would like to thank the brewers who gave their time to discussing their histories and plans for the future and who welcomed me to their breweries and gave me tours of their plants. Particular thanks are due to Rick Bailey, chairman of the IFBB, and Caroline Nodder, the press and publicity officer, for their help and their enthusiasm for the project.

I F ∘ B B
INDEPENDENT FAMILY BREWERS OF BRITAIN

The rise and resilience of Britain's family brewers

THE ROOTS of the family brewers of Britain lie in the Industrial Revolution, a turbulent period of the island's history that transformed it socially and economically. From the 1760s, Britain moved from an agrarian economy to a manufacturing one and it became the powerhouse of the world with a large trading empire. The country made textiles on a vast scale for domestic use and for export while a new industrial working class dug coal, forged iron and steel, and built ships. They also brewed and consumed beer in enormous quantities to slake thirsts created by long hours of back-breaking labour.

Demand outstripped supply

In the Georgian period brewing was a small-scale occupation. It was conducted by 'licensed victuallers' – publicans who paid a licence fee to brew on their premises, usually the cellars of their pubs – and in private houses. But as workers poured into rapidly expanding towns and cities to work in factories, mills and foundries, demand outstripped supply. Commercial or 'common' brewers sprang up to produce beer in unprecedented volumes.

By the late 18th century there were 746 common brewers registered in the country and the number grew during the following century. When Queen Victoria came to the throne in 1837, commercial brewers in England and Wales produced around 55 per cent of beer output, licensed victuallers 33 per cent and beerhouses around 12.5 per cent. By the end of Victoria's reign in 1901, commercial brewers accounted for 95 per cent of production.

Almost without exception, the new commercial brewers were family businesses. The famous names of the 18th and 19th centuries, such as Allsopp, Barclay Perkins, Bass, Charrington, Courage, Greene King, Truman, Whitbread and Worthington, started out as family concerns until the need to expand turned them into public companies.

The increase in the amounts of beer produced reflected the growth in population, which in England more than doubled from 8.3 million in 1801 to 16.8 million by 1850, and then grew to 30.5 million by 1901. Apart from in isolated rural areas and some small towns, it was impossible for publican brewers and beerhouses, relying on small wells and rudimentary

equipment, to meet the insatiable demand from consumers. In sharp contrast, the commercial brewers not only grew apace but were able also to make beer of greater quality and consistency, using new technologies unleashed by the Industrial Revolution.

With the rise of pale ale brewing in Burton upon Trent in the 19th century, this small Midlands town could vie with London as a major brewing centre. By the end of the century, Burton-based Bass was producing close to one million barrels a year and for a time, before the rise of commercial lager brewing in central Europe and the United States, was the biggest brewer in the world.

Corinthian Tom and Jerry Hawthorne make free with the drinks in an illustration by George Cruikshank, 1821

The 1830 Beer Act

A further reason for the rapid growth of family-owned commercial breweries came with the 1830 Beer Act, which enabled householders who paid an annual fee of two guineas to turn their premises into a beerhouse where they could brew their own beer.

Within eight years, the number of beerhouses rose to 46,000 and added substantially to the stock of 51,000 licensed inns, ale houses and taverns that existed before the Act. In 1836 beerhouse producers accounted for 13.4 per cent of total production, but the figure had fallen to less than 10 per cent by 1860.

'Tom and Jerry houses', named after two dissolute characters in a popular novel of the time, acquired a bad reputation for often insanitary conditions and poor beer. Many beerhouse keepers, who struggled to produce a decent pint, turned to commercial brewers for help. They responded by offering better quality beer and loans to improve premises, but each house became tied to the supplying brewery.

A new Beer Act in 1869 rescinded the free-for-all in the supply of beer. As beerhouses went out of business, unable to pay back their loans, commercial brewers snapped them up, intensifying the growth of the tied house system.

Tough times in the early 20th century

The early years of the 20th century presented brewers of all sizes with unprecedented challenges. During the First World War, the government nationalised breweries in areas where munitions were made and restricted pub opening hours. The strength of beer was reduced substantially in order that supplies of grain could go to the bread industry while excise duty was massively increased: the total rise in beer duty between 1914 and 1920 was 430 per cent.

Relief after the war was short-lived. The industry slowly recovered but was then hit by the economic crisis created by the collapse of the American stock

The Hook Norton brewery team at the turn of the 20th century

market in 1929. Between 1930 and 1931 the Labour Chancellor of the Exchequer, Philip Snowden, raised beer duties by more than a third. Consumption fell throughout the 1930s and family brewers were especially affected. Bigger brewers had sufficient resources to improve their production methods, to use motorised transport to move beer around the country, to invest in bottling lines and to advertise their brands. Smaller brewers lacked the finances to expand. Many were unable to pay dividends in the straitened times and the result was a spate of mergers to consolidate resources.

The number of brewers fell from 2,464 in 1921 to 1,502 in 1928 and then to only 840 by 1939. The bigger breweries had gone on the takeover trail. Whitbread, for example, bought a number of family brewers in the 1920s, including the Notting Hill and Forest Hill breweries in London and two brewers in Kent, Frederick Leney & Co and Jude, Hanbury & Co.

The Second World War presented brewers with similar problems to the first. Prime Minister Winston Churchill was determined that the brewing industry should receive sufficient raw materials to supply both the domestic market and troops fighting overseas. Nevertheless, excise duty was once again increased and by the end of the war duty rates were 486 per cent higher than at the outbreak.

The arrival of keg

There was little respite for family brewers after the war. A food crisis in 1946 meant grain had to be directed to bread makers and brewers were ordered to reduce their output and lower the strength of beer to 3 per cent alcohol. These restrictions were soon lifted but family brewers faced the challenge posed by a new type of beer.

During the war, many experienced publicans had lost their lives either during bombing raids at home or while on military service. New publicans often lacked the skills to look after cask-conditioned beer that for a while was so weak that it rapidly became sour. As a result, drinkers switched to bottled beers, which were stronger and, as they were filtered and pasteurised, had a longer 'shelf life'. By 1959, bottled beer accounted for 36 per cent of total beer production with the sector dominated by Guinness and such brands as Double Diamond and Mackeson: in 1959 bottled Mackeson accounted for 50 per cent of Whitbread's production.

The big national brewers drew the conclusion that if drinkers enjoyed carbonated beer in a bottle then they should be offered a similar product on draught. The result was keg beer, so-called because it was stored in a sealed container and driven to the bar by extraneous carbon dioxide. The beer was filtered, pasteurised and gassy but very profitable due to its long shelf life. Such brands as Watney's Red Barrel, Flowers Keg, Double Diamond, Whitbread Trophy and Worthington E were trunked all around the

country and advertised to a mass audience with the arrival of commercial television. The total advertising budget for all Britain's brewers in 1977 was £70 million and most of that was devoted to keg beer and another style, previously much less common on these shores: lager. In 1959, keg beer accounted for one per cent of beer sales; by 1970 it had grown to 63 per cent.

Family brewers were in an impossible situation. They lacked the funds to invest in keg production, which required new and expensive metal containers, chillers, filtration and pasteurisation units, plus cylinders of carbon dioxide that had to be supplied to pubs. Neither could they afford to advertise their products, especially on television. Many small brewers decided to call it a day. Others had no option but to sell the keg beers produced by the big brewers. By 1980 only 81 brewers were left in Britain: the decline was due not only to keg beer but also what has been called the 'merger mania' of the 1960s and 70s.

Merger mania

The City of London was awash with cash and property tycoons were on the lookout for acquisitions. Breweries were a prime target as they owned between them 70,000 licensed premises. One company, Grand Metropolitan, formed a brewing division that included Watney, Mann and Truman in London and Wilson's in Manchester. Grand Met flooded the brewers' pubs with wine, spirits, Coca-Cola and Carlsberg lager.

Pub ownership became highly profitable as baby boomers in the 1960s and 70s went to pubs in increasing numbers. Beer consumption increased from 24.6 million barrels a year in 1958 to 42.1 million in 1979, a rise of 71 per cent.

It was not only property companies that were creating large brewing groups. Bass Charrington, a merger of the Burton and London brewers, also owned several regional brewers including Mitchells & Butlers in Birmingham, Stones in Sheffield, Hancock's in Cardiff and Tennents in Glasgow. Cask beers such as Draught Bass and Charrington IPA were sidelined as the group put all its financial muscle behind promoting Carling Black Label lager.

Whitbread created an 'umbrella scheme' in which the company took a stake in many family brewers with the aim of saving them from takeover by outsiders. It was a false prospectus as most of the brewers that huddled under the umbrella were closed not by property tycoons but by Whitbread itself. The first edition of CAMRA's *Good Beer Guide* in 1974 listed the following family and small regional brewers who were members of the Whitbread scheme: Bentley, Brickwood, Chesters, Duttons, Fremlins, Nimmo, Rhymney, Starkey, Knight & Ford, Strong, Tennant, Threlfall, West Country and Wethered. All eventually closed. A popular CAMRA T-shirt listed all the breweries closed by the group with the title 'The Whitbread Tour of Destruction'.

Fremlins, Strong, Threlfall and Wethered were all 'protected' by Whitbread's 'umbrella scheme' but later closed by the national brewer

The Campaign for Real Ale, founded in 1971, played a crucial role in encouraging many family brewers to stay in business and to concentrate on cask beer. Fuller, Smith & Turner, the major family brewer based in Chiswick, West London, had taken a decision to switch to carbonated beer. It changed its mind following lobbying by CAMRA and inspired by the determination of the nearby London family brewer Young's of Wandsworth to remain loyal to cask. Fuller's went on to become one of the most successful cask beer producers in the country.

With a resurgence of interest in cask and sales of keg beer in free fall – Double Diamond's sales slumped by 60 per cent between 1972 and 1978 while Watney's revamped Red was such a disaster that it was withdrawn in 1979 – the national brewers concentrated instead on promoting their poor imitations of European lager. Conditions remained tough for the family brewers as lager was heavily promoted and began to take a greater share of the beer market.

It seemed some improvements were to hand with the publication in 1989 of a report by the Monopolies & Mergers Commission (MMC) into the supply of beer in Britain. The report was a coruscating critique of the six national brewers: Allied, Bass, Courage, Scottish & Newcastle (S&N), Watneys and Whitbread. The MMC said they acted as a cartel, fixing beer prices, overcharging for their products and keeping smaller breweries out of their tied houses. The Big Six, as they were known, controlled 75 per cent of the beer market and owned the overwhelming majority of pubs. The national brewers also dominated much of the free trade through loans that required those running the pubs to take beer only from them.

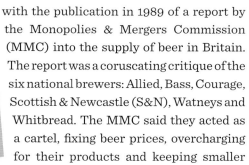

The MMC report recommended that no brewer should be allowed to own more than 2,000 pubs. This would require the Big Six to sell off some 22,000 licensed premises. The government of the day responded in 1991 with the Beer Orders, which instructed the national brewers to turn the bulk of their pubs into free houses, allowing access to family and regional brewers.

For a while this enabled the family brewers to supply a range of pubs that had been previously closed to them. But the change was short-lived. The nationals decided that if they couldn't tie pubs, they would leave brewing. One by one the nationals packed their bags, the biggest exits coming in 2000 when both Bass and Whitbread sold their breweries. Of the Big Six, only S&N remained and is today owned by Heineken with its Star Bars & Pubs division. The other national brewers were replaced by non-brewing pub companies, known as 'pubcos', which are free from the Beer Orders and can tie their outlets. The three biggest pubcos, Enterprise Inns (now called Ei), Punch Taverns and Mitchells & Butlers, own as many pubs as the old Big Six and are equally adept at restricting choice for drinkers. But in recent years, as a result of persistent campaigning by CAMRA, the Society of Independent Brewers (SIBA) and the Independent Family Brewers of Britain (IFBB), the major pubcos have grudgingly allowed some slight relaxation of the tie.

Squeezed in the middle

Further government legislation in 2002 proved another double-edged sword for family brewers. Chancellor Gordon Brown introduced Progressive Beer Duty, which cut by 50 per cent the duty paid by the smallest brewers producing no more than 5,000 hectolitres (300 barrels) a year. The system is now known as Small Brewers Relief and incorporates a taper that gives lesser relief up to 60,000 hectolitres (36,000 barrels). The system was greeted with joy by small brewers and their umbrella organisation SIBA, but one leading family brewer described it as an 'unmitigated disaster'. As duty relief started to take effect and more small breweries were launched, the family brewers found them themselves squeezed in the middle. The small brewers could sell beer more cheaply due to duty relief while global brewers – AB InBev, Heineken and Molson Coors – used economies of scale to offer heavily discounted products to both pubs and supermarkets.

To add to the problems, there had been hints from Brussels that the European Union was taking a close look at the tied house system with a view to declaring it 'a restraint of trade'. The family brewers knew that without their ability to run tied estates they would eventually be driven out of business. Leaders of several of the family brewers formed an organisation, the Independent Family Brewers of Britain (IFBB), to help protect their share of the market. The aims of the IFBB were to promote cask beer – the bedrock of their business – defend the tie and to call for better training of licensees in order to ensure that cask beer is served in first-class condition. With more than 30 members, the organisation was responsible for producing 700 beer brands, owned more than 4,000 pubs and gave employment to 46,000 people.

The IFBB has led a vigorous campaign in defence of its aims, but the beer market has remained difficult for its members. The duty problem has taken its toll and several IFBB members, including Batemans, Brains, Everards, Hydes, McMullen, Thwaites and Wells, have either reduced their output to qualify for Small Brewers Relief or have closed their existing plants and have built or are building new smaller ones.

In 2019, the industry was rocked by the news that Fuller's had sold its brewery and brands to Asahi of Japan and would become a pub retailer. The Fuller's sale underscored the problems facing the 'squeezed middle' of family brewers. In its last financial year, the company had made healthy profits of £43 million but only 10 per cent of the profits came from brewing. Despite owning such big-selling brands as London Pride and Extra Special Bitter, the burden of beer duty was making brewing almost marginal to the overall business.

In September of that year, a further shock came when Greene King announced it would be bought by a Hong Kong property company. While Greene King is no longer a family brewer, it's an old and revered English business founded by Suffolk families and its future is worrying. Will the new owners be interested

Everards is downsizing to its new Meadows site, which when it opens in spring 2021 will have a capacity of 16,000 barrels a year

solely in the brewery's vast pub, restaurant and hotel side and abandon brewing? And are all breweries with successful brands and pub estates now at risk from takeover?

The questions were given additional impetus in May 2020 when a merger was announced that created the Carlsberg and Marston's Brewing Company. While Marston's is a large national brewer with several plants, and such leading brands as Pedigree and Hobgoblin, it has 40 per cent of the new company, with Carlsberg the main player with 60 per cent. The deal will mean that Carlsberg will have access to Marston's estate of 1,700 pubs and the two brewers can combine forces to supply beer to both free trade pubs and supermarkets, restricting sales from smaller brewers.

On the plus side, the threat to the tie has evaporated and it seems unlikely that a future British government outside the EU would take action on this issue. As many family brewers now take guest beers in their pubs, the perceived restrictive nature of the tie has largely disappeared.

Craft vs cask

But the squeeze on middle-ranking brewers has intensified. Small brewers have morphed into what are called craft brewers, a term that has no definition or legal standing. Many of the new craft beers are a modern type of keg, and though they tend to be unfiltered or unpasteurised, they are served at a cooler temperature than cask.

Wadworth's Horizon is available at regular cask temperature and in a colder format

The protagonists of craft make much of the fact that their beers are more popular with younger drinkers than cask ale, but despite the noise and brouhaha surrounding craft beer, it commands a far smaller section of the ale market than cask. Family brewers, however, are aware they must reach out to younger drinkers. They are conducting research into lower serving temperatures for cask ale and are investing in smaller casks in order that beer can be served within two to three days while in peak condition.

On the duty front, there's discussion taking place on whether the British government, once Britain is outside the EU, could introduce preferential rates of duty for cask beer to boost its popularity and claw back sales from heavily discounted supermarket brands. One suggestion is that draught beer in pubs should have the same lower rates of duty as cider.

Change is vital if family brewers are to continue attracting consumers to their pubs by offering beer at prices which can offset the appeal of cheap alcohol from supermarkets. Currently it's impossible for pubs to compete with the off-trade, where beer is sometimes sold for as little as a bottle of water. CAMRA has argued that charging lower rates of duty on draught beer will strengthen the role of community pubs, enabling them to offer a warm welcome and friendly environment to everyone regardless of their income.

The need for reform has become critical as the global and national brewers tighten their grip on the off-trade. Marston's says its merger with Carlsberg will double its sales to the off-trade, meaning less room on supermarket shelves for smaller brewers.

The family brewers, however, have survived and overcome many challenges over the past three centuries, including Spanish Flu in 1918 and Coronavirus in 2020, and will use their best endeavours to keep the beer flag flying for the future.

THE
PIONEERS

SHEPHERD NEAME · SAMUEL SMITH · HALL & WOODHOUSE

BRAKSPEAR · PALMERS · ELGOOD'S

OMMERCIAL or 'common' brewers who opened for business in the Georgian period coincided with the first stirrings of the Industrial Revolution that would change Britain out of all recognition. As towns, cities and the population grew, publicans who brewed on their premises struggled to keep pace with the demand for ale, leading to a rapid rise in the number of common brewers.

Brewing, by the standards of the following centuries, was primitive. Mashing temperatures were judged by the brewer placing his elbow in the vessel or waiting for the steam to clear so he could see his face reflected in the liquid. Daniel Fahrenheit invented the mercury thermometer in Amsterdam in 1714 but brewers were slow to use it and many older brewers refused to accept such a modern contraption.

The hydrometer or saccharometer was also invented in the 18th century: this simple device allowed brewers to accurately measure the amount of fermentable sugar in their mashes, but it was not until late in the century that its use became widespread. When a brewer from Hampshire, James Baverstock, urged Samuel Whitbread in London to use a hydrometer, the biggest brewer in the country dismissed him contemptuously with the instruction to 'go home and not engage in such visionary pursuits'.

Fermentation was especially primitive. As commercial brewing developed, bigger brewers installed large wooden fermenting vessels, but smaller brewers fermented the beers in casks placed above troughs. The violence of fermentation would drive yeast and liquid out of open bung holes and into the troughs where the yeast would be collected and reused in subsequent brews. It wouldn't be until the late 19th century that Louis Pasteur and other scientists unlocked the mysteries of yeast and were able to develop pure strains for both ale and lager brewing. Until that time brewers stood in awe of what they called 'God-is-Good' – the magic froth that turned a sugary liquid into a life-enhancing drink.

Most beer at this time was brown in colour and it got darker as the 18th century unfolded. The reason was simple: grain was cured or kilned over fires fuelled by wood and the result was brown and sometimes charred malt. Pale beer did exist but it was expensive. Kilning used coke rather than wood and the costs involved meant that pale beer was bought in the main by the aristocracy and the gentry.

The main types of beer consumed by working people were mild and stale: mild was a fresh brown beer, stale the same beer matured for several months during which time it picked up some lactic sourness from wild yeasts and bacteria in wooden storage vessels. Many drinkers liked to mix the two beers, just as 20th-century consumers had a taste for light and bitter or mild and bitter mixes. Beer was also blended in the brewery before it left for the ale house. A type now called 'country beer' can still be seen at Greene King in Bury St Edmunds where Strong Suffolk Ale is a blend of 5 per cent BPA (Best Pale Ale) and 12 per cent Old 5X, the latter aged in wood for a year.

A new type of beer that was to change brewing out of all recognition appeared early in the 18th century. Porter and its stronger version stout porter was first brewed in London, but its popularity and profitability led to brewers producing the style throughout Britain and Ireland. Porter was the response to drinkers developing a taste for what they dubbed three threads or three thirds: a blend of pale, brown and stale beers. Three threads had to be mixed in pub cellars from three casks and to avoid this labour brewers produced a beer with the character of three threads but served from one cask or butt. Brewers called the beer Entire Butt, but it became better known as porter because of

its popularity with the large army of porters working the streets, markets and docks in London. Porter, rich in proteins and nutrients, was a healthy as well as a refreshing drink.

Porter was a phenomenon. To keep pace with demand, bigger and bigger breweries had to be built to cope with the insatiable clamour for the beer. Samuel Whitbread was the major porter brewer in London and by 1758 he was producing 64,000 barrels a year in the Barbican, followed by the neighbouring Calvert's Peacock Brewery with 61,800 barrels and Ben Truman's Black Eagle Brewery in Brick Lane, White-chapel with 55,000 barrels. As the names suggest, they were all family-owned breweries, passed on from generation to generation. The founders all became fabulously wealthy, lived in grand style in country mansions and were ironically dubbed 'the Beerage'.

So many barrels of porter and stout were exported to Ireland that brewers there, notably Arthur Guinness in Dublin, started to brew the beers themselves, as did brewers in Scotland, Bristol and Norwich. As the chapters in this section show, smaller family brewers in country areas such as Kent were also quick to jump on this fast-moving bandwagon. Shepherd Neame in Faversham used imported Spanish liquorice to give both colour and flavour to its version of porter.

New technology began to bring improvements to breweries' working practices as the 18th century progressed. The introduction of steam engines, invented by James Watt, enabled the grinding of malt, the stirring of the mash and the general movement of beer and ingredients to be carried out mechanically, and the sad sight of horses trundling for hours round mash tuns came to an end. Towards the end of the century, the use of attemperators – metal coils through which cold water was pumped – enabled the temperatures of mashing and fermentation to be controlled. Until then, brewing was a seasonal affair as summer temperatures caused beer to spoil. Attemperators were the first step towards brewing becoming an all-year-round, and therefore more profitable, business.

Shepherd Neame

1698 · FAVERSHAM · KENT

SHEPHERD NEAME is steeped in history. It is Britain's oldest brewery, dating from before the Georgian period and the birth of commercial brewing. At a time when most beer was produced by publicans in their cellars, Shepherd Neame grasped all the opportunities offered by the developing Industrial Revolution to make innovative new ales and sell them far beyond its heartland in Kent.

When you visit the offices and brewhouse in Court Street, Faversham, you are immediately aware of the antiquity of the enterprise. There are oak-panelled rooms, creaking floors and timber framing, with paintings and photos of the founding fathers and their successors adorning the walls. Along with old brewing vessels and steam engines from the 19th and early 20th centuries, they all point to the company's rich past.

And yet there's almost an air of mystery about Shepherd Neame. When did the brewery actually start producing beer? The year 1698 is much used in promotions but it's not certain this is the true date. Historians, including the brewery's own archivist John Owen, believe the brewery's origins to be as early as 1573. Of equal interest is the fact that, despite the company name, the Shepherds and the Neames were only in partnership for 12 years: the company has been owned solely by the Neame family since the late 19th century.

Faversham's long brewing tradition

Faversham has the advantage of a plentiful supply of water with a high calcium content that makes it well suited for making beer and it has a long brewing tradition. The town was not an isolated country backwater. Compared to many parts of England, the roads were tolerably good and, as brewing developed, beer was taken by horse-drawn wagons to other towns in Kent and as far as London. Ships also linked the town with the capital.

The town was well thought of by the aristocracy: Faversham Abbey, for example, was endowed by King Stephen and Queen Matilda in the 12th century. The abbey, in common with most abbeys of the time, had a malt house and brewhouse to make ale for the monks, the abbot's guests and pilgrims.

The earliest surviving list of brewers in Faversham dates from 1327 and records 87 brewsters – women brewers – operating in the town. Beer was an important element of the nation's diet at the time. Tea and coffee were unheard of, while milk was full of bacteria and could cause tuberculosis. Water was also insanitary – unless it was boiled, as it was during the brewing process. Brewing then was a domestic occupation, largely carried out by women, with local people invited into the brewsters' homes to enjoy the ale. As the brewsters paid tax it's clear their work was a commercial activity, albeit it on a modest scale.

Nevertheless, beer making made an important contribution to Faversham's economy. In that year of 1327, 60 per cent of the town's income came from taxes on brewing.

Anything but common

The brewery that became Shepherd Neame was known in the 17th and 18th centuries as a 'common brewery', but there was nothing common about the families that founded it and went on to run it. The Faversham Brewery was bought by an officer of the local militia, Captain Richard Marsh, who paid the highest taxes on beer in the town in 1678. Marsh took part in the arrest of James II and kept him prisoner in the brewery: the monarch was attempting to escape to France and avoid William of Orange, who succeeded James in the Glorious Revolution of 1688.

It's possible that the date of 1698 for the founding of what is now Shepherd Neame was the result of Marsh taking over the brewery in Court Street that year. 1698 and the name Shepherd Neame were first mentioned more than 160 years later in 1865 in an advertisement in the *Kentish Gazette*. The advertisement was later reproduced as a lithograph showing the much-enlarged brewery which was said to produce Mild, Stock Ale, London Porter and Stout.

Richard Marsh died in 1726 and his son, also Richard, died the following year. Richard's widow,

HOPPY ALES IN THE 9th CENTURY?

A discovery made in 1970 of the remains of a boat in the mud of Graveney Marshes on the edge of Faversham has thrown up an intriguing question as to whether this small coastal town was several centuries ahead of the rest of the country where brewing was concerned. The boat, possibly English, dated to around AD 900 and it contained a large quantity of hops. As Faversham was a leading port, importing and exporting to mainland Europe as well as London and East Anglia, is it possible the hops had been brought from Europe where the plant was first used in brewing in the 9th century?

The counter argument is that hops were cooked and eaten as a delicacy at the time, rather like asparagus, while the long stems or bines of the plant were used to make ropes that were used in the shipping trade. Official histories claim that hops were not used in brewing in England until the 15th century and ale brewers balanced the sweetness of malt with herbs and spices. But the question hangs tantalisingly in the air: was Faversham using hops far earlier than previously thought?

Mary, married Samuel Shepherd in 1732 and he then took over the running of the brewery.

The Shepherd family were farmers, owning substantial amounts of land and Samuel was involved in making malt as well as brewing. The brewery in Court Street was across the road from another brewer, Rigden, which also had a plant in Canterbury. Competition between the two companies was fierce and Shepherd started to buy and tie pubs in the town and surrounding areas in order to have regular outlets for his beer. Samuel Shepherd's son Julius not only expanded the trade but also modernised the brewery. In 1789 he installed a steam engine built by Boulton & Watt, the first engine to be used in brewing outside London: Whitbread had bought a Watt engine for its London brewery four years earlier. The engine drove the machines and pumps that ground grain and moved water and wort around the brewery. Shepherd proudly called his modernised plant the Faversham Steam Brewery.

The Shepherd partners

The Shepherd family had a succession of partners, first Hilton and then Mares. The arrival of John Henry Mares was critical, for the brewery ran into financial difficulties in the 1840s. Many businesses struggled at that time due to the wars with Napoleon's France and the high taxes and inflation that resulted. Shepherd had to mortgage some of its property and John Henry Mares arrived with an investment of £5,000 – close to £300,000 in modern terms – and set about restoring the fortunes of the brewery and expanding sales with the aid of the railway. He also married the sister of Percy Beale Neame, the son of a prosperous tenant farmer who was to play an important role in the future of the company.

Faversham became an important junction for the new railway, with links to Canterbury and Dover and all the main towns into London. In 1865 the brewery described itself in an advertisement as 'East India Pale Ale Brewers' and 'begged to call special attention to their FAMILY BITTER BEER which from the

delicacy of its flavour and pureness of tonic qualities has gained so great a reputation in the estimation of the public; and also their STOCK AND MILD ALES which they are now sending out in high perfection.' The brewery opened stores in Bromley, Canterbury, Ramsgate and Sheerness to drive sales on.

Many brewers produced beers they called Table or Family, meaning they were comparatively low in strength and suitable for consuming with family meals. Stock Ale was similar to London's Stale, a strong beer aged in wood for several months that was often used for blending with weaker beers. It's significant that the company in 1865 described itself as 'East India Pale Ale Brewers', indicating that the brewery was up-to-date with all the latest developments in the brewing industry in London and Burton upon Trent. Unlike the London and Burton brewers, however, Shepherd & Mares and later Shepherd Neame did not export IPA to the outposts of the British Empire.

The use of the term bitter is also interesting as it didn't come into popular use until the early 20th century.

John Henry Mares died in 1864 aged just 45. Shortly before his death, he and Henry Shepherd had brought Percy Neame into the brewery to protect the Mares' financial interests. Henry Shepherd, grandson of Julius, died in 1875 and, at the young age of 28, Percy was suddenly in charge of a company worth, with its brewery, pubs and stock, more than £5 million in today's money. Percy eventually bought everyone else out and became the sole proprietor of the business. The new age of Shepherd Neame had arrived and it was cemented by the arrival of Percy's three sons to help run the company.

Output rose at the brewery from 13,000 barrels in 1859 to 21,000 in 1863/4. By the end of the century, production was running at close to 40,000 barrels a year. As well as its own beers, Shepherd Neame bought porter and stout from Meux and Truman in London and began to brew its own stout in the 1860s.

During that decade a new mash tun, liquor tank, fermenters and hop back were added to boost volumes. A refrigeration unit was installed, indicating how advanced the brewery was in adapting to new technology. New pubs were opened and by the 1870s the brewery owned almost 100 outlets. The tied pubs were essential due to the rivalry between Shepherd Neame and fellow Faversham brewer Rigden. Rigden followed its rival in enlarging and modernising its plant in the 1870s to attack the Kent and London markets. Such was the level of the rivalry that the two families never socialised and met only during the annual hunt.

Henry Shepherd

Percy Beale Neame

The brewhouse, c.1890

Bucking the trend amidst wars and recession

When Percy Neame died in 1913, he handed on the business to 10 children. He had bequeathed a plentiful supply of Neames to keep the brewery in family hands in the 20th century. Their task was not only to build the business by brewing more beer, acquiring more pubs and expanding the free trade but also to steer the brewery through the turbulence of two world wars and a recession in between.

The brewery fared better than many others in the first years of the 20th century. Despite massive increases in duty, the company recorded sound profits and managed to buck the recession of the late 1920s and early 30s by producing some 60,000 barrels a year. The brewery also began to target the large and potentially lucrative club trade in Kent and surrounding areas. In the first decade of the century just 27 clubs – often working men's clubs – were supplied but the number grew to more than 150 in the 1920s.

The brewery responded to an increased demand for bottled beer in the 1930s by investing in modern bottling lines. This has been a theme throughout the 20th and 21st centuries and today Shepherd Neame is unusual among family brewers in producing more packaged beer than draught.

The Second World War brought many problems for the brewery. Once again duties were raised to painfully high levels and ingredients were in short supply. As the war raged in the skies over Kent, pubs and stores were damaged or destroyed, while many members of staff and publicans were called up for military service, some failing to return. Nevertheless, in 1944 the chairman, Jasper Neame, was able to report 'a record year in every respect'. Barrelage of 82,000 was the highest on record, due in no small measure, Jasper added, to the presence of large numbers of British and Allied forces stationed fortuitously in the brewery's trading area.

Nellie Jemmett bottling in 1939

Expansion and adaptation

The post-war years saw a continued drive by the brewery to buy more pubs and extend its free trade into clubs and off-licences. In 1956 Shepherd bought the Waterside Brewery in Maidstone, which added 50 pubs and eight off-licences to the stock. In the 1960s, as merger mania raged in the brewing industry (see p.10), Shepherd Neame invested substantially in its tied estate. This investment was also made necessary by changes in society. Pubs could no longer be the sole preserve of working men. Women and families, many with cars, wanted to go to attractive pubs that offered food and wine as well as beer.

Rigden over the road had also bought and improved its pubs, but it was less successful than Shepherd Neame in seeing off the piranhas encircling the industry. In 1948 Rigden had been bought by the big Maidstone brewer, Fremlins. The substantial number of tied houses attracted Whitbread in London: it was keen to expand sales of both its keg beer and Heineken lager, which it brewed under licence. Whitbread bought Fremlins in 1968 and closed the Faversham site in 1990. It's now a supermarket.

Charlie, Shepherd Neame's last drayhorse, retired in 1968

THE SECRET IN THE CELLAR

The intensity of the rivalry between Shepherd Neame and Rigden came to light in 2012 with a remarkable discovery in the cellars at Shepherd Neame. In a dark corner, archivist John Owen found old leather-bound books from the 19th century, covered with dust and cobwebs, which contained recipes for beers. John wasn't able to read the recipes as they were written in code. It appears the Neames were worried that a disgruntled member of staff, perhaps one who had been dismissed, might cross the road and hand over the recipes to Rigden.

John sat down with brewer Stewart Main and they attacked the recipes with all the zeal of code-breakers at Bletchley Park during the Second World War. The work took several months as they painstakingly unravelled the ingredients of two

beers. Double Stout, 5.2 per cent, and India Pale Ale, 6.1 per cent, were both brewed in the 1860s.

The recipes were divided into columns and included such groups of letters as GBX, JBX and SBX written in faded copper-plate writing. Stewart's experience told him the letters referred to the malts and hops used in each brew along with the amounts. John and Stewart tried all possible permutations of the letters until they were satisfied they had managed to unravel the recipes. Stewart then proceeded to brew the two beers in a pilot plant used to try out new beers.

Double Stout is brewed with roasted malts alongside pale malt and the hop is East Kent Goldings. IPA is brewed with pale and crystal malts with Fuggles and East Kent Goldings: the hops are added three times during the copper boil.

The bottled beers have labels and crown corks that are replicas of the ones used in the 19th century. Draught versions are produced as seasonal brews.

Shepherd Neame survived the onslaught of property tycoons and giant national brewers but it knew it had to adapt to changing consumer demand by adding keg beer to its portfolio. The chairman's elder son, Robert Neame – always known as Bobby – was given the paltry sum of £1,000 to create a keg plant and buy containers. He bought two 20-barrel tanks from a man named Roberts in a yard in North London behind Tottenham Hotspur football club's stadium. Bobby described the experience as being like an episode of the TV series *Steptoe & Son* which chronicled the dodgy exploits of two rag-and-bone men. The deal to buy the tanks was sealed with a meal of greasy lamb chops on a 'tablecloth' of old newspapers.

In the brewery, keg beer was pasteurised by a rudimentary system of lowering the kegs into baths of boiling water. The result was beer of inconsistent quality, but as sales grew the brewery was able to install an automatic keg washing and racking line. In the 1970s lager was added following a deal between Shepherd Neame and the Swiss brewer Hürlimann. This was a successful arrangement, though in recent years the Swiss beer was joined by the Japanese Asahi lager. Shepherd Neame now owns the Hürlimann brand, but the contract to brew Asahi ended in 2016 and the brewery developed its own lager brands including Spitfire Lager and Bear Island Triple Hopped Lager.

The brewery didn't ignore traditional beer. It added two new beers that made an excellent contribution to sales. In the 1950s it launched Bishops Finger, a strong 5.4 per cent ale, named after ancient Kentish roadside finger boards pointing pilgrims to Canterbury cathedral and the tomb of Thomas Becket. In 1990 it added a beer that was to become its cask and bottled flagship. Spitfire (4.2 per cent in cask, 4.5 per cent in bottle) commemorates the Royal Air Force pilots and crews that had fought the Nazi Luftwaffe over Kent during the Battle of Britain.

The beers came to the aid of the brewery when the European Union's relaxation of border controls in

the 1990s led to 'booze cruises'. British drinkers crossed the Channel to buy French beer at prices considerably cheaper than in Britain due to far lower rates of duty in France. Shepherd Neame, close to the Kent ports, suffered more from the cheap imports than other companies. It hit back by exporting its ales to France, where Bishops Finger became a cult beer. It also improved its pubs to attract drinkers back from the sofa, the TV and cheap French lager. Many pubs now have top-quality food and accommodation.

The brewery also added to its pub estate. As the national brewers started to divest themselves of pubs, Shepherd Neame in the 1990s bought or leased more than 100 outlets from Allied Breweries, Bass, Courage and Whitbread.

Over 300 years old and still going strong

Shepherd Neame celebrated its 300th anniversary in 1998 and twenty years on the family remains in firm control. Jonathan Neame, the son of Bobby, joined the brewery in 1991 and rose through the ranks to become chief executive in 2003 when Bobby retired and became honorary president. He died in 2019.

In 2003 Bobby Neame had a major bust-up with his cousin Stuart Neame, who was vice-chairman and aged 58. He said Bobby, coming up to his 70th birthday, should stand down and allow younger members of the family to take over. Stuart criticised the low profits of £8.7 million and said too much money had been spent on an advertising campaign for bottled beers. The campaign was called the Bottle of Britain and played on memories of the Battle of Britain and the role of the Spitfire in defeating the German Luftwaffe. Supporters of Bobby Neame said

Jonathan Neame, chief executive

Stuart wanted to become chairman himself and when he recognised that he didn't have sufficient backing from the board he resigned.

The brewery has forged ahead since then. It produces some 200,000 barrels a year and exports to Australia, Brazil, Chile, Mexico, Russia, Finland, Italy and Scandinavia. The pub estate now numbers an impressive 323 outlets and more are being sought, including in London where the Samuel Pepys opened in 2018 near St Paul's, followed by the Savoy Tap off the Strand and the Cheshire Cheese in Little Essex Street. There are some 2,000 free trade outlets as well.

The beer range has been refreshed and extended. A number of beers, bottle and cask, have been introduced using the Whitstable Bay name and they include an organic beer and a Red IPA. In 2019 the brewery launched the Cask Club, with a new cask ale produced every month. The club marks an important contribution to the cask sector at a time when some family brewers are bemoaning its decline.

The brewery has always prided itself on using English ingredients, especially the prized Kentish hops. Eighty per cent of the hops used come from Kent, including what Jonathan calls 'the peerless East Kent Golding'. Shepherd Neame has invested in the National Hop Collection near Faversham where 70 English varieties are housed (see feature on p.273).

The brewery itself is being turned into a major visitor attraction. Visitors can see both ancient and

The cask plant team

modern sides of the business, from the old steam engines, malt store, and the artesian well that supplies water for brewing, to the greatly extended brewhouse and fermenting rooms.

Three hundred years or more since it was founded, Shepherd Neame is well set for the future.

Shepherd Neame, 17 Court Street, Faversham, Kent ME13 7AX · 01795 532206
www.shepherdneame.co.uk
Tours available

Regular cask beers:

Master Brew (3.7%)
Whitstable Bay Pale Ale (3.9%)
Spitfire Gold (4.1%)
Spitfire (4.2%)
Bishops Finger (5%)

Mike Unsworth, head brewer

Samuel Smith

1758 · TADCASTER · NORTH YORKSHIRE

WHAT IS IT about Yorkshire brewers that they fall out so spectacularly? First the Smiths in Tadcaster and then the Theakstons in Masham have had disputes that have shaken dynasties to their cores. In Tadcaster, the split in the Smith family has never healed and has been made worse by the fall from grace of John Smith's brewery. While it is far bigger than Sam Smith's, it had the misfortune to be taken over first by Courage, then by Scottish & Newcastle and finally by Heineken UK, which is now Britain's biggest brewing group. To adapt the words of Lady Bracknell in Oscar Wilde's *The Importance of Being Earnest*: To be taken over by one national brewer may be regarded as a misfortune, to be taken over by three looks like carelessness.

Meanwhile, Sam Smith has remained fiercely, even fearsomely, independent, proud of its standing as Yorkshire's oldest brewery. Beer is fermented in traditional slate Yorkshire squares, coopers build and repair wooden casks, and local deliveries are made by horse-drawn drays. It owns some 200 pubs, with such architectural gems in London as the Chandos at Charing Cross, the Swiss Cottage in Hampstead and the Olde Cheshire Cheese in Fleet Street: the last-named was once the haunt of Johnson, Dickens and other members of the literati.

From coaching inns to the Old Brewery

Tadcaster has been an important brewing town for centuries. It stands on the old Roman road that linked London with York. When 50 coaches thundered north and south daily on the Great North Road, inns in Tadcaster refreshed weary travellers with good ale. Brewing was aided by the fact that the town, in common with Burton upon Trent, has mineral-rich hard water, ideal for producing sparkling ales.

The brewery that became Samuel Smith's Old Brewery was created in 1758 by two partners called Backhouse and Hartley who had run a successful coaching business in the town and had taken over the White Horse, the leading inn. As the Industrial Revolution swept across the north of England it brought the railway in its wake and the 'iron horse' quickly drove coaching inns out of business. Shorn of its valuable coaching business, Tadcaster went into decline and Backhouse and Hartley's brewery struggled to survive. When they died, the brewery passed to Hartley's widow, Jane, and it was bought from her by John Smith in 1847.

Chimneys of both Samuel Smith's and John Smith's breweries seen from the River Wharfe

The Smith family came from Leeds where Samuel Smith the First had a few businesses, including tanning and running the Bull & Mouth, the oldest coaching inn in the city. John Smith was financed by his father to buy the Tadcaster brewery from Jane Hartley, and was joined by his brother William. They threw their energies into transforming the almost derelict site into a thriving business. When John died in 1879, he left his property, including the old brewery, to his brothers William and Samuel and stipulated that when they died the brewery should pass to their heirs.

Salt in the family wound

William was a bachelor and as a result had no heirs, which meant the brewery would be owned by Samuel and his successors. To maintain his grip on the business, William arranged that his share would go to his sister Sarah Riley and her children: his nephews Frank and Henry Riley were already working for him. William and the Rileys started to build a new brewery cheek-by-jowl with the old one. To enhance their control and to rub a large amount of salt into the family wound, the Rileys changed their name by deed poll to Riley-Smith to ensure the name Smith would continue to dominate brewing in the town.

Samuel Smith the Third, William's nephew, inherited not only an empty brewery but also no trade, as this was now controlled by the Riley-Smiths. But Sam was made of true Yorkshire grit and in 1886 wrote to his lawyers: 'It is probable I shall reopen the Old Brewery within the next few weeks… and that if I do reopen the Brewery it will be my endeavour to turn out not only as good but rather better an article than my neighbour.'

In September that year, two weeks after the death of his uncle William Smith, Samuel wrote to Henry Herbert Riley:

> Dear Harry, I should feel obliged if you will hand me over to-morrow all the deeds belonging to the properties left me by my Uncle John. If you will wire me in the morning where I can meet you to take them over any time after 1pm [sic]. At the same time if this time is not convenient to you I shall be glad if you will appoint one. Trusting you are quite well. Your affect. Cousin, Sam Smith.

ALL SQUARE IN YORKSHIRE

The Yorkshire square fermentation system is now rare but is still used by Sam Smith and Black Sheep. The system tackles not only the problem of cleansing yeast from beer but also the nature of the difficult yeast strains used in the north of England. Yorkshire yeasts are highly 'flocculent'. This means yeast cells clump together and separate from the beer. Unless the yeast is roused or aerated on a regular basis, the finished beer will have a high level of unfermented sugar and will be unacceptably sweet.

The square is a two-storey vessel. The two chambers are connected by a manhole with a raised rim or flange and also by 'organ pipes'. The top deck, known as the barm deck, is open: barm is a dialect word for yeast. The bottom chamber is filled with wort and yeast. As fermentation gets under way, wort and yeast rise through the manhole. The yeast is trapped by the rim of the opening while the wort drains back into the bottom chamber via the organ pipes. Every two hours or so, wort and yeast are pumped from the bottom chamber to the top via a fishtail spray. This aerates the wort and mixes in more yeast. When fermentation is complete the manhole is closed

and the 'green' or raw beer is left in the bottom chamber for two days to condition and purge itself of off-flavours before being racked into casks. Yeast is recovered from the top chamber and stored for further use. Beers brewed in Yorkshire squares are notably full bodied due to the presence of some residual malt sugar.

It's not known if this meeting ever took place: if it did, it would certainly have been interesting to have been a fly on the wall.

In the 1950s, the chairman of John Smith's, WH Douglas Riley-Smith, commented: 'The results of these disagreements left a legacy of ill-feeling which affected a generation – our Victorian forbears were pretty forthright individuals and were not averse to showing their feelings.'

Sam Smith used his inheritance to rebuild and stock his plant, which he named the Old Brewery to avoid any legal dispute with the adjacent company. The centrepiece was – and is – formed by the Yorkshire square fermenting vessels that give a unique character to the beers brewed in the region and help create the thick collar of foam on a pint expected by drinkers.

Steadfastly traditional

While many family brewers are looking to the future, developing new beer styles for a modern audience and redesigning pubs to meet the needs of all age groups, Sam Smith is content to remain firmly traditional. Its yeast strain dates from the 19th century and is thought to be the oldest in use in the country. Pure brewing water is drawn from an 85-feet (26m) well dug when the brewery first opened. Most of the beers are hopped with the two most traditional English varieties, Fuggles and Goldings, which date from the 18th and 19th centuries respectively. They are used in whole flower form rather than pellets. Smith's single cask-conditioned beer, Old Brewery Bitter, is served from oak casks built and repaired by two resident coopers and the casks are delivered in the Tadcaster area by horse-drawn drays. If you suggested to the chairman of the company, Humphrey Smith, that he should produce a beer in collaboration with a rock group, as others have done, he would have apoplexy.

His pubs are both penny plain and tuppence coloured. He spends generously to restore such Victorian masterpieces as the Princess Louise in London's Holborn. Other outlets are more utilitarian. Most are

multi-roomed, echoing an age when pubs had clear distinctions between public and saloon bars. The pubs are not branded: Humphrey Smith took the decision to remove the name of the brewery from all signage and only the beers on the bar will tell you that you're in a Sam Smith's outlet. The brewery doesn't deal with other companies: wines, spirits, soft drinks, peanuts and crisps all come from Tadcaster. There's a common menu for all pubs, with strict 'portion control'.

Much controversy but beautiful beers

In one area, Sam Smith is in touch with modern demands. It was the first brewery to register with the Vegan Society and its bottled Imperial Stout is suitable for vegans. Several of its bottled beers use only organic malts and hops. While only the strong Yorkshire Stingo is bottle conditioned, the likes of Taddy Porter, Pale Ale, Nut Brown Ale, India Ale, Oatmeal Stout and Organic Wheat are of the highest quality. A range of fruit beers are all organic and are brewed at the Sam Smith-owned All Saints Brewery in Stamford, Lincolnshire (see below). At a time when most British lagers were parodies of the real thing, the Sam Smith's lager, brewed in conjunction with the Ayinger brewery in Bavaria, was praised for its authentic taste and proper brewing methods, with supplies of yeast sent regularly from Germany. But in 2005, Humphrey Smith ended the relationship with Aying and now makes Pure Brewed Lager to his own specification.

With so much fascinating history on its side and a brewery that upholds traditional skills, it's a pity that too often the company is dogged by controversy. It took legal action against the small Cropton brewery

over its use of the White Rose of Yorkshire symbol. Sam Smith has long had the symbol as its logo and took action when Cropton also used it for a beer called Yorkshire Warrior, with the proceeds going to the local regiment's benevolent fund. Smith won the case. Humphrey Smith has banned live music in all his pubs, which means he saves on the Performing Rights levy. He has prohibited mobile phones, laptops and tablets, and most recently has issued an edict to his publicans to refuse entry to bikers, whom he describes

ALL SAINTS BREWERY

The Melbourn Brothers' All Saints Brewery is based in Stamford, Lincolnshire, a town famous for its mellow limestone and timber-framed buildings and the home of the aristocratic Cecil family. William Cecil, later Lord Burghley, was Elizabeth Tudor's First Minister. Largely untouched by the Industrial Revolution, Stamford's Georgian elegance makes it a popular venue for film and TV productions.

The brewery dates from 1825 but beer may have been made earlier on the site. It is largely unchanged since the 19th century, with power created by steam engines and the production process carried out in wooden or copper vessels. It was bought by Sam Smith's in 1974 and was closed but then reopened in 1998 to make a range of fruit beers. In common with the fruit lambic beers made in Belgium, the All Saints' products are made by spontaneous fermentation, allowing wild yeasts in the atmosphere to turn the malt sugars into alcohol. This gives the finished beers a lactic sourness, balanced by the fruit. The beers are made with organic barley, wheat and hops.

The beers are trunked to Tadcaster where they are conditioned and organic fruit juices added. The range includes apricot, cherry, raspberry and strawberry. They can be enjoyed in the All Saints pub adjoining the brewery, which is open for guided tours.

All Saints Brewery,
21–22 All Saints Street, Stamford,
Lincolnshire PE9 2PA · 01780 752186

as 'undesirables'. He has fallen out with the GMB trade union by surcharging his licensees if they over-fill glasses with beer and in 2017 told licensees they must evict any customers heard swearing. In July 2019, the Cheshire Midland pub in Hale, Greater Manchester, was closed when representatives from the brewery found a man using a mobile phone. He claimed he was sending an urgent text message, but he was told to leave the premises. The pub was then closed and the stock was removed the following day.

Samuel Smith is not the only pub-owning company to prohibit live music or mobile phones, but the list of edicts and fines give an unfortunate image of an out-of-touch company.

The beers, however, are marvellous.

STINGO – ancient style lives on

Yorkshire Stingo belongs to a style in 'God's Own County' of strong barley wines given the generic name of Stingo. Sam Smith's version, 8 per cent, combines the skills of brewers and coopers. The beer is aged in oak casks, some more than 100 years old, which have been built and repaired by the resident coopers. Stingo is brewed with pale malt and cane sugar: the sugar is needed to reach the required level of alcohol. The beer matures in the bottle and has rich aromas and flavours of malt, hops, treacle toffee, raisin fruit, Dundee cake and oak.

Samuel Smith, The Old Brewery, High Street, Tadcaster, North Yorkshire LS24 9SB · 01937 832225
www.samuelsmithsbrewery.co.uk

Regular cask beer:
Old Brewery Bitter (4%)

Bottle-conditioned beer:
Yorkshire Stingo (8%)

Hall & Woodhouse

1777 · BLANDFORD ST MARY · DORSET

'ALE is the lifeblood of the brewery,' Mark Woodhouse proudly declares. Standing in the spacious brewing hall of the new plant that opened in 2012, Mark is a member of the seventh generation of his family to run the brewery. The gleaming stainless-steel vessels can produce lager as well as ale, but Badger Best Bitter and the large range of other ales remain the heartbeat of the company.

Hall & Woodhouse – better known as Badger from its logo and leading beer – brings a new meaning to downsizing, as the new brewery has a substantial capacity of 80,000 barrels a year. It has been designed not for tax reasons but to meet the *realpolitik* of the modern beer world. The company sold its free trade business in 2008 and the new plant enables it to concentrate on its core estate of 200 pubs that stretches from Bristol and Exeter to London and Brighton. The new plant replaces the old site, which opened in 1900 and was known as 'the new brewery' to distinguish it from the first one founded in 1777. The 20th-century plant had an impressive capacity of 300,000 barrels a year, but that level of brewing is now consigned to history.

The start of a dynasty

Charles Hall, the son of a farmer, brewer and maltster, built the first brewery in the village of Ansty near Dorchester. He flourished as a result of being granted a licence to supply troops stationed at Weymouth during the Napoleonic Wars. The troops, on stand-by, were bored by inactivity and the sale of beer to them was described as 'brisk'. Charles was joined by his son Robert, who took over when his father died in 1827. George Edward Woodhouse – known as Edward – started work at the brewery in 1838 and laid the ground for the Hall & Woodhouse dynasty. He was made a partner in the business when he married Robert's niece and he became the sole owner when Robert died in 1859. Robert's family had little interest in the business and he left his share of the brewery to Edward, making the Woodhouses the dominant power.

Charles Hall

Robert Hall

Edward Woodhouse

Blandford Brewery, c.1900

1875 was a key year in the history of the brewery. Edward Woodhouse died after vigorously building the company by buying a number of new outlets for his beers. His sons George Edward and Alfred took over as partners and introduced the badger trademark by which the brewery has been best known ever since. The partners used the symbol of the much-loved animal to stress Hall & Woodhouse's commitment to Dorset with hearty ales that accompany a bucolic way of life. The partnership was strengthened in 1893 when Frank Woodhouse joined the business and was to stay for 59 years, living to the remarkable age for the time of 90.

Conflagrations and new beginnings

When the company bought Hector's Brewery in Blandford St Mary in 1882, it was preparing the path for its own move to the area some years later: Blandford St Mary is a suburb of the town of Blandford Forum, reached by an impressive arched bridge across the River Stour. Plans for a new brewery in Blandford were drawn up in the 1890s but were hit by a financial crisis. In 1898, Godwin Brothers Brewery in Durweston was bought, adding an additional 26 pubs to the estate,

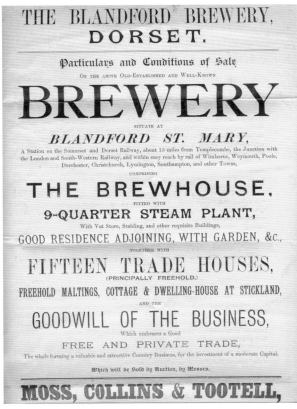

The Blandford Brewery sale in 1882

which then stood at 105. But the takeover caused a cash crisis that was resolved when the partners – following the example of other breweries – formed a limited company in order to raise capital. Once sufficient funds were in place, the new brewery was designed and building work started in August that year.

When the Hector's Brewery buildings burnt down in 1900 before the new plant was ready to open, this proved to be a blessing in disguise. The insurance money covered a substantial £7,000 overspend on the brewery, which was completed at a cost of £28,000.

The town of Blandford had suffered a number of conflagrations over the centuries but the Great Fire of 1731 was the most catastrophic, destroying more than 90 per cent of the town. The fire started in a candlemakers' workshop in a building that is now the King's Arms pub. An Act of Parliament decreed that Blandford must be rebuilt and subscriptions were raised to help with the reconstruction. The king, George II, donated £1,000, a considerable sum for the time. Blandford rose from the ashes within ten years, the new town designed by two architects, John and William Bastard. Despite their less than propitious name, the Bastards created a town of such Georgian elegance that people flock to this architectural gem from around the world.

Investment and expansion in troubled times

Hall & Woodhouse, firmly ensconced in their new Blandford home, entered the 20th century, when beer cost twopence a pint, by buying the Fontmell Magna Brewery. The new technologies of the time were eagerly embraced: telephones were installed at the brewery with the number of Blandford 9, while three Foden steam engines, named Fox, Badger and Hare, replaced horse-drawn drays.

In common with all breweries, Hall & Woodhouse faced the rigours of the First World War, with severe restrictions on opening hours for pubs and punitive increases in duty. During the war, George Edward Woodhouse, who had played such a pivotal role in the growth of the business, died and Frank Woodhouse replaced him as chairman. The company marked the end of hostilities in 1918 by making its first free trade loan to a Mr Jones – first name unknown – who had bought the Crown Hotel in Blandford from Lord Portman. Thirteen years later, in 1931, the brewery bought the hotel from Jones for £14,000 and the attractive brown stone building, with elegant restaurants and bedrooms, just across the river from the brewery, became the Hall & Woodhouse flagship. It remains so today, with award ceremonies and gatherings for staff and publicans held there on a regular basis.

X MARKS THE SPOT

In the 19th century, long before marketing and branding came into play, Hall & Woodhouse produced two main beers, labelled simply X and XX. The current head brewer, Toby Heasman, believes both were types of mild ale, popular at the time with agricultural workers. The recipes included pale, crystal and amber malts, suggesting the beers were not as dark as mild ales brewed in other parts of the country.

There's no evidence from the brewing books that the brewery

produced an India Pale Ale in the 19th century. But by the early part of the 20th century, the range of beers included mild, a stronger mild ale labelled XXX, stout, pale ale and XXXX, a strong premium beer. In the 1970s, IPA had made a belated appearance while mild, XXX, pale ale and stout were still produced. Bottled beers at the time included XXXX, described as 'Old English Ale', Badger Light Ale, Martyrs Ale, Stingo – a type of barley wine – and Badger Brown, which was mild ale in a bottle.

The first brewery in the village of Ansty near Dorchester

The 1920s were a time of economic and political turbulence. The General Strike in 1926 saw 1.7 million workers down tools in support of coal miners demanding better wages and conditions, while the Wall Street crash in 1929 sent shock waves around the world. Added to these, a high level of unemployment should have seen a fall in demand for beer, but Hall & Woodhouse not only rode out the crises it also expanded its pub estate, which grew to 135 houses.

In 1935, in order to keep strict control of the brewery in family hands and to see off any takeover bids, it became a private limited company, with restrictions on the sale of shares. In the same year, the Wimborne Brewery, with 15 pubs in Bournemouth and Poole, was bought.

The Second World War created problems for all brewers, with restrictions on ingredients – barley in particular – and heavy rises in duty. But Hall & Woodhouse had the additional problem of being in a major war zone, with preparations for the D-day invasion of Normandy by Allied troops taking place on its doorstep. The problem was underscored when Harold Woodhouse was killed during a raid by the German Luftwaffe on Blandford Camp. On a more cheerful note, the brewery, mirroring its support for troops in Weymouth in the late 18th century, supplied American servicemen based in Dorset. It's not recorded what the Americans, raised on cold lager, thought of warm Badger ale.

New brews on the horizon

In 1952, Frank Woodhouse, known to family, friends and staff as 'Uncle', died aged 90 and his cousin Charles became chairman. The post-war years were a difficult time for brewers who had had buildings, including pubs, destroyed by enemy action and many employees and publicans killed on active service. As consumers switched to bottled beer and big brewers began to introduce keg beer, many smaller producers sought safety through mergers, but Hall & Woodhouse was determined to remain independent: 'Offers of amalgamation from other breweries were politely declined' was its oblique comment.

The years 1957 and 1959 saw major changes in the brewery's business model. It launched a soft drinks department with products that were later named Panda: Panda Pops were sold widely and made a sizeable contribution to the company's income. In 1959 the brewery launched its first lager beer, called Brock, an old country name for badger. The brand lasted for 30 years despite being launched with a slogan – 'Brock Around the Clock Tonight' – that would meet with stern disapproval by today's Chief Medical Officer. It was a punning reference to Bill Haley and the Comets' hit of the time 'Rock Around the Clock'.

The brewery had made a number of attempts over the years to buy Matthews Brewery in Gillingham and was finally successful in 1963. Panda soft drinks were

made at Gillingham but were moved to Blandford in 1973. This important part of the business ended only in 2005 when the Panda brands were sold to the manufacturers of Vimto.

The 1980s saw the brewery move to strengthen both its ale and lager categories. With golden ales growing in popularity, head brewer John Woodhouse fashioned a new 4.7 per cent cask beer that was given the name Tanglefoot as a result of John supping several tankards of the new beer, which caused him to trip over his feet. The beer, both on draught and in bottle, became so popular that the name was used as branding for a select group of the company's pubs.

While the brewery had both Brock and a second lager called Skona, the directors were keenly aware they needed a beer with genuine European credentials to improve their performance in this growing sector. As a result, David Hart, the company's first managing director from outside the family, approached the world-famous Hofbräuhaus in Munich to discuss brewing its lager under licence in Blandford.

The Hofbräuhaus tavern was opened in 1589 by Duke Wilhelm of Bavaria as an extension to the royal court brewery. It was opened to the public in 1828 and both brewery and tavern were taken over by the state when the royal family lost power at the end of the First World War. Although the tavern was destroyed during

The seventh and eighth generations of the Hall & Woodhouse family, Mark, Anthony and Lucinda

the Second World War, it was rebuilt in all its Gothic glory and is one of Munich's major tourist attractions.

David Hart was successful in his talks with the Bavarian state government, which still owns the brewery, tavern and brands, and Hall & Woodhouse was able to add the Hofbräu 'Helles' or pale lager to its range, served in distinctive glasses bearing the letters HB.

REMEMBERING THE MARTYRS

A moving and memorable event took place in the small Dorset town of Tolpuddle in 1971 when the Hall & Woodhouse pub the Crown was renamed the Martyrs Inn. The change commemorated the Tolpuddle Martyrs, six agricultural labourers who had joined forces in the early 19th century to campaign against a cut in wages for all farm workers. They were judged to be in defiance of the Combination Acts, which outlawed the swearing of oaths and attempts to form trade

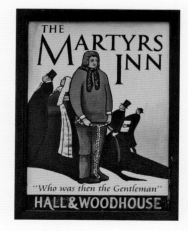

unions. In 1834 the six were put on trial, found guilty and transported in chains to Australia to serve seven years in penal colonies. Demonstrations in Britain and a petition signed by 800,000 people won the six a pardon in 1836 and they returned home as heroes.

The Martyrs Inn was officially opened by Vic Feather, the general secretary of the TUC, and a new beer, Martyrs Ale, was brewed for the occasion and became a regular beer for several years.

Success, controversy and sadness

In 1990 the family tradition was strengthened when David and Mark Woodhouse joined the board. It was a decade of both success and some controversy. The company for decades has been the biggest regional brewery in the bottled beer sector and this was marked in 1998 when Golden Champion won the first Tesco Challenge staged by the supermarket group. Hall & Woodhouse went on to win the challenge no fewer than three times and the winning beers were promoted as 'the Badger Sett'.

On the debit side, there was some consumer criticism when the brewery bought the Gribble Inn, a home-brew pub in Oving in West Sussex. Eventually, in 2005, the pub was sold back to the owner, but Hall & Woodhouse retained the rights to Gribble's Fursty Ferret, a popular bittersweet ale.

On a much larger scale, in 2000 the company bought King & Barnes in Horsham, West Sussex. The brewery dated from 1800 and its range of cask beers was highly prized. Hall & Woodhouse retained some of the brands and added 55 pubs to its estate, which grew to 250 outlets. The Horsham site was demolished to the distress of beer lovers, but they were unaware that King & Barnes had been in talks about a possible buy-out. Discussions with Shepherd Neame had broken down but the Blandford brewery was more successful.

In 2000 David Woodhouse took over as managing director and he drove the brewery forward with considerable energy. To build sales in both the on- and off-trades, a new bottling and canning line was installed and the racking cellar for draught beer was refurbished at a total cost of £1.5 million. In 2002 a Community Chest scheme was launched in north Dorset that offered funds and help for voluntary organisations. It was later extended to the whole of the county and finally to West Sussex.

The momentous decision was made in 2008 to sell the brewery's free trade business and this paved the way for the move to the new brewery. But all the work at the brewery was overshadowed that year when David Woodhouse, aged just 48, died of a heart attack while out walking in the countryside near his home. It was shattering news not only for his family and colleagues but also for the wider brewing industry. Mark Woodhouse and his cousin Anthony became joint managing directors, but their jobs were reshuffled the following year, with Mark becoming chairman and Anthony the sole Managing Director.

A modern and sustainable approach

Work started on the new brewery in 2011. Cheek-by-jowl with the old brewery, it offers a startling change of style. Designed by head brewer Toby Heasman and built by Musk in Derbyshire, it's a modern interpretation of brewing. In place of the mash tuns, coppers and open fermenters of the old plant, the new one is European in concept, based on mash mixers and lauter

HOP CHOICES

Hops for the main ales are Fuggles and Whitbread Goldings, though the flagship Badger Best Bitter has a modern twist with the Slovenian varieties Celeia, Bobek and Dana. Tanglefoot has Challenger, Goldings and Whitbread Goldings hops, and the varieties used in Wicked Wyvern, an American-style keg IPA, are Amarillo, Cascade and Mosaic from the United States. The hops in the new Forum Lager are Hallertau Blanc and Huell Melon from Germany, with a yeast culture from the renowned Weihenstephan brewery and school of brewing near Munich.

The new brewery opened in 2012

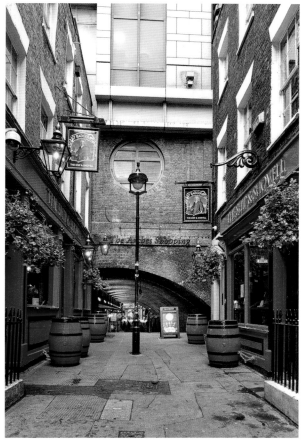

The pub that serves most pints of Badger ales is the Ship & Shovell, Craven Passage, London WC2. It's close to Charing Cross station, is Grade II-listed and has the unique distinction of being on both sides of the street, linked by an underground cellar. It's named after Sir Cloudesley Shovell, an Admiral of the Fleet in the 17th century.

tuns where the wort is clarified then boiled with pellet hops in a kettle and clarified in a hop whirlpool. Fermentation takes place in conical vessels. The one constant between the two plants, old and new, is the spring water filtered through the Cretaceous chalk downs and drawn 120 feet (37m) from the brewery's own well.

The new brewery has an energy recycling system to trap steam, which it uses to help heat the following brew prior to boiling in the copper. The brewery treats its waste water before discharge and from this process it recovers biogas to generate electricity, which is fed back into the grid. The new packaging hall has PV panels on the roof that also feed electricity into the national grid. With four new warehouses and a bottling line, the new complex has cost £18 million, and a pilot brewery gives Toby Heasman the opportunity to try new recipes for possible future beers.

From small bucolic beginnings in a village in 1777, Hall & Woodhouse is now a thoroughly modern company, well equipped for the challenges of the 21st century.

Hall & Woodhouse
Bournemouth Road, Blandford St Mary,
Blandford Forum, Dorset DT11 9LS
01258 452141 · www.hall-woodhouse.co.uk
Brewery tours are available

Regular cask beers:
Badger Best Bitter (3.7%)
Fursty Ferret (4.1%)
Tanglefoot (4.9%)

Brakspear

1779 · HENLEY-ON-THAMES · OXFORDSHIRE

WHAT'S IN A NAME? In the 18th century, when spelling could be idiosyncratic, Robert Brakspear, founder of the brewing dynasty, was first called Breakspear while other branches of the family preferred Breakspeare or Breakspere. When Robert moved to Henley-on-Thames and joined the brewery run by his uncle Richard Hayward, he changed the spelling to Brakspear, but the correct pronunciation remains *Breakspear*.

However spelt, the name gives the family and its beers an ecclesiastical connection, for they were distant relatives of Nicholas Breakspear from Hertfordshire. He was the son of a humble monk at St Albans Abbey but rose to become, in 1154, the first and to date only English Pope, Adrian IV. He chose as the symbol on his mitre the image of a bee to stress the first letter of his family name. Brakspear the brewers underscored the link by adopting the bee as their company logo.

Robert Brakspear and William Henry Brakspear

A more modern conundrum is the confusion caused today by two companies both using the name Brakspear. Most of the beer branded Brakspear, draught and packaged, is produced not in Henley but at the large Wychwood brewery in Witney owned by the national group Marston's. This is the result of WH Brakspear in Henley making the fateful decision in 2002 to close its brewery and become a pub company. It leased the beers and brands to Refresh UK, which owned Wychwood. Refresh was bought by Marston's in 2008. The deal included moving all the brewing equipment from Henley to Witney: the brewing kit plays a critical role in the story (see 'A special drop' on page 47).

In 2006 the Brakspear pubs were bought by another pub company, JT Davies, for £106 million. It merged all its pubs under the name of Brakspear and in 2013 it restored brewing at the Bull pub on Bell Street, the site of the original brewery in the 18th century. While neither brewery has any connection with the Brakspear family, the Bell Street plant in Henley is family-owned and deserves a place in this book in order to record its fascinating story.

Bell Street in the 18th Century

Henley-on-Thames is famous today for its annual rowing regatta, elegant Georgian villas fronting the river, and literary and artistic connections with *The Wind in the Willows* and William Morris. In the 18th century it was a thriving market town with a corn exchange at its heart. Grain was bought and sold there,

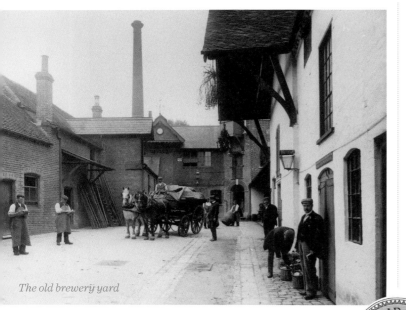

The old brewery yard

Robert came from an impoverished background. His father was a tailor who was too poor to leave a will. Despite a lack of funds, Robert was determined to succeed in life and was largely self-educated. He was born in Faringdon but moved to Witney in 1769, where, at the young age of 19, he became the landlord of the Cross Keys inn. It's likely he brewed on the premises as by 1777 he was selling ale to other publicans in the town. He also regularly visited his Uncle Richard in Henley and gave some part-time help in the running of the Bell Street site. He was clearly well-versed in the skills of brewing when he took up full-time work in Henley in 1779.

Exacting standards

When Richard Hayward retired, he gave the bulk of the business to Robert, who eventually bought out a third partner and became sole owner of the brewery in 1803. Where brewing practice was concerned, Robert was ahead of his time. He brewed all year round when most brewers stopped production between June and August as warm weather made it difficult to control fermentation. In common with the London brewers, Robert used a thermometer to check temperatures and a hydrometer to measure the specific gravity of his beers – the amount of fermentable sugars prior to fermentation. He also added an attemperator to control the temperature of the fermenting wort: this was a coiled copper pipe placed in the fermenting vessel, with cold water pumped through the pipe to maintain the correct temperature at which yeast could convert malt sugars into alcohol.

Early in the 19th century, Robert Brakspear's main products were strong ale, an amber strong with the addition of well-roasted amber malts and a weak 'small beer', thought to be around 2.8 per cent alcohol. The stronger beers accounted for four-fifths of

turned into malt by local maltsters and used by brewers in the town and its vicinity. Grain was also taken by barge along the Thames to London. Beers brewed in the capital would make the return journey, offering good choice for drinkers and sharp competition for the local ale makers. In the 1720s the people of Henley were said to be 'generally Meal-men, Maltsters and Bargemen, who by carrying Corn and Wood to London, enrich the Neighbourhood and pick up a comfortable Subsistence for themselves'.

In the 1760s there were two 'common' or commercial brewers in the town, one in Bell Street, the second in New Street close to the river. The Bell Street brewery was founded in 1711 by the Brooks family, who had been maltsters in Henley for several hundred years. The brewery prospered and in 1768 Brooks took on a partner, Richard Hayward. Just four years later, Hayward bought out Brooks and in 1779 employed his nephew, Robert Brakspear, who became a partner in 1781.

his annual production. He also made a few barrels a year of an 'amber porter' to offer drinkers a distinctive local version of the dark porters and stouts brewed in London and exported by barge to the Thames Valley. These styles had dominated London for most of the previous century but tastes started to change in favour of lighter beers, which may have accounted for Brakspear's paler version of porter.

In every respect, Brakspear's production was small beer compared to his London rivals. In the year 1784–85 he brewed 4,497 barrels while four London brewers, Barclay Perkins, Calvert, Truman and Whitbread, produced more than 100,000 barrels each. By 1811, Brakspear was producing an average of 6,250 barrels a year. His production may have been small but in every way he was a meticulous brewer whose brewing books detailed all aspects of each brew, from the malts and hops used to the temperatures of mashing, boiling and fermentation, and the action of yeast. He was especially fascinated by fermentation and recorded the variations in time from one brew to another and noted why occasionally one batch would turn sour. In order to prevent his recipes from being stolen and passed to rival brewers, he invented his own form of shorthand code.

At a time when Burton upon Trent was being celebrated as the country's major brewing centre, Brakspear was scathing about the beers from the town and surrounding areas: 'The French very justly call this Beverage Barley Soup, satisfied that a weak stomach will as soon digest Pork or pease soup as Burton, Yorkshire and Nottingham ales. They make excellent bird lime and when simmered over a gentle Fire, make the most excellent Sticking plaister for old Strains.' Fortunately, the outposts of the British Empire had a higher opinion of the beers from Burton.

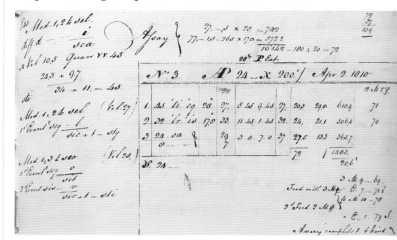

Robert Brakspear's brewing book with his own shorthand code

Brewers' war

The quality of Brakspear's beer was critical, for what was called 'the brewers' war' broke out in Oxfordshire and neighbouring Berkshire early in the 19th century. As well as the rival brewery in New Street, Robert Brakspear faced competition from breweries in other towns and villages, including the substantial Simonds company in Reading. Besides buying pubs, the brewers bought their way into other outlets by offering publicans cash inducements and loans. A few decades before it took hold in London, the brewers in Oxfordshire were laying the grounds for the development of the 'tied house' system. By 1812, when Brakspear merged with the brewery in New Street owned by Appleton, Shaw and Benwell, the two companies owned, leased or had a substantial interest in 44 pubs, around a third of all the pubs in the area.

When Robert retired due to ill health, he left a substantial fortune but he had a pressing problem: his eldest son had no interest in the business and his younger son, William Henry, was only 10 years old. In order to maintain the Brakspear name in the town, Robert negotiated the merger with the New Street brewery. One clause in the agreement stipulated that William Henry should join the company at the age of 20, by which time he would have learnt the skills of brewing as a pupil with another brewery. Production

The Brakspear maltings c.1890s

continued at Bell Street for a few more years, but the plant was eventually closed with all production centred at the large and attractive New Street site overlooking the Thames. Within a few years of joining the company, William was able to buy out his partners and he became the sole owner of what was renamed WH Brakspear & Sons; the family now put down its roots in New Street where it remained until the early years of the 21st century.

Troubles and technical advances

William faced a turbulent time. The 1830 Beer Act, detailed in the Introduction, led to the opening of scores of rudimentary and often squalid beerhouses. The Act was accompanied by the abolition of beer duty and the country was suddenly awash with cheap drink. The result was regular outbreaks of drunkenness, which the police, with inadequate resources, were unable and, in many cases, unwilling to tackle. There was riotous behaviour in the large town of Reading and even genteel Henley didn't escape.

Further riots were organised by Captain Swing, the leader of an army of impoverished and often destitute agricultural workers who demanded an increase in their wages and an end to new machines that threatened their jobs. It was a measure of the fear felt by the populace that William kept a blunderbuss and swords at his house in the brewery.

Brakspear's profits fell heavily in the 1830s and early 40s but they recovered when the Beer Act was reformed and the beerhouses themselves came under the strict control of local magistrates. Commercial brewers started to supply good quality beer to the beerhouses, replacing the often-rancid brews made on the premises. And as beerhouses declined and closed, brewers like Brakspear were able to buy them and add them to their stock of tied houses.

While William assiduously built the pub side of his business, he emulated his father by adopting the new technologies of the period to maintain the quality of his beers. New Street was extended, with storage space for more than 1,100 barrels while the transport depot had stabling for 10 horses. By 1836 William had installed a refrigerator to control the temperature of the beer. A new boiler house was built and in 1865 a steam engine provided all the power to move ingredients and beer around the plant. An artesian well was sunk to provide a constant supply of pure, hard water, ideal for brewing the pale ales that were becoming increasingly popular, despite Robert Brakspear's contempt for Burton-style beers. Nevertheless, traditional strong amber ales still accounted for around 85 per cent of annual output, which by 1880 had risen to 14,300 barrels a year, with the addition of stout and extra strong ale. Small beer went into decline as the drinkers of south Oxfordshire showed a marked preference for potent ale.

William was a hard taskmaster. By the middle of the 19th century he employed around 100 men and he brought in a series of fines for any misdemeanours, with the money raised donated to a hospital in Reading. He even fined himself if he was late for work or forgot the keys to the premises. The amounts were meticulously noted in a ledger and included one shilling paid by the chief clerk, George Wright, when he left his keys in his desk. Green 'drunk on premises' had to hand over a shilling, Hutton 'intoxicated at Reading' paid 8½ pence and was later fined a shilling for not being 'civil to customer'. Harris had to pay one shilling and sixpence for 'being asleep and denying it'. The largest fine was paid by William's son Archibald when, aged just 18 and unused to brewery discipline, he was fined two shillings and sixpence for being 'too late morning' and was charged a double fee of five shillings when he was late again a few months later. At a time when the average wage was 12 shillings a week, the fines were not trivial.

Enjoying the fruits of William's labour

William died in 1882 at the venerable age (for the time) of 80 and left a remarkable legacy. He started his reign at the brewery by borrowing extensively to both expand the site and buy pubs but when he died,

FAREWELL TO THE HORSES

The stables and the horses became redundant in the 20th century as they were replaced first by a steam wagon called the Busy Bee and then by petrol vehicles. One of the great sights in Henley disappeared. Fred Sadler, who worked for the brewery for 50 years, starting in 1909, recalled the days of the horse-drawn drays as follows:

Lined all up New Street, loaded up with beer, ready for going off; the dray men used to start at half past five, feed their horses and clean them, go for breakfast, put the horses in the dray and off they'd go; and you'd see them coming over Henley Bridge, Reading Road, Bell Street, 10, 11 and 12 at night, poor old devils. [The drivers] used to live on beer and bread and cheese and onion, no dinner all day, and they were all fit and well, you know… they were satisfied and happy, although they got a bit tipsy; they had a pint before they started, you see, every pub they delivered at they got another pint – a dozen pubs a day, a dozen pints.

he had discharged all his debts and left a well-run brewery with an estate of 80 pubs. It was said of his sons, Archibald and George, the third generation of the Brakspear dynasty, that 'they enjoyed the fruits of their father's labours'. They both lived comfortable lives as country gentlemen and the day-to-day running of the company was left to the staff, but the sons did continue the policy of adding to the pub estate. With the demand for beer increasing at a fast rate in the 1880s, they could hardly fail and profits increased substantially.

Archibald and George did have to make some major business decisions in the 1890s. They had a rival in Henley, Greys Brewery. It was badly run, was constantly teetering on the verge of collapse and many of its pubs were former beerhouses that were in a poor state of repair. To fund a takeover, the Brakspear brothers decided to follow in the path of some of the bigger breweries such as Guinness that had become limited companies listed on the Stock Exchange. Brakspear's brewery and pubs were valued at £157,000. In 1896 shares were issued, with the family controlling

the majority, and the company added 'Limited' to its name. In November that year Greys Brewery was bought for £57,000 and the Brakspear estate grew to 150 pubs.

The brewery now had sufficient capital to not only improve its pubs, especially those bought from Greys, but also to update the brewery site. A three-storey malt house was built with stables while a new tun room was installed. Profits from brewing and retailing grew impressively until the period before and during the First World War. In common with all brewers, Brakspear was badly affected by the impact of the temperance movement, which was strong in Henley, and the savage increases in beer duty imposed by the government during the war.

The Chalcrafts arrived

At the top level, one generation of Brakspears followed another but few had the dedication of Robert or William. They were content to leave the running of the business to the senior staff and handed over much of the key decision-making to a new family, the Chalcrafts, who had been brewers in Hampshire. In 1914 John Chalcraft moved to Henley and worked for Brakspear for 41 years. When he retired, he was followed by his son Michael as managing director while members of the Brakspear family took on the titular role of chairman. But the family was determined to maintain the independence of the brewery in the turbulent times of the 1950s and 60s.

Family breweries were falling like ninepins and the Brakspears and the Chalcrafts noted with dismay the decline of brewing in their own area. In the 1950s, Wethered of Marlow was taken over by Strong of Romsey, which in turn was bought by national brewer Whitbread. Another national brewer, Courage, bought Nicholson of Maidenhead and Simonds of Reading, both in 1960. Later, Morrells family brewery in Oxford closed in 1998 and most of its 132 pubs were bought by Greene King. In 2000, Morland of Abingdon was bought by Greene King, which closed the site.

A SPECIAL DROP

A fascinating example of new brewing methods of the late 19th century was the 'double drop' fermentation system introduced at Henley. The date is not certain but was probably in the 1880s. This was a time when brewers were keen to follow the success of the Burton brewers with pale ales. As glass replaced pewter, drinkers were unimpressed with cloudy beers and expected crystal-clear pints.

Clarity was achieved by removing excess yeast from the finished beer. Burton developed the 'union' system of fermentation, with fermenting beer driven into collecting trays above oak casks, while further north 'Yorkshire square' two-storey fermenters acted in a similar fashion.

At Brakspear, the method involved oak vessels arranged on two storeys, with round ones on the top level and rectangular ones below. The vessels were originally lined with copper but this was later replaced with stainless steel or polypropylene. Fermentation starts in the upper storey and when a rocky head of yeast has formed on top and around half the malt sugars have been consumed by the yeast, the wort drops from the top vessels to the ones below. This leaves behind what is known as trub – dead yeast cells, spent hops and unwanted protein.

According to Peter Scholey, the last head brewer at New Street, the drop aerates the wort and encourages a vigorous further fermentation and the creation of pleasant flavours. One of the flavours is known as diacetyl, which gives a rich butterscotch note to the beer. Modern brewers do everything they can to avoid diacetyl in their brews but it was Brakspear's signature. Deliveries further afield than south Oxfordshire meant the beers in London and elsewhere were older and had a lower diacetyl character, while younger versions sold in pubs close to Henley had a profound butterscotch note.

The double drop vessels are now used at the Marston's plant in Witney but following an arrange-ment with JT Davies, owners of the Brakspear brewery at the Bull, yeast is shared with the Henley plant. As the Witney beers are trunked in bulk to Burton and Wolverhampton to be racked into casks, these versions are likely to have a softer diacetyl note than Brakspear Special brewed in Henley. To enjoy the flavour of a true Brakspear beer, it's necessary to go to its historic source.

The vultures were circling around Brakspear too. Feeling vulnerable in the 1960s, Bill Brakspear and John Chalcraft, chairman and managing director, approached Whitbread for support. The national group bought sufficient shares in the Henley company to see off the speculator. In return, Whitbread was given two seats on the board and Brakspear agreed to sell its bottled beers. Fortunately Brakspear avoided the fate of other brewers under Whitbread's 'umbrella' scheme who were eventually taken over and closed by the group itself.

Far from ordinary

Brakspear's survival was in large part due to the quality of its beer. While other family brewers had followed the Big Six down the route of keg beer, Henley stayed true to cask. Its range included XXX Mild, Bitter, Special and XXXX Old Ale: Old Ale was Special with the addition of coloured malts. The brewery also produced two bottle-conditioned beers. The beers were much admired, especially Bitter, which was better known as Ordinary, a puzzling name as it was far from ordinary.

In 1986 John Mortimer, the author and playwright who lived near Henley, said of Ordinary in an article for the *New York Times*: 'Brakspear's draught bitter is undoubtedly the best to be had in England. It is not, of course, clear and cold or thin and gaseous. It is flat, opaque, warmish and tastes of hop fields in the English summer. It also has the supreme advantage of making you slowly, but not too slowly, drunk.'

People at the brewery must have winced at the final sentence and no doubt preferred the accolade from the celebrated beer writer Michael Jackson, writing in the *Independent* in 1993: 'In its delicate malty sweetness, teasing yeasty fruitiness and hoppy bitterness, Brakspear's "Ordinary" is lightly refreshing, gently sociable, more-ish and appetite-arousing, the perfect companion in a bitter. The hoppiness is its salient feature.'

While other small breweries struggled, Brakspear flourished. Michael Chalcraft, the managing director who had followed his father, and Paul Brakspear, the son of Bill, increased production and added around 30 free houses in London and the Home Counties at the same time. In 1975, sales of Special doubled and in that same year, when total UK beer production fell by three per cent, Brakspear's rose by 14 per cent.

A puzzling decision

By 2002, when the brewery closed, output had increased to an impressive 45,000 barrels. So why did such a successful brewery close? By then the chairman was Michael Foster, who had joined the brewery from Courage, one of the Big Six. When the closure was announced, he blamed declining sales, an inability to compete with the heavily discounted products of the national brewers, and the introduction of Progressive Beer Duty (PBD) for small producers.

The claim that sales were declining sits oddly with a substantial increase in production, while PBD was brought in by the government in 2002 and took several years to make an impact. There is another possibility: the Henley site was estimated to be worth £10 million, a fact not lost on the shareholders, especially the major ones. So to the distress of beer lovers, the historic Henley site closed and is now, with spectacular insensitivity, called the Hotel du Vin. The brands were bought by Refresh UK, which had the beers brewed for a time at the Thomas Hardy Brewery in Lancashire before moving them, with the brewing equipment, to Wychwood in Witney. Wychwood was subsequently bought by Marston's.

Back in Bell Street

Today the Brakspear pubs and the microbrewery at the Bull on Bell Street in Henley are in the hands of another dynasty. The pubs were bought in 2006 by JT Davies, a family company that started with one London pub in 1875 and grew quickly with more pubs and later wine shops. In the 1990s Davies sold its wine shops to concentrate on running pubs. It now

Tom Davies and brewer Malcolm Mayo

owns 105 pubs, all branded Brakspear, with an estate that covers Oxfordshire, Essex, Kent, London and Warwickshire.

Tom Davies, the chief executive of Brakspear, says he has a good relationship with Marston's who brew Brakspear Bitter and a new beer, Oxford Gold, at Witney. Marston's didn't have

sufficient throughput to also produce Special and as a result it agreed to allow Brakspear to brew Special back in Henley along with Mild and Old Ale plus a range of seasonal beers.

The brewing equipment at the back of the Bull pub was installed in 2013 and is run by Malcolm Mayo, who has a connection with both sides of the fence as he brewed with Ringwood in Hampshire, now owned by Marston's. The kit, which can be seen from the bar, is a small brewhouse with attractive wood-panelled mash tun, copper and hot liquor tank. Three fermenting vessels are in a separate room and can handle three brews and 14 casks a week. Malcolm uses whole hops with hard brewing water from the public supply and says the yeast supplied by Witney works well in his fermenters.

Special, 4.3 per cent, is brewed with a blend of Maris Otter and Optic pale malts with crystal malt and a touch of black malt. The hops are Bramling Cross, Pilgrim, Savinjski Goldings from Slovenia, and Whitbread Goldings.

Other Brakspear beers back in Henley are the 2.9 per cent Mild and 4.3 per cent Old Ale. Hooray Henry, first brewed to celebrate the wedding of Prince Harry and Meghan Markel, has since been subtly renamed Hooray Henley. There are some seasonal brews as well. Marston's distributes the beers to Brakspear pubs along with its own Wychwood brands.

Special sampled in the bar at the Bull is a delight, a rich and complex blend of honeyed malt, spicy, fruity and peppery hops and the famous rich butterscotch note. It's history in a glass.

The Bull, Bell Street, Henley-on-Thames, Oxfordshire RG9 2BA · www.brakspear.co.uk

Regular cask beer:
Brakspear Special (4.3%)

Henley River & Brewing Museum (Mill Meadows, Henley RG9 1BF) has a first-floor cabinet with a display of old Brakspear bottles – Pale Ale, Brown Ale, Light Ale and Strong Ale – with a sign for the Row Barge pub above the cabinet.

Palmers

1794 · BRIDPORT · DORSET

YOU COULD BE forgiven for thinking that Palmers' brewery in Bridport is based in a sleepy backwater. It's on the Jurassic Coast, the UNESCO World Heritage Site that stretches from Devon to Dorset, and today the town is a tourist destination offering superb sea views, broad beaches, towering cliffs packed with fossils… and some fine pubs with excellent beer.

But Bridport has a turbulent history, caught up in the Napoleonic Wars of the 19th century and the two world wars of the 20th. As well as brewing, the town had a vigorous industry based on textiles, sailcloth, webs, ropes and netting, all supplied to the Royal Navy. Bridport Harbour, now called West Bay, and home of the brewery, played a major role in times of both war and peace.

Bridport has a long tradition of brewing. The town records of 1267 show that ale prices were linked to the price of barley and had to be strictly adhered to. If, for example, the market price for barley was four shillings per quarter then ale had to be sold for a penny per four quarts: two pints equalled one quart. If the rule was infringed, the perpetrators were carried round the town in a tumbrel, a cart frequently used to take prisoners to a place of execution.

Until the arrival of a commercial brewery in the town, brewing was carried out by both publicans and householders. By 1614, possibly earlier, the Bridport Town Brewhouse and Malthouse was producing beer. It prospered thanks to a ruling by the town council that forced publicans to buy beer from the brewhouse rather than brewing at their own premises. Houses in the town were mainly thatched and were subject to frequent fires. While the brewhouse was also thatched, the councillors thought the risk of fire would be reduced if brewing took place in just one building.

The brewery became an important part of the town's industry. As well as producing beer, it malted grain that was used not only for its own purposes but also by local people brewing at home. An inventory of 1650 shows the brewery was well equipped with 'a furnace pan, four cool backers (coolers) and three large vats'. In that same year, the brewery was taken over by the town council, with some of the profits going to support the poor and needy in the town.

The Old Brewery is born

The brewhouse reverted to private hands early in the 18th century and was run by a series of partnerships, several of them involving the Gundry family, leading textile makers in the town. When the brewhouse once again came under the control of the 'cofferers' or town treasurers, Samuel Gundry VI and a partner bought a meadow called Five Yards on the outskirts of the town in 1794 and built a new brewery. It was known, somewhat oddly as it was a new enterprise, as the Old Brewery. It still stands today and is now JC & RH Palmer.

Gundry's family textile business made handsome profits from the Napoleonic Wars, funds that helped create a modern brewery utilising all the new technologies of the age. The substantial buildings housed a malt house, brewhouse, fermenting room, cellars for racking ale and storing it, stables, a carpenter's shop and an area for cask washing. Gundry bought several pubs in both Bridport and the surrounding area in order to have regular outlets for his beer, though brewing remained a seasonal activity from October to June: it wasn't until refrigeration arrived in the 19th century that brewing was possible in the summer months.

The protracted wars with France were good for brewing as well as textiles. The British fleet used Torbay as a harbour and between 1799 and 1800 more than 1,000 barrels of Gundry's porter, worth some £1,800, were shipped to the fleet from Bridport. This profitable trade came to end in 1802 with the Treaty of Amiens and the British fleet moved away from the West Country. Gundry turned his attention to local trade and bought additional pubs in Bridport and neighbouring areas. He also managed to prosper from the notorious 1830 Beer Act, which allowed householders to turn their premises into rudimentary pubs. The number of licensed properties in Bridport doubled and it was claimed that on South Street, a major thoroughfare, every other house was a pub. Few of them brewed, however, and Gundry supplied them with ale, his output doubling to some 6,000 barrels a year.

Gundry became a partner in the Bridport Bank and he transferred his shares in the brewery to his son Samuel Bowden Gundry. The young Gundry ran the brewery with a series of partners, expanding production and buying further pubs. The arrival of the railway in Bridport in 1857 enabled Gundry to expand trade still further, while the opening of the Railway Tavern, the Railway Inn and the Railway Terminus in the town stressed the importance of the new mode of transport. To keep pace with demand, Gundry invested heavily in the brewery to take advantage of all the new equipment and brewing methods available. The brewhouse had two mash tuns made of English oak, complete with rotating sparge arms that

washed out remaining sugars at the end of the mash. When the wort left the mash tun it went via an oak underback to three coppers. Following the boil with hops in the coppers, the hopped wort flowed into an underback built with Polish timber. A refrigeration unit cooled the liquid, which then transferred to fermenters. The green beer was left to condition for a week in a 100-barrel cleansing back made of deal. Finally, the beer was pumped to cellars where it was racked into oak casks. The only signs of antiquity were the original thatched roof and the impressive water wheel that provided power until the arrival of a steam engine. The wheel, 18 feet in diameter and weighing six tons, is still in place.

From boom to bust

Brewing books from the middle of the century show the beers being produced were X, XX, Ale, Table Beer and Porter. By 1862 an astonishing amount of beer was being made for export from a relatively small brewery in an equally small town. Twelve different beers were produced, with Burton-style ales proving popular: the owners were clearly well-aware of the development of brewing in London and Burton upon Trent. A new pale ale was shipped to Calcutta, India, and also Brisbane and Melbourne in Australia. In 1863, 25 hogsheads – giant oak casks, each containing 54 gallons of beer – were sent to Vancouver for a visit by the French Emperor Napoleon III. Some 150 barrels

of Best Bitter were brewed for the Newfoundland trade and were carried there annually on the same ship that took nets and lines for the fishing industry made by Bridport's textile firms, including the one owned by the Gundry family.

Despite this considerable success, the Old Brewery faced severe financial problems in the 1860s, caused to some extent by the emergence of big national brewers such as Bass and Whitbread. Their production was enormous – Bass at one stage was brewing close to one million barrels a year – and they could undercut smaller rivals. A decision was made to refashion the ownership of the Bridport brewery, which in July 1864 became the Bridport Old Brewery Company Limited and the age of Gundry control came to an end. The new owners, mainly from the London area, set about improving the brewery to compete more effectively

The brewery in the 1890s

in the market. A new beer store was built and the tied trade was expanded by leasing six new pubs.

At first the company was successful, reporting healthy profits of £4,500 in 1865. But sales fell dramatically the following year, due mainly to the collapse of the export trade. Losses amounted to £10,000 and were projected to rise to £20,000. The directors had raised £60,000 but half of that sum had disappeared and creditors were demanding their money. The company's accountant told the directors they must stop trading and liquidators were appointed. For a short period, the brewery was run by the Leggs, a farming family, but it continued to trade badly and the Leggs were happy to hand over ownership to members of the Palmer family in 1896, though the 'late Job Legg' and 'established 1794' appear on posters promoting JC & RH Palmer.

The Palmers have a taste for brewing

The Palmers came from North Perrott near Yeovil in Somerset. John Palmer was a farmer who joined the Royal Navy during the Napoleonic Wars, rising to the rank of captain. Following the war, he returned to farming near Taunton, and following his death in 1828 the family moved yet again, this time to West Bexington on the Dorset coast. Robert Palmer, John's fourth son, decided to dip his toes in the brewing business and he held discussions with Henry King, owner of the Odiham Brewery in Hampshire, with a view to buying the business. King was willing to sell and Robert paid close to £30,000 and installed his son Cleeves, 40 years his junior, to run the brewery.

Cleeves had a taste for brewing. He rapidly built both production and profits at Odiham. He was ambitious and in the 1890s he was offered the chance to buy the Old Brewery in Bridport. It was a difficult decision to make as Odiham was financially sound while the Old Brewery had experienced troubled times, but the challenge of running a much bigger brewery was too tempting to reject and in 1896 Cleeves and his younger brother Henry took over the Bridport

business. It was hard going at first. While the Palmer brothers had sold Odiham for £30,000 they had to pay £82,000 for the Old Brewery and the gap was covered by mortgages.

The Palmers' enthusiasm for brewing carried them through a difficult period in Dorset. Agriculture was in crisis and impoverished farm labourers were hard pressed to buy beer, turning instead to cheaper cider. Demand for nets and ropes was in decline and two makers in Bridport went out of business following a crisis in the fishing industry in Newfoundland. Shipbuilding was also in decline and the population of the West Bay harbour area, where the brewery was based, halved between 1870 and 1901 to just 250 people. Changes in society also had an impact on the brewery. The temperance movement was in full swing and people were being encouraged to watch football and cricket rather than sit in pubs.

Cleeves Palmer, c.1896, with his eldest son, Bob (standing), and two younger sons, Eddie and Leslie, who were both killed in the First World War

Bottled success

Undaunted, the Palmer brothers ploughed on. They celebrated Queen Victoria's Diamond Jubilee in 1897 by selling crates of a dozen bottles of Best Bitter for just one shilling and sixpence per crate. The brothers built on sales of bottled beer by installing a bottling line. At first Palmers bought beer in cask for bottling from Bass, Marston's, Salt and Worthington in Burton, as well as Guinness stout, but the brewery soon added its own products in bottled format.

Against the odds, the brewery made healthy profits and major investments were made to keep pace with both demand and improved technology. A 40-barrel refrigerator was installed in 1901 and replaced ancient coolers, enabling beer to be brewed without the threat of infection from wild yeasts. A new mash tun was purchased in 1907 and the malt mill was renewed in 1912. Palmers branched out into wines and spirits, which proved an important income stream. The income from wine, for example, increased from just £200 in 1896 to £500 by 1914, with private clients accounting for around half the sales. Wine has remained an important part of the business to the present day, with the current wine department considered one of the finest in the country.

At war

Cleeves Palmer was a keen supporter of the Tory Party and he went to war with the new Liberal government that won power in 1906. Urged on by the teetotal Lloyd George, the Liberals were determined to crack down on pubs and drinking. As a result of pressure from the temperance movement, Palmers had to close several pubs in Bridport and Cleeves was determined to prevent further closures. In 1908, he took a party of 150 people to London in support of a major protest against government plans for further restrictions on pubs and brewing. The party went by train from Bridport station and joined a crowd of 150,000 who heard 70 speakers on 20 platforms.

The attrition between brewers and parliament ended with the outbreak of war in 1914, which led to the swingeing restrictions on brewing and pub opening hours described in the Introduction: patriotic brewers had to toe the government line. Palmers renamed its King of Prussia pub the King of the Belgians in recognition of Belgian refugees who came to Bridport to work in local factories.

The war proved to be a boon for the struggling rope and nets industry in Bridport, but it had the reverse impact on the Old Brewery. With around 1,600 men from the Bridport area called up for military service and no thirsty troops stationed nearby, the demand for beer slumped. Despite having beer-loving Belgians in their midst, Palmers' production fell during the war to 70 per cent of the pre-war levels and by 1917 only 6,000 barrels were produced. Alongside this, the massive increases in duty caused the price of a pint to double.

New generation

Cleeves Palmer was taken ill with bronchitis in 1926 and died two years later. His brother Henry took over the running of the brewery and was joined by Cleeves' son Bob, who had learned the brewing skills at a number of breweries, including another coastal one, Adnams of Southwold in Suffolk. Henry died in 1933 and Bob became the sole owner of the brewery. He prepared his two sons, Cleeves and Tony, to join him. (The number of Palmers called Cleeves reflects the close links by marriage with the Cleeves family who were also based in Somerset.)

The new generation faced tough times. The industrial unrest of the 1920s was followed by economic depression in the next decade. The local textile trade was once again badly affected and beer sales fell at Palmers. Undaunted, Bob bought new pubs in Axminster, Bridport, Charmouth and other towns, and invested further to make them attractive to the tourist business that was boosted by growing car-ownership.

At war again

The Second World War had a quite different impact on Bridport than the first. British, then Canadian and finally American troops were stationed in the area,

The yard and drays in 1938

with the Americans preparing for the vital D-day landings. Tourism declined as Bridport was bombed twice but some 800 evacuees from London and other cities were billeted in the area. The new arrivals helped keep beer sales buoyant even though many locals were called up for military service. Pubs became convivial meeting places for a mix of locals, Cockneys and servicemen from overseas. Bob Palmer took the lead in getting the Brewers' Society to designate

LASSIE CREATES A LEGEND

A Palmers' pub and a loyal dog helped create a film legend. German U-boats attacked ships bringing essential goods, such as grain for brewing, from North America to Britain. The plan was to starve the country into submission. HMS *Formidable* was sunk in 1915 and bodies of seamen were brought ashore at Lyme Regis and laid out on the floor of Palmers' Pilot Boat inn.

The landlord had a collie called Lassie and as she moved among the corpses, she licked

the face of one supposedly dead sailor. He was Able Seaman John Cowan, who sat up and proved to be very much alive. The event was reported widely and was picked up by British writer Eric Knight who had moved to Hollywood to work as a scriptwriter. He wrote a short story in 1938 about a collie who crossed hundreds of miles to find the boy who owned her. The story was turned into a best-selling novel called *Lassie Come Home* and was filmed with a young Elizabeth Taylor among the cast.

brewing an 'essential industry' and this enabled Palmers to keep skilled staff at the brewery.

During the Second World War, the government once again restricted the supply of malt and hops and dramatically increased duty. Despite these difficulties, Bob Palmer made some important investments in the plant. He installed two New Zealand pine fermenters along with a bottle-washing plant and a second-hand steam engine. Plans for a new beer conditioning room were started and completed when war ended.

Tragedy struck the family. Bob Palmer's elder son Cleeves joined the Royal Engineers but in 1940 contracted peritonitis and died, aged just 24. Tony, Bob's younger son, was called up for the Royal Artillery, leaving Bob to manage the brewery single-handed until the war ended. He nevertheless found time to join the Home Guard to help defend Bridport: a photo of him in Home Guard uniform shows him looking remarkably like Captain Mainwaring in *Dad's Army*.

Bob Palmer

Sparging of the malted barley in the mash tun

The immediate post-war years were difficult ones for Palmers. Grain supplies were still restricted and beer consumption fell by around 25 per cent until the end of the 1940s. But the brewery was able to ward off the threat of takeover and merger. The 1950s and 60s saw considerable contraction in the industry and in the south-west Arnold & Hancock was swallowed by Ushers of Trowbridge, Mitchell & Toms was bought by the large London brewer Charrington, and Starkey, Knight & Ford was bought by an even bigger London company, Whitbread. In Dorset, Devenish and Groves in Weymouth merged.

Loyal to cask

The brewery set its face against the major development in this period: keg beer. Palmers remained true to cask ale and simply did not have the resources to invest in the expensive equipment needed to brew and serve beer that was filtered and pasteurised at source, and served chilled and by gas pressure in the pub. In 1953 it added draught IPA to its range and, as beer sales in general started to revive, the new beer quickly became Palmers' most popular beer, accounting for around 70 per cent of total production.

Cleeves and John Palmer

Bob Palmer retired in 1958 and Tony Palmer became the owner of the business until it became a limited company in 1976. His staunch defence of cask beer paid dividends when CAMRA arrived with a blaze of publicity and beer festivals that championed the cause of real ale. At the same time, Tony Palmer overhauled his pubs, making them more welcoming to visitors and introducing improved food.

John Palmer took over from his father Tony as managing director in 1983 and he was joined by his younger brother Cleeves as sales and marketing director. The fourth generation of the family have continued their father's modernisation of beer and pubs. While some under-performing pubs have been closed, the brothers have looked further afield for sales and have bought outlets in Devon and Somerset. Head brewer Darren Batten has brought strict quality control to the beer range, which was rebranded in 2008 with pumpclips declaring all the beers as 'cask conditioned'. The beers include: Copper Ale, an easy-drinking 'lunchtime pint'; Best Bitter, or IPA as it's also known; Dorset Gold, introduced to meet the popularity of paler beers; 200, which celebrated the double centenary of the brewery; and a strong dark ale, Tally Ho! In 2018 it finally entered the keg market with Dorset Pale. It now produces close to 10,000 barrels a year, of which 95 per cent is draught.

With local industries in West Dorset in terminal decline, the popularity of Palmers' beer has been aided by growing tourist numbers following the Jurassic Coast being chosen as a World Heritage Site by UNESCO in 2001. Publicity surrounding filming in the area has also helped. The television series *Harbour Lights* was filmed in West Bay and Hugh Fearnley-Whittingstall's *River Cottage* series about food and cooking was also shot locally. More recently, the crime series *Broadchurch*, starring David Tennant and Olivia Colman, was filmed in and around West Bay.

The success of both Palmers' beers and pubs can be measured by the large number of awards it has picked up in the 21st century. They include trophies

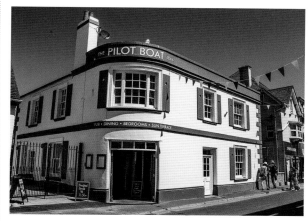

The Pilot Boat in Lyme Regis

from both CAMRA and SIBA for Tally Ho! and Gold, awards from Taste of Dorset, and further awards from CAMRA and SIBA for the company's pubs, including the campaign's Best Pub Refurbishment for the Pilot Boat in Lyme Regis. The brewery also won Best Tenanted Pub Company in the annual Publican awards.

Palmers has survived many ups and downs over its long history, but has adapted well to changing demands from a vastly different society in the 21st century. Between them John and Cleeves have six children and family ownership is assured.

Palmers, The Old Brewery, West Bay, Bridport, Dorset DT6 4JA · 01308 422396 · Brewery shop www.palmersbrewery.com · Tours available

Regular cask ales:

Copper Ale (3.7%)
Best Bitter or **IPA** (4.2%)
Dorset Gold (4.5%)
200 (5%)
Tally Ho! (5.5%)

Elgood's

1795 · WISBECH · CAMBRIDGESHIRE

ELGOOD's is wrapped, cocooned and steeped in history. The striking Georgian facade stands proud alongside the fast-flowing River Nene in the ancient Fenland market town of Wisbech in Cambridgeshire. Four acres of gardens, open to visitors, offer some of the oldest trees in East Anglia, with a lake and a maze: to emphasise the links to the brewery, the maze is shaped like a yard of ale glass. The brewhouse is achingly traditional, reached up narrow, creaking stairs, with a wood-jacketed mash tun and burnished copper, while the malt store is jealously guarded by a black-and-white cat: rodents beware. Fermentation takes place in high-sided wooden vessels.

But Elgood's is proof that breweries in the 21st century cannot live in the past. Managing director Belinda Sutton, who with her sister, company secretary Jennifer Everall, are the fifth generation of the Elgood family to run the brewery, says: 'We had a choice: to just brew our traditional beers and quietly

Elgood's Georgian brewery façade, 1909

decline or innovate to stay alive. Our future – our heart – is in brewing. We don't want to become a pub company. But the future is about being a niche brewery. We will continue with our main beers, but sour and wheat beers are what a lot of people want to drink today.'

Change was vital. Belinda Sutton, who has worked at the brewery for 35 years, says Elgood's was once the only brewery in Cambridgeshire; today there are more than 20. Wisbech is near to the borders with both Norfolk and Lincolnshire, with more breweries in close proximity, while Adnams and Greene King are both powerful forces in East Anglia.

But sales have increased for Elgood's at home and abroad, and this welcome success is due to bringing back into use some antique brewing vessels that had been no more than a visitor attraction for decades. The vessels, known as coolships, have allowed antiquity to combine with the needs of a brewery facing the challenges of the new century.

The early days

The brewery stands on a site that was first run by a wool comber in the late 17th century. The wool trade was vital to Wisbech's economy, with fleeces sent by river and sea to Hull and then on to the Yorkshire mill towns. But in the 18th century, the site had become a tannery. This was a trade that required a great deal of water and the owner dug a series of wells on the site that proved essential when another change turned the buildings into a brewery by the end of the century.

George V's Silver Jubilee, 1935

The site was sold to Thomas Fawsett on Christmas Day, 1795. The North Brink Brewery is believed to be the first classical Georgian brewery built outside London and it was designed by a partnership of Dennis Herbert of Biggleswade and John Gooch, described as a 'common brewer' from Wisbech. It was built with 30-inch solid brick walls and was designed to last. Herbert and Gooch bought four local pubs and they were followed in 1801 by a new partnership of William Watson and Abraham Usill who rapidly developed a tied house estate of 40 pubs that provided the brewery with regular and reliable outlets for its beer.

The brewery and pubs were sold to a new partnership in 1836 that quickly foundered. The business was then bought by the Phillips family who sold it in 1877 to another partnership of John Elgood and George Harrison, who paid £38,965 for both brewery and pubs. It was a large amount of money to find and after nine years Harrison was declared bankrupt.

The start of the Elgood era

John Elgood came from a St Neots family and his father had been a merchant. John sold his maltings in Godmanchester to take sole ownership of the brewery and his family has been in control ever since. The company logo of a greyhound with a key in its mouth is based on the Elgood coat of arms: permission had to be granted by the College of Arms for it to be used commercially.

Successive generations of the family installed new equipment to meet the growing demand for beer in the 19th and 20th centuries. Most of the current plant was put in place either side of the Second World War, but older pieces of equipment survive, including a mash tun from the early 1800s and, critically, two coolships from the 1920s.

A coolship renaissance

Coolships are large, open copper trays where hopped wort – the malt extract from the mash tun that has been boiled with hops – can cool prior to fermentation. They have gone out of favour as the wort is wide open to infection from wild yeasts. Today, coolships are mainly confined to Belgian brewers who make the style known as lambic and who welcome the action of wild yeasts from the atmosphere. The result is beer with a sharp, tangy and acidic character. Lambic beers are brewed only in warmer periods of the year when wild yeasts are active.

As Elgood's is surrounded by gardens with fruit trees and vegetation, the brewery positively invited wild yeasts to attack the beer. Thus, the coolships were abandoned decades ago, and every precaution was then taken to keep the house yeast culture pure and unsullied.

Later, artisan brewers in both Britain and the United States took an interest in lambic and decided to brew their own interpretations. As lambic beer is protected by both Belgian and EU law, brewers couldn't use the term and instead call their beers 'sour'.

Bob Leggett of Artisanal Exports in Texas, who sells Elgood's beers in the US, said when he saw the redundant coolships at Wisbech: 'You should brew lambic'.

Chairman Nigel Elgood, Belinda and Jennifer considered his advice along with head brewer Alan Pateman, and it was eventually decided that they should go ahead.

John Elgood

WELCOMING WILD YEASTS

It was a momentous day for Elgood's on 12 November 2013 when the first batch of beer was made using the coolships, which can both hold 27 barrels of beer. At the end of the copper boil, Alan Pateman called out: 'Open the taps!' Boiling hopped wort gushed from pipes attached to the copper and eddied and flowed into the coolships, with billowing steam filling the room. When the vessels were full and the steam cleared, Alan Pateman's last words to his brewing team were: 'Make sure you leave the windows open when you leave.' Decades of brewing practice were set aside to create the new beer. In order to encourage a good build-up of wild yeasts and other microflora, Alan took planks from an oak tree that had been cut down for safety reasons in the brewery gardens and placed the planks above the coolships.

It takes 18 months to make a batch of lambic beer, which is called Coolship at Elgood's. Most of the beer is aged in tanks on a bed of woodchips, the rest is placed in oak casks bought from the French wine industry. Beer from both sources is then blended. Coolship is made from a combination of malted barley and unmalted wheat. The hops are Styrian Goldings from Slovenia and are two years old. They have lost most of their bitterness: bitterness doesn't combine well with the spicy aroma and flavour imparted by wheat, and the hops are used for their preservative qualities.

Alan laconically commented: 'I've spent 25 years keeping wild yeasts out of the place and now we want them back again!'

Elgood's sour, Coolship, created a good deal of attention when it was launched in 2014 and sales at first were brisk in the US. Belinda Sutton says sales have since declined there as a result of the large number of American craft breweries producing their own versions of sour beer. But Coolship is sold throughout the UK and exported to Europe and Scandinavia.

In the manner of Belgian lambic brewers, Alan Pateman has added fruit versions of Coolship, including Mango and Fruit, the latter a blend of berry fruits. Coolship has picked up some major awards, including Best Sour in Europe in the prestigious World Beer Awards and a Gold medal from SIBA for Coolship Mango. Coolship Fruit was named Champion Speciality Beer in the 2017 International Beer Awards.

Using a small pilot brewery he installed for short-run beers, Alan has developed a range of fruit wheat beers, including apple, cherry, banana, strawberry, mango and raspberry. He also uses the pilot plant to produce beers for export, including 8.7 per cent Rex and Blonde and 9 per cent Scotch for Italy.

Cask is still vital

In spite of the success of Coolship and wheat, Elgood's isn't ignoring its traditional range of cask and bottled beers: cask is vital to its tied and free trade in eastern England, while bottles are part of the export package. The beers are available in Europe, Canada, Chile and Russia and can be found on P&O liners.

Nigel Elgood, who became managing director in 1968, recalls the changes to the beer range over his long career with the brewery. Thirty years ago, EB, which stood for Elgood's Bitter, was renamed Cambridge Bitter and has become the brewery's best-selling ale. Mellow Mild was renamed Black Dog 25 years ago and, despite many other breweries delisting mild ales, remains a popular member of the range: the roasty character and intriguing name help. Black Dog or

Nigel Elgood with his wife, Anne, in the brewery gardens

Sisters Jennifer Everall, Belinda Sutton, and Claire Simpson. Claire, who helped design the brewery gardens, died in 2019.

Black Shuck is a famous ghostly hound that's alleged to haunt the Fenlands.

Golden Newt has been added to the portfolio along with Double Swan and Warrior bottled ales. Plum Porter and Blackberry Porter, available in cask and bottle, are further recent additions. There's also a rolling programme of monthly seasonal cask beers, ranging from dark ale at Christmas to spritzy summer refreshers.

Nigel Elgood is keen to point out that the brewery was the first in the country to brew a low alcohol beer back in 1985 when the breathalyser was introduced. Highway was 0.5 per cent alcohol and was produced by a system known as reverse osmosis in which a membrane separates the alcohol from the liquid. It won an award in 1986 in the Food from Britain competition.

n Pateman

No corners are cut where beer quality is concerned. Alan Pateman draws most of his barley from farmers in North Norfolk who specialise in the acclaimed Maris Otter variety. Hops include such English varieties as Bramling Cross, Challenger, East Kent Goldings and Fuggles along with American Cascade, Chinook and Willamette. Brewing water is medium hard and is filtered through a chalk aquifer.

A fine reputation

Since Nigel Elgood took over in the 1960s, a great deal of effort has gone into improving and modernising the brewery's pubs. They now number 29. Although a few isolated Fenland outlets have closed due to the low throughput of beer, other pubs are flourishing. It has two pubs in the major town of Peterborough and a flagship outlet, the Reindeer, in Norwich. The Reindeer has built a fine reputation for both food and beer in a city where there's keen competition from many other pubs. The Duck in Stanhoe near Burnham Market in Norfolk was named one of the country's Top 50 gastro pubs by the *Sunday Times*. 'It sells a lot of beer!' Belinda is quick to point out.

Elgood's in 2020 is a modern, forward-thinking brewery in a superb historic setting. And there are six Elgood children waiting in the wings to take over and ensure the family business survives for many more generations.

The brewery gardens

Elgood's, North Brink Brewery, Wisbech, Cambridgeshire PE13 1LW · 01945 583160
www.elgoods-brewery.co.uk

Tours available throughout the year.
The visitor centre includes a small museum featuring brewery memorabilia and items from the Elgood family history. The brewery gardens are also open all year and can be hired for weddings and corporate events.

Regular cask beers:

Black Dog (3.6%)
Cambridge Bitter (3.8%)
Golden Newt (4.1%)

The Reindeer, Norwich (top), and the Duck, Stanhoe (bottom)

THE EARLY 19TH-CENTURY BREWERS

HARVEY'S · McMULLEN · HOOK NORTON · EVERARDS

Beer and drinkers' preferences began to change in the early part of the 19th century in step with the innovations of the Industrial Revolution. Once coke was made on an industrial scale, it was possible for brewers to use substantial amounts of pale malt in their brews.

Coke fires in kilns were easier to control than wood fires and the resulting pale malt had higher levels of the enzymes that convert starch to brewing sugar. This meant that brewers needed less malt to make beer, leading to a reduction in costs.

Pale malt was used to produce porter and stout though the style became darker in colour when a device, similar to a coffee roaster, was invented to make roasted malts. 18th-century porters and stouts, brown in colour, were then replaced by the jet-black beers we know today. Porter also changed from being produced 'entire butt' in a brewery, to being mixed by the publican from mature beer and fresh mild ale. Mixing was aided by the invention of the beer engine that enabled publicans to draw beer from the cellar with the use of a handpump, avoiding the labour of mixing beer in the pub cellar.

Porter and stout reached the zenith of their popularity in 1823 but sales then started to fall by as much as 20 per cent by 1830. Consumers were moving away from the tart and acidic nature of porter, switching instead to sweeter, fresh mild ale. Whitbread, whose fortunes had been made by porter and brewed nothing else until 1834, started to produce mild. The other major family brewers in London, such as Barclay Perkins and Truman, followed Whitbread's lead while traditional ale brewers Charrington and Courage saw a massive increase in demand for mild: Charrington's output rose by close to 250 per cent between 1831 and 1851.

The popularity of mild ale was a boon for the brewers. They no longer needed to store beer for months in vast oak tuns and could deliver freshly brewed mild to pubs within days of it leaving the fermenting vessels. Mild chimed with the times. As the population of Britain soared, a growing army of both industrial and agricultural workers welcomed the ability of mild to refresh them and restore lost energy.

The style was not confined to London and was a popular beer in such industrial heartlands as the

Black Country in the Midlands and the mill towns of Manchester and Lancashire. As this section shows, family brewers throughout the country made large amounts of mild, often with a range that included pale as well as dark versions. McMullen in Hertford had a number of milds branded with letters on the casks and one of those, AK, is still a popular beer today. In Oxfordshire, Hook Norton refreshed both farm labourers and quarrymen with its milds and later in the century had a new thirsty audience when railway navvies drove a line through the village.

Dark beers – mild, porter and stout – were drunk in the main by the working class. In the early 19th century, a new type of pale beer emerged that satisfied the growing ranks of the middle class in Britain. The pale ale that later became known as India Pale Ale (IPA) was initially developed for export to the Indian subcontinent.

George Hodgson, an East London family brewery at Bow Bridge, close to the East India Docks, in common with many London brewers, exported dark beers to India for the British soldiers and civil servants based there. Hodgson heard that the Raj were demanding a more refreshing beer and he, along with a few other East London brewers, developed a pale ale based on an existing style known as October Beer. October Beer, brewed in the autumn with the first malts and hops of the harvest and then stored for a year before it was drunk, had been designed for members of the gentry who didn't wish to drink the dark beers associated with the hoi-polloi.

Hodgson's pale beer may not have been exceptionally pale: London's brewing water at the time was best suited to producing dark beer. It was probably just paler than mild or porter. It was strong and heavily hopped as alcohol and hops kept the beer in good condition on the long sea journeys, lasting up to six months, to India. Hodgson estimated that the journey would age the beer well and it would arrive in drinkable condition. He was proved right and soon members of the Raj were revelling in the new beer sent to them.

But Hodgson was quickly eclipsed by brewers in Burton upon Trent. The Midlands town had long been renowned for the quality of the beers made there, thanks in no small measure to the remarkable qualities of Trent Valley water. It's rich in sulphates such as calcium and magnesium, which enhance the flavour of beer, and it proved ideal for brewing pale ale.

Brewers in the town were desperate for new markets. They had for many years exported a brown beer known as Burton Ale to Russia and the Baltic States. But the interminable wars with Napoleon's France had led to the Baltic ports being blockaded by the French and Burton's beer couldn't get through. The East India Company, which controlled trade with the sub-continent, came to Burton's aid. It encouraged family brewers such as Allsopp and Bass to follow Hodgson's lead and within a few years their superior beers outsold London versions of IPA.

When IPA became available to the domestic market, drinkers found it too strong and hoppy and brewers responded with a lower strength version called simply Pale Ale. The beer's popularity with the new, aspiring middle class was aided by the arrival of the railway. Trains could take batches of Burton pale ale to London and other parts of the country in a few hours, whereas horse-drawn wagons would have taken days or weeks to cover the same distances.

IPA and pale ale were described as 'the beers of the railway age' and family brewers in rural areas were quick to add pale ale to their portfolios. Dark beer wasn't in decline, but its hegemony was being challenged by a new pale interloper.

In the middle years of the 19th century, the pub trade was changing too. The Beer Act of 1830 (see p. 8) saw a rapid increase in the number of licensed premises. The social problems that followed in the wake of the act, including increased drunkenness and violence, saw the legislation reined in later in the century. But, as many of the gimcrack beerhouses failed due to bad management and poor beer, they were snapped up by family brewers and thereby the roots of the tied house system were laid.

Harvey's

ESTABLISHED 1790, BREWING BEER SINCE THE 1820s

LEWES · EAST SUSSEX

'WE believe in evolution, not revolution at Harvey's,' Miles Jenner says. Is there a twinkle in his eye as he then hands me a glass of Tom Paine Ale? It's brewed every July to celebrate both Independence Day in the United States and the life of Paine, who lived and worked in Lewes from 1768 to 1774. He was the author of the *Rights of Man* and was an active supporter of both the American and French Revolutions.

Lewes, too, has a reputation as a 'rebellious little town'. It has often been in conflict with the government and the monarchy. The Second Barons' War of 1264 took place in Lewes, with the result that Simon de Montfort's forces defeated Henry III, turning de Montfort into the most powerful man in England.

The history is at odds with Miles Jenner's support for evolution. But what the joint managing director and head brewer of Harvey's means is that his company takes a measured approach to brewing, avoids fads and concentrates on doing what it knows best: producing award-winning ales, of which Sussex Best Bitter is the outstanding success.

In common with the town, Harvey's has had its fare share of turbulence. It has been flooded twice and has also been the victim of a major fire. But the turmoil of the past is belied by the imposing view as you approach Harvey's by the Cliffe Bridge over the River Ouse. The Grade II-listed site includes a tall chimney alongside a red-brick main building with arched windows, topped by a pagoda-style roof and weather vane, with the name of the brewery picked out in gold lettering. The brewery dates from 1838 but the current design was the work of the famed architect William Bradford, who refashioned Harvey's in the 1880s in the 'tower brewery' style also seen at Hook Norton in Oxfordshire.

Miles Jenner and his team are not turning their backs on modern trends in the beer world. 'We've got to remain relevant,' he says. 'We see some weird and wonderful new beer styles, but we expect there will be a drift back to more traditional styles.' In recognition of the demand for 'craft keg', Harvey's has a new range

Founder John Harvey

Harvey's brewery in 1881

of keg beers, including Wharf IPA, Black Stout and Gold Bier. The brewery reached out to both traditional and newer beer lovers at the 2019 Great British Beer Festival with a groundbreaking comparative tasting of cask and keg beers, conducted by Miles.

But the modern world cannot mask the rich history of Harvey's. It's the oldest independent brewery in Sussex and today is controlled by the eighth generation of the family, with five descendants of John Harvey working at the brewery.

Wines, spirits, ale and coal

John Harvey's family were Londoners but moved to Lewes where they sold wines and spirits and purchased a few local inns: the founding date of 1790 is when the Harveys began to trade in Lewes. John turned to brewing to supply the inns with ale and, after working at Thomas Wood's plant in the town, he established the Bridge Wharf Brewery on its present site by the Ouse.

Harvey kept a journal that gives a fascinating insight into the practice of a Georgian brewer and the problems he faced at a time when temperature control was primitive and making beer could be difficult in the extreme. 'Warm day for brewing, worts cool badly,' he noted one spring day, while on a day in January he recorded the air was 'cool and frosty' and he was obliged to 'put a fire round the tun to bring it on in heat.' In December 1833, while brewing at Wood's, he had an especially bad experience, reporting: 'Pipes broken again. Obliged to brew from the river water. First brewing today very thick and muddy.' A later entry in 1834 said: 'First brewing from our spring again after waiting three months and obliged to use dirty water all the time.'

In 1838, Thomas Wood died and John Harvey moved to the Bridge Wharf site, which he bought for £3,707. Its location close to the river was ideal for transporting malt, hops and coal. John built a brewhouse at a further cost of £1,100 that included bell-shaped oak vats with a storage capacity of 650 barrels. The open copper and liquor backs were coal-fired and a steam engine pumped brewing water and drove the malt mill. The mash tun, hop back, wort coolers and fermenting vessels were all built of oak and cooling was achieved by immersing copper tubing into the vats and pumping cold water through the tubes.

John Harvey traded as a brewer, wine and spirit merchant and coal merchant. He brewed between 15 and 20 barrels of beer a day and supplied 14 tied houses and a growing free trade. The beers, by modern standards, were powerful, between eight and nine per cent alcohol. This was the norm for the time when most people were engaged in heavy manual labour and could comfortably work off the effects of strong liquor.

The start of a dynasty

In later years, John was joined at the brewery by his three sons William, Henry and Edwin. A dynasty was being created. John died in 1862 and the brothers expanded the business, increasing brewing capacity by 50 barrels. When Edwin and Henry died within days of one another, William entered into a partnership with his son-in-law John Maxfield Smith and hired Henry Barrett as their head brewer.

Barrett came from Wethered's brewery in Buckinghamshire and at first he regretted the move, saying it was 'a great sacrifice on my part, leaving a 40 quarter plant where everything worked like clockwork, to brew in a small brewery where mashing operations were performed by four men in a very primitive way, mashing with oars.' (A quarter was the measurement used for malt: a quarter of malt equates to approximately 320 pounds.) Despite his early doubts, Barrett worked well with the partners. They eagerly took on board new brewing techniques and installed a Steel's Masher, a device that accurately blends grain and water before they hit the mash tun.

Water continued to be a major headache for the brewery. In 1875 typhoid fever in Lewes killed 30 people as a result of contamination of the Lewes Water Company's supply. Henry Barrett recorded – somewhat alarmingly – that he examined the brewing

Workers outside the brewery, c.1870

water each morning prior to mashing and found it was covered in scum. 'This had to be skimmed off daily,' he wrote in his log. 'Of course, we used it in brewing, purifying it by boiling, fermenting, etc, turning out a pure beer.' Nevertheless, a desire for a better source meant a bore hall was sunk at the wharf. Water was struck 60 feet (18m) below ground and the same supply is used today, pure water that has filtered down from the chalky Sussex Downs.

Barrett recorded that he was brewing ale and 'Old Best the Stout'. He doesn't specify what type of ale but by the late 19th century it may well have been pale ale as consumer preferences changed following the success of IPA from Burton upon Trent. He was without doubt producing mild ale as well, as it remained a staple at Harvey's and is still brewed today. Old Best the Stout may not have been a black beer, as we would expect now, as stout was then a generic term for the strongest or stoutest beer produced: Old Best may have been strong old ale, matured for several months.

The most profound change at the brewery came in 1881 when William Bradford was commissioned to design a new 15-quarter brewery. The project cost £8,000 and the new brewhouse was situated at the northern end of the yard alongside the fermenting room, enabling brewing to continue on the old plant until the building was finished. During the course of the work, Bradford visited Lewes no fewer than 48 times. His fees amounted to £440, 10 shillings and a penny, but he left behind the architectural gem and striking façade that still dominate the Cliffe Bridge area of the town.

Women steer ahead

Economic difficulties at the start of the 20th century led to three breweries in Lewes closing. Harvey's traded well but its future was cast in doubt as a result of the death of John Maxfield Smith. His widow Alice and her son Howard ran the brewery for a while but when they died control passed to Howard's three sisters, Alice-May, Elise and Nora. From 1912 to 1980, women continued to administer the brewery, with Alice-May Harvey-Smith taking up the role of chairman in 1929. The sisters went on to make some astute appointments that ensured the brewery's survival.

Alice-May Harvey Smith

The First World War had a similar impact on the brewers in Lewes as elsewhere, with duty rising, the strength of beer falling and supplies of grain strictly rationed. Harvey's fared better than its main rival in the town, Beard's. All its employees had to join the Sussex Yeomanry Reserve and when they were called up for army service only the head brewer was left and he had to use Harvey's plant twice a week to produce beer for Beard's pubs and free trade.

In the 1920s, the three ruling sisters saw the need to look to a new generation to run the brewery. Their sister Beatrice had a son, Eric Carlyon Rundle, who was working in India. He agreed to return home in 1923 and after training as a brewer he became managing director. With Alice-May as chairman advising him, he steered the company through the difficult time of recession and unemployment that saw many other brewers fall by the wayside.

A major turning point in the history and fortunes of the brewery came in 1938 when Rundle appointed a new second brewer, Anthony Jenner. He came from Jenner's family brewery in Southwark, London, which had closed and he needed a job. Following the Second World War, Tony Jenner was promoted to head brewer. He forged a close relationship with Rundle and since then the brewery has been run by members of the two families. The two men put their hearts and souls into the brewery and kept it afloat during the turbulent times of the 1950s and 60s when mergers and takeovers had a devastating impact on both the industry and drinkers' choice. Their most lasting decision was to launch Sussex Best Bitter in 1955, which today is the flagship beer. It has won many awards and is considered by connoisseurs to be one of the finest examples of a traditional best bitter.

The changing times and good fortune brought to the company by Sussex Best Bitter are reflected in the following statistics. In 1945 75% of production at Harvey's was Mild Ale, with IPA accounting for 25%. When Best Bitter was launched in 1955, Mild still accounted for 74% of annual production. By 1985, the figures were Mild 8%, IPA 7% and Best Bitter 85%.

Equipping for survival

The closure of many breweries did have one good result for the companies that survived: a large amount of redundant brewing kit came up for sale. Harvey's had had no new equipment for 40 years and the mash tun was in a state of collapse. In 1954, when Page & Overton's Brewery in Croydon closed, Tony Jenner attended the sale of its equipment and found himself in competition with men from the scrap metal business. When the mash tun and grist case came under the hammer, Jenner and one dealer fought to buy it with considerable acrimony. At one stage the dealer shouted across the room at Jenner: 'You'll never bleedin' well place it!' The chairman of Charrington, the large London brewer, came to Jenner's defence, telling the men in the room: 'Gentlemen, I would have you know that Mr Jenner is not a dealer, he is a brewer and requires the plant to brew with at Lewes.' The dealer backed down and called out: 'Ah well, that's different, mate. Let 'im 'ave it!'

Subsequently, more kit was bought from a number of closed breweries and, together with a new refrigeration and filtration plant, Harvey's entered the 1960s with a modern and well-equipped brewery and bottling hall, essential requirements if it were to survive in a period of great difficulty. Bigger brewers were circling like sharks to buy and close smaller operators and Harvey's could feel their hot breath on its neck when Watneys bought the Brighton brewer Tamplin's in 1969.

Harvey's hunkered down. 'We survived because we wanted to,' the current chairman and joint managing director Hamish Elder says. 'We were approached on a monthly basis by bigger brewers who wanted to buy us but we posted a notice: "Not For Sale".'

Nevertheless, the brewery was forced to make concessions to survive in a fiercely competitive environment. The company had previously reached an agreement with Beard's, the other remaining Lewes brewery, to produce their beers while Beard's closed and became a wholesaler, supplying its pubs and the free trade. And in 1964 Harvey's took the momentous decision to move into keg production at a time when the likes of Watneys Red, Double Diamond and Worthington E were surging to success. Within four years, Sussex Keg Bitter accounted for a quarter of the brewery's production and, with bottled beers included, grew to 50 per cent.

Catastrophe and good fortune

In 1960, it was nothing short of a miracle that Harvey's was able to brew any beer at all as the plant was hit by a massive flood, with Cliffe High Street under water for close to a week. The brewery staff struggled on as best they could but there was serious disruption to the plant for some time, especially as the mill room is on the ground floor close to the river.

Harvey's had better fortune in 1968 when it won an unprecedented six prizes at the International Brewers' Exhibition in London. It was the biggest number of awards made to a brewery at the contest.

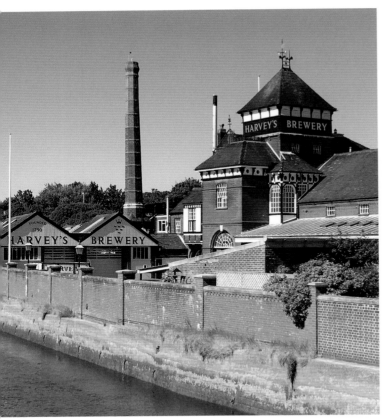

Three awards were for traditional draught beers, the remaining three for bottled beers, one of which won the prestigious Championship Gold Medal.

The awards received a great deal of media attention, which was repeated the following year when Watneys discontinued production of Tamplin's Sussex Bitter. Reporters asked Eric Rundle if he planned to phase out his traditional cask ales and whether, inevitably, the company would be swallowed by a national group. He replied pithily and in similar terms to Hamish Elder today: 'We survive because we want to. All the big firms have tried taking us and I have told them all the same thing: "Nothing doing, chum". Harvey's has nothing to fear or we should not be here now. We are doing quite nicely, thank you, and aim to stay that way.'

The tide turned dramatically for Harvey's and all other family brewers with the arrival of CAMRA in 1971. Miles Jenner recalls: 'By 1973 sales of our cask-conditioned beers were soaring and for a decade averaged a growth rate of 10 per cent a year. After years of austerity it was more than refreshing to see the fermenting room working to capacity and orders flooding in.'

To cope with the demand, the brewery had to be extended. Additional fermenting capacity was needed and three new 120-barrel vessels were installed in the 1970s and early 80s. Fermenting capacity doubled as a result and a second copper and a new hop back were also added. The final stage was building a second brewing line to meet the continuing surge in demand for cask beer. A new brewery tower and loading dock had to mirror the original design of William Bradford and, due to the careful use of cast iron and other building materials, the finished work was awarded a Civic Trust Commendation.

The brewery was hit by a further catastrophe in 1996 when a raging fire caused £2 million of damage to the offices and shop on the High Street. The office had to be temporarily moved to an empty restaurant across the road that is now the John Harvey Tavern. The damaged buildings were restored in 1998 but many crucial historic files were lost. To thank the fire brigade for their work in tackling the blaze, the brewery produced a special beer called Bonfire Boy.

Further devastation followed in 2000 when the Ouse flooded for a second time, with yet again £2 million of damage. An eyewitness recorded that the hop backs on the ground floor had just been filled with 50 barrels of wort when the Ouse smashed into the building. The insurers said the brewery wouldn't be back in operation for nine months but brewing started again within nine days, thanks to help from other breweries, such as Shepherd Neame in Kent. Beer that survived the flood was bottled by Shepherd Neame and sold as Ouse Booze, with the proceeds going to the Lewes Flood Appeal. Visitors to the brewery today can see the tide mark, more than six feet (1.8m) high, on the doors in the yard. A flood wall has now been built, which should prevent any repetition occurring.

Miles Jenner

History and the future in family hands

A tour of the brewery with Miles Jenner is a walk through brewing history. One wood-jacketed mash tun dates from 1926, the second from the same decade – and was the vessel Miles's father bought in the Croydon auction. A 60-barrel copper is a relative youngster from 1999, the second copper came from the long-closed Chelmsford brewer, Gray's. You clamber down narrow wooden stairs to the fermenting room, dating from the 1870s and built before the Bradford redesign. The room bursts with nose-tingling, fruity aromas as yeast turns wort into beer. There are 12 fermenters, ranging in size from 30 barrels to 120 with a total capacity of 1,000 barrels. Most of the vessels were producing Sussex Best, far and away the biggest brand. It was runner-up two years running in 2005 and 2006 in the Champion Beer of Britain competition.

'In the 1980s we were told we brewed the hoppiest beer in Britain,' Miles says. Sussex Best has 38 units of bitterness, modest by some modern IPAs, but still sufficient to tickle the taste buds. Miles uses Maris Otter as his base malt but buys all his hops from local growers in Kent, Surrey and Sussex. He uses Bramling Cross, Fuggles, Goldings and Progress in whole hop versions. His yeast is 60 years old and came from John Smith's in Tadcaster. As well as the regular beers, Miles has a programme of monthly seasonals, including wheat beer and stout, with a Christmas beer blessed by a local vicar.

The brewery has a capacity of 45,000 barrels but is currently using 80 per cent of that capacity. Miles Jenner says volumes are under pressure as a result of the intense competition from the new wave of smaller breweries, with between 65 and 70 in Sussex and a total of 150 if you include Kent and Surrey. Sales to the free trade account for 90 per cent of production. Harvey's owns 43 pubs: most are in Sussex, with the remainder in London, Surrey, Kent and Berkshire.

Harvey's core bottled range

SHIPWRECKED IMPERIAL TREASURE

Harvey's Imperial Extra Double Stout only accounts for 30 barrels a year and yet it's arguably the most fascinating beer in the brewery. It's a brilliant recreation of a style brewed in the 18th and 19th centuries by London brewers for export to Russia and the Baltic States.

The major brewer was Barclay Perkins, which later became Courage. When Courage discontinued production, the style became just a footnote to brewing history until a batch was discovered on the seabed. The consignment from London was on a Prussian boat called the *Oliva* that was shipwrecked in 1869. In 1974 divers brought bottles from the wreck to the surface and they were found to carry the mysterious name of A Le Coq. Research revealed this was a Belgian called Albert Le Coq who had earned a living exporting stout to Russia. He had been granted an imperial warrant from a grateful Tsar when he donated bottles of the stout to Russian soldiers wounded in the Crimean War. The warrant enabled the London brewers to call their export stouts 'Imperial'.

Early in the 20th century, Le Coq's company built a brewery in Tartu to increase the supply of stout and avoid tariffs on English exports. But following the Russian Revolution in 1917 the brewery was nationalised and converted to lager.

Back in England, Courage continued to brew small batches of Imperial Russian Stout until it became part of the Scottish &

Newcastle group, now Heineken UK, which stopped production.

An American import company, B United, approached Harvey's to see if the brewery would be interested in reviving the beer.

The Americans had managed to find descendants of Le Coq and were given carte blanche to brew the beer again. Lewes was the ideal town to launch the beer as in 1929 secret talks were held in the White Hart pub between representatives of the British and Soviet governments to explore the resumption of diplomatic relations between the two countries.

Miles Jenner spoke to a number of brewers, including some who had worked at Courage, to design an authentic recipe for the beer. Finally, in 1999 the first batch was brewed with Maris Otter pale malt, amber, brown and black malts, and hopped with East Kent Goldings and Fuggles. It was launched, fittingly, in the Russian Tea Rooms in New York City.

The bottle-conditioned beer has a driven cork stopper. Miles says early batches were bottled too soon and tended to explode. The beer is now kept in tank for a year before it's bottled. It has won many awards, including the World Beer Award and Champion Bottle-conditioned Beer in the Champion Beer of Britain competition. Sales are mainly domestic as there are many imperial stouts now produced in the United States.

It has a rich bouquet of vinous fruits, fresh leather, tobacco, smoky malt and peppery hops. Dark fruit, hop resins, liquorice and roasted grain dominate the palate, with a long and complex finish with warming alcohol, dark fruit, fresh tobacco, roasted grain and spicy hops to the fore.

The company remains firmly in the two families' hands, with chairman Hamish Elder a direct descendant of the founder, John Harvey, and Miles the son of Tony Jenner. Two of the eighth generation, Zoë Prescott and Peter Nicholas, work at the brewery in senior positions and there are four ninth generation family members waiting in the wings. Miles is a respected figure in the industry: he has been named Brewer of the Year by the Parliamentary Beer Group, Brewer of the Year by the British Guild of Beer Writers and has been given a special award by CAMRA for outstanding services to the brewing industry.

Miles and Hamish are determined there will be a brewery for their descendants to work in. Despite fierce competition and the imbalances of the current beer duty system, there are no plans to downsize to micro status. 'We would be destroying our heritage,' Miles Jenner says emphatically.

The Queen and Prince Philip, here being greeted by Hamish Elder and Miles Jenner, visited Harvey's in 2013 to start the mash for a batch of Elizabethan Ale, which is brewed to commemorate the coronation in 1953.

Harvey & Son, Bridge Wharf Brewery, 6 Cliffe High Street, Lewes, East Sussex BN7 2AH
01273 480209 · www.harveys.org.uk
Tours by arrangement. A brewery shop has beer to take away along with clothing and memorabilia.

Regular cask beers
Sussex XX Mild (3%)
IPA (3.5%)
Sussex Best Bitter (4%)
Old Ale (4.3%)
Olympia (4.3%)
Armada Ale (4.5%)

Bottle-conditioned beer
Imperial Extra Double Stout (9%)

Hamish Elder, chairman

McMullen

THE STORY of McMullen is a classic one of poacher turned gamekeeper. Early members of the family included one denounced as a 'rogue and a vagabond' while one son behaved so badly, he was sent packing to the United States and was never seen again. Scroll forward to the 20th and 21st centuries and all has changed, with the family honoured as pillars of the establishment. Several members won awards for bravery in the world wars and the family united after the Second World War to save the company from the threat of death duties and closure. Four generations, most recently David and Fergus McMullen, have served as High Sheriff of Hertfordshire and Deputy Lord Lieutenants.

Most importantly, McMullen has kept the beer flag flying in a county that once had 44 breweries but was reduced to just one before the rise of the new generation of small craft breweries. Today, as joint managing director Tom McMullen acknowledges, the company has to run hard to keep abreast of changing consumer preferences. Tom, Fergus's cousin, represents the sixth generation of the family to run the business, and his main task is to carefully expand the pub estate in East Anglia, London and the Home Counties. While McMullen is principally a managed house company and avoids running gastro pubs, Tom says food now plays an increasingly important role in attracting customers. The beer side of the company has changed out of all recognition in recent years. Sales of cask ale are in decline and a micro plant in Hertford produces a range of new styles to please the younger generation of drinkers.

Hard times in Hertford

As the name suggests, the McMullens are of Scottish and Irish origin. William McMullen was born in Co Down in 1756 and worked as a gardener for the Marquess of Downshire. When the marquess moved to Hertford, William followed and he was recorded in 1791 as a member of a fellowship society, a type of private social security system that supported members falling on hard times as there were no state handouts. William received his payments at the White Hart inn in Hertford, a pub the family would buy 118 years later. He and other recipients were told firmly they would be fined sixpence if they were found 'disguised by liquor' – a euphemism for being drunk.

Mill Bridge Brewery, Hartham Road

William sired 11 children. The eldest, James, drowned while it was Arthur McMullen who behaved so disgracefully that he was packed off to the US. Peter, the fourth son of the family, was apprenticed as a cooper but was dismissed in 1817 for 'neglect of duties and bad behaviour'. A year later he was fined £5 for poaching. His brother Charles was convicted for being 'a rogue and a vagabond' for 'being abroad', which probably meant being away from home rather than out of the country.

The first brews

Peter McMullen married Sarah Manning in 1820. She described Peter as 'a somewhat unruly lad in his youth' and while she attempted to 'steady him' he continued to flout the law. In 1827 he started to brew illegally without a licence in a house in Railway Street, Hertford, but with the passing of the Beer Act in 1830 he was able to brew legitimately with an annual payment of two guineas for a licence. Peter flourished as a brewer. In 1832 he bought land on the site of the current Woolpack pub and founded what he grandiloquently called the William IV Brewery, claiming to operate with the patronage of the king. The name honoured the monarch who signed the Beer Act into law but for Peter McMullen to claim royal patronage was stretching credulity.

Peter McMullen, founder

In an advertisement for the brewery, Peter went to war with other, older brewers in the area, saying 'he will challenge any monopolists of the old school or any of their minnows to sell at the same price a more wholesome, pleasant-flavoured, strength combined, clear, nutritional beverage, with all their artificial means and manoeuvres'.

Peter was a remarkable man for his time. He overcame hardship and poverty and became literate, articulate and successful at his new-found trade. In 1833, just one year after founding his brewery, he launched a beer called AK that became his flagship brew and it has remained McMullen's leading brand to this day (see p.82).

In the early 1840s, aware of developments in London and Burton upon Trent, he added IPA to his range. Though there is no evidence he engaged in the export market, he would have been aware of the East India Company, which handled trade with the sub-continent and whose administrators were trained in Hertford. With the River Lee at hand, Peter could have sent beer down to the East London Docks with ease, but the London brewers had the lucrative India trade locked for their sole benefit. Instead, Peter turned to his bucolic roots with a beer called Farmer's Ale launched in 1851, a beer that is still brewed today as No1 Pale Ale.

A growing business

When Peter McMullen retired in 1860, he passed to his sons Alexander and Osmond Henry a thriving brewing business with a small estate of four pubs. The brewery, with less braggadocio, had been renamed the more prosaic Mill Bridge Brewery, possibly because William IV hadn't been a respected monarch: he was known as the Sailor King as he spent more time on his yacht than on the throne. His legacy of the Beer Act had caused many problems, including increased drunkenness and beerhouses with a reputation for poor beer. Osmond H McMullen reflected the unpopularity of the 'Tom and Jerry' beerhouses when he attacked 'the indulgence of home-brewing, where cats make their beds in the pockets of hops and several rats are drowned in the fermenting square'.

The success of the brewery, now called P McMullen & Sons, can be measured by the vastly improved lifestyle of the family and the growth of the business. In 1887 Alexander, who was three times mayor of Hertford, moved with his family into the medieval splendour of Hertford Castle, where his grandfather had once worked as an itinerant gardener. His daughter Nora met and married Andrew Mellon, the American ambassador to Britain, US Treasury Secretary and owner of the Mellon Bank, but the marriage ended in divorce as Nora preferred the social life of Hertford to Pittsburgh.

In 1891, a new brewery was commissioned and was designed by the celebrated William Bradford, who also worked for Harvey's, Hook Norton and Tolly Cobbold. Three wells were sunk on the site at a depth of 140 feet (43m), the height of Nelson's Column in Trafalgar Square. The same water supply is used today, filtered through a natural chalk aquifer.

The 19th century ended with McMullen owning close to 100 pubs, including what became its flagship outlet in Hertford, the Salisbury Arms. It was brewing substantial amounts of beer to feed the pub estate and the main brands were AK and DS. DS stood for Double Stout, but its sales were hindered in the new century by the popularity of Guinness and eventually the Irish stout replaced DS in McMullen's pubs, a position Tom McMullen says he would love to reverse.

At the start of the 20th century, there were 30 breweries in Hertfordshire and McMullen had risen to become the second biggest, outgunned only by Benskins of Watford. The success was dented by discord between Alexander and Osmond H – the first but not the last family dispute. The row was over Alexander's handling of Peter McMullen's will, Peter having died in 1881. The dispute was settled by Osmond H buying Alexander's share of a business valued in total at £173,618, and turning the company into McMullen & Sons Ltd.

In common with all family brewers, the early years of the new century were lean ones for McMullen. Ownership had passed from Osmond H to his son Osmond Robert who was faced with increases in duty, cuts in the strength of beer, noisy opposition to drinking from the temperance movement and the absence of family members who were fighting the war overseas.

Drays old and new: top from the late 1920s, and below from 2020

The wartime activities of John McMullen must have been a source of inspiration for the Biggles adventure novels: the author, Captain WE Johns, was born in Bengeo, close to Hertford, and would have been well aware of the McMullen family's adventures and misadventures. John McMullen, aged 51 and already commissioned as an officer, applied to join the Royal Flying Corps, forerunner of the RAF, but was turned down on the grounds of age. He served instead as an ambulance driver at Gallipoli and was awarded the MBE. But he was determined to fly and he finally managed to join the RFC and was due to receive his 'wings' just as the war ended. Undaunted, he obtained a private pilot's licence aged 69 and in 1935, at the age of 72, became the first man to fly a gyrocopter across the Irish Sea.

When trading conditions improved in the 1920s, McMullen expanded its pub estate. In 1922 it bought the rival Hope Brewery in Hertford, with 20 pubs, and three years later built the Woolpack on the site where Peter McMullen had first started to brew. The brewery began its move into London, where it is now firmly established. In 1927 it bought the Nag's Head in Covent Garden for £7,500 – £406,000 in today's money. The imposing, multi-storey pub opposite the Underground station, worth millions today, had a complicated history. It was leased to Whitbread and wasn't fully operated by McMullen until 1982. The brewery also bought the Stafford Hotel in Green Park in 1927 for £27,500.

In the mid-1930s a bottling line was installed at the brewery. This enabled McMullen to develop a

AK – WHAT'S IN A NAME?

In 1933, McMullen celebrated 100 years of brewing its main beer, AK. It remains its core draught ale while the name continues to intrigue both drinkers and writers. There have been some fanciful notions about the name, such as misspellings All Klear and All Korrect.

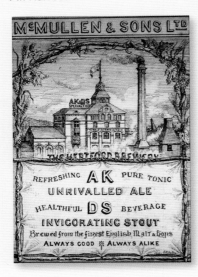

But the most likely reason for the name is simple: cask marks.

In Victorian Britain, before marketing and branding, brewers branded their wooden casks with simple markings for their beers. Worthington E, for example, was the result of the Burton brewer giving its range of cask beers branding marks from A to E.

A number of breweries, including Fremlins in Kent, produced beers called AK. Most brewers produced more than one version of both mild and bitter beers and branded them with either Xs or Ks.

AK indicated the first in a range of milds. In the case of McMullen, AK was a 'light mild', with an amber colour, in sharp contrast to darker versions of the style.

To further confuse the matter, McMullen rebranded AK in the 1980s as bitter, but in 2019 it went back to basics and new pumpclips proclaim it as 'Original Mild'.

new income stream, but with its growing tied estate draught beer remained its core business. The importance of draught beer was measured by the Woodman pub in Welwyn Garden City, which sold 1,400 barrels in 1939.

Future threatened

Colonel Peter McMullen returned from the Second World War to lead the brewery and was soon embroiled in a dispute that threatened the very future of the business. New inheritance tax rules introduced by the government meant that Revenue & Customs made such swingeing demands on Osmond R's estate that some members of the family said there was no alternative but to sell the brewery and pubs, and cease operations. Peter McMullen refused. He said the family had a duty to its workers, many of whom had, like him, served their country in the war.

Fortunately, for all those who relied on the business for their jobs, the wartime record of four cousins, who had been decorated with many awards for gallantry along with one knighthood, created a formidable challenge for the taxman. In order to meet the demands of the tax authorities, Peter McMullen sold his family home and contents. They were, he said, 'desperate times'. Fortunately, inheritance tax was scaled down and the family was able to settle the bill in 1956. The Stafford Hotel in London was a later casualty, sold to fund the required working capital of the business, which was on its knees.

With worrying times behind them, family and brewery were able to grasp all the new opportunities of the post-war world. In 1954 the company moved into the off-licence trade, which would eventually account for sales of 10 million bottles a year. There was considerable investment in the brewery. Peter McMullen was a forward thinker in all areas of the business. As well as responding to demands for keg beer and lager, he argued the case for modernising pubs, saying as early as the 1960s that they had to move from being drinking dens for working men and open up to families who wanted good food as well as alcohol. Both he and his successors, though, have maintained areas in their pubs where people can just enjoy a good pint, and the brewery still has a number of 'wet pubs' for dedicated drinkers.

John McMullen, who joined the business in 1953, led the response to changing demand for both cask and keg beer. £300,000 was spent in 1968 on a new bottling hall and a kegging plant was added three years later. By the time the company celebrated its 150th anniversary in 1977, it owned 162 pubs and turnover passed £10 million for the first time, with profits of £1.2 million. As a sign of the times, a second kegging plant was added in 1978, three years after McMullen launched its first lager, Steingold, with conical fermenters making an appearance at the brewery. But traditional beer was not ignored and Country Best Bitter had been introduced in 1964, adding a more robust companion to AK in the brewery's pubs.

In 1982 McMullen finally got total control of the Nags Head in Covent Garden, giving it a totemic outlet for its own beers, rather than Whitbread's, in

The Nags Head, in London's Covent Garden

the heart of London. Two years later, the Spice of Life at Cambridge Circus in London's theatreland joined the estate. The pub is decked out with fascinating photos of leading actors and memorabilia of the stage. The only setback in a period of dynamic growth was a law in 1974 banning retail price maintenance. This led to massive undercutting of prices in several areas, including food and drink, and McMullen responded by selling its off-licences.

The family refreshes itself

In 1978, David McMullen was encouraged by Colonel McMullen to leave a career in the City and join the brewery. He was followed in 1984 by Fergus McMullen, who was well versed in the drinks business after working with the leading cider maker, Bulmers. Both were to play vital roles in helping the brewery survive at a time of profound change in the industry at the end of the 20th century.

The Beer Orders, which flowed from the Thatcher government's review of the brewing industry in the late 1980s (see p.11), saw the national brewers leave the industry, to be replaced by pub companies with a strategy of selling mainly national brands bought with heavy discounts from national suppliers. The impact on regional and family brewers was severe, with a number deciding the game was no longer worth the candle and closing down. In 2002, some members of the McMullen family wanted to follow suit and argued

the case for selling up and retiring on the proceeds. After more than 170 years of making fine beer and running a wide range of pubs, the only brewery left in the county town of Hertfordshire was on the brink of closing.

The fightback was led by David McMullen, at first from a minority position. His strength was that many of his supporters in the family worked or had worked at the brewery. As with the trials and tribulations of the post-war tax affair, there was mutual loyalty between shareholders and employees, forged from working together on a daily basis. David, who spent a vast amount of time dealing with the media, who were convinced McMullen was finished, won the day. A compromise was reached, the opponents were paid off and the brewery continued in business.

But the business was to continue in a very different manner. In 2004 McMullen downsized beer production dramatically. The management closed the Hartham Road site and moved a short distance to a much smaller new plant at Old Cross, designed by Fergus McMullen and head brewer Chris Evans. The assumption was that the company had reduced production to around 10,000 barrels a year in order to qualify for the new lower levels of duty brought in by the Labour government's Progressive Beer Duty (PBD).

Tom McMullen counters this argument. 'We had a brewery with a 60,000-barrel capacity at a time when

Tom, Fergus and Alex

overcapacity and a shift in bargaining strength meant supermarkets were starting to squeeze the margin out of production, particularly for weaker brands. The smoking ban also led to a decline in beer drinking in our pubs. Quite simply, we couldn't fill the brewery in a profitable manner. PBD was a subsequent benefit but it wasn't the rationale for the move.'

The old brewery had featured in an episode of *Inspector Morse*. Ironically, it was portrayed as a big brewery attempting to close down an older and more traditional one, represented by and filmed at Brakspear in Henley-on-Thames. The Hartham Road site was sold to Sainsbury in 2007 and the sheer size of the supermarket gives an indication of how big the old brewery was.

Undaunted by the changes in brewing, McMullen continued to buy pubs and to build new ones, some a distance from Hertford, such as the Prince George in Milton Keynes. It continued to expand its London base with the Lord Moon of the Mall in Whitehall.

Tom McMullen joined the brewery in 2010. Before working in corporate tax law, he had cleared land mines in the army in Somalia, Afghanistan and other war zones, a useful training, you might think, for dealing with the turbulence of the modern brewing industry and pub trade. In 2016 he was joined by his brother Alexander who had worked for Price Waterhouse Coopers in London and was an experienced accountant. A new generation was taking over the reins.

Awards and breathers

Despite a rocky period, the brewery won several awards. Macs No 1 bottled beer won a gold medal in the Monde Sélection competition in 1991 and in 1995 it was named the top British brewery by the Parliamentary Beer Club. Two years later Stronghart won the barley wine category in CAMRA's Champion Beer of Britain competition and in 2010 Country was named Champion Beer of East Anglia.

The CAMRA awards were all the more pleasing as the brewery and the campaigning group had had a long-running dispute, lasting 24 years, over the use of a device known as the cask breather. Instead of being vented to the atmosphere, casks are attached to cylinders of carbon dioxide. As CO_2, produced by secondary fermentation, leaves the cask it's replaced by an equal volume of gas from the cylinder. McMullen argued that the breather stopped beer oxidising and

going stale while CAMRA responded that the system stopped beer developing properly and could taste 'green' or immature.

The brewery's use of breathers led to it being barred from the Great British Beer Festival and its pubs were not listed in the *Good Beer Guide*. The dispute was finally settled in 2018 when CAMRA's annual meeting lifted the ban on the system. Nick Boley, a member of CAMRA's national executive who is responsible for technical matters, said: 'I've tried to work out the chemistry of why cask breathers were wrong. I couldn't and I'm still scratching my head.'

The new plant at Old Cross is called the Whole Hop Brewery. Production director Fergus McMullen and head brewer Chris Evans both believe passionately that the whole flower of the hop plant delivers better bitterness and aroma than pellets or oils. Only English hops – Fuggles, Progress and Whitbread Goldings Variety – are used in the cask ales with the exception of IPA which has Cascade, Dana, Mount Hood and Summit. Exotic imported hop flavours are found in the new range of craft keg beers and lager that come from a micro plant within the brewery. Known as Rivertown, the range includes Pale Ale, Pilsner and Eight Hop Beer.

The family mission is to revive the fortunes of cask beer. 'We're fighting back but turning round the cask ship is a long process,' Tom McMullen says. All his pubs must sell cask beer, but he points to the problem faced with sales figures for one of the company's leading outlets, the Peahen in St Albans. This handsome, galleried old coaching inn in the city centre and close to Roman Watling Street, sells twice as much keg beer as cask, with a keg IPA the top seller along with imported lagers.

'The challenge comes from strongly-hopped American-style keg beers,' Tom says. 'Will drinkers come back to cask? We've got to engage younger drinkers. But the likes of AK, IPA and Stronghart have to survive. They are our heritage.'

McMullen & Sons, The Whole Hop Brewery, 26 Old Cross, Hertford SG14 1RD · 01992 584911 www.mcmullens.co.uk

Tours available.

Regular cask beers:

AK (3.7%)

Cask Ale (3.8%)

Country Bitter (4.3%)

IPA (4.8%)

Hook Norton

1849 · OXFORDSHIRE

WHENEVER I visit the Hook Norton Brewery, I'm reminded of that old Gene Kelly musical *Brigadoon* about a Scottish Highland village that mysteriously appears for just one day every 100 years.

The brewery is an equally magical experience. To find it you drive through the picture-postcard village of Hook Norton in Oxfordshire – all winding narrow streets with many thatched cottages built of local ironstone – until you find the Pear Tree Inn.

You turn up Brewery Lane and suddenly out of a mist of steam and inviting aromas of malt and hops you are confronted by one of the most enduring and inspiring visions of brewery architecture, the Victorian tower brewery of Hook Norton.

The first brewery dates from 1849 and was built by a farmer, John Harris. He grew grain and malted it to supply pubs in the area that brewed their own ale. It's likely that Harris also brewed on his farm for his family and labourers. In 1856 he installed fermenters and other equipment and he became a serious brewer as well as maltster.

Harris the brewer flourished. It may seem remarkable and even incongruous that a brewery existed in this rural idyll, but in the late 19th century the Industrial Revolution was going full throttle. The brewery had not only farm labourers in abundance eager to drink its beer, but the village also had an ironstone quarry that produced building materials between 1884 and 1948. The railway came to the village in 1887,

the line dug out of hills by an army of navvies with an insatiable need for refreshment. Today, the quarry and the railway line are both long gone.

By 1872, Harris had built a three-storey brewery on the farm and when he passed the business to his relations, the Clarkes, they commissioned the leading brewery architect of the day, William Bradford (see also Harvey's), to construct the present majestic site.

John Harris, founder

The massive expansion underway in the 1890s

A rich history

The new brewery buildings, now Grade II-listed, opened in 1900, a fitting year to launch a new plant for a new century. Visitors today can revel in the marvels of an old steam engine, and oak-lined mash tuns and coppers. The Buxton & Thornley engine was installed in 1899 and for many years it was the heartbeat of the brewery, huffing and puffing as it drove the mill that ground the malt, then sent brewing water and grain to the mash tuns, coppers and fermenters. Today it's used as back-up, but it's switched on for the first Saturday of the month for visitors to see and admire.

Brewing vessels have changed over the years, with some acquired from companies that have fallen by the wayside. The current mash tun, where malt is mixed with pure hot water to start the brewing process, came from Ruddles of Rutland. The copper, where the wort is boiled with hops, was bought from another defunct and famous brewery, Flowers of Cheltenham, which used the head of Shakespeare as its logo, recalling his words in *The Winter's Tale* that 'a quart of ale is a dish for a king'.

The most fascinating piece of kit lies beneath the brewery roof. It's an open wort cooler or coolship (see also Elgood's p.61). It's no longer in use but was used to cool the hopped wort prior to fermentation. The wort was pumped to the top of the brewery and settled in the large open pan. Louvred windows allowed cool breezes to enter and lower the temperature.

Managing director and former head brewer James Clarke says: 'It's astonishing to think we were using

The Buxton & Thornley steam engine installed in 1899

The coolship is no longer in use

As I approached the brewery on my most recent visit, right on cue the Hook Norton brewery dray appeared with a driver in traditional garb that includes a bowler hat. The delivery that day was being made to the Pear Tree down the lane, scarcely an arduous trip, but the four dray horses stabled on site can travel

further, taking beer to some of Hook Norton's 47 mainly rural pubs. One horse is called Roger – but not in my honour.

While the brewery is firmly rooted in its rich history, it's not living in the past. James Clarke is a member of the founding family and has worked at the brewery for close to 30 years. He became head brewer in 1998 and then managing director following the death of his father. He is busily expanding the business, not only developing a range of new beers

the coolship to try and keep a clean, uninfected wort while across the Channel in Belgium the same type of vessel is used to inoculate wort with wild yeasts to make lambic beer. It's a better use of the kit but a couple of our brewers want to try it out again.'

Today, when the wort has been cooled it drops down several storeys into fermenting vessels. They are a joy to behold, circular wooden vessels known as 'rounds', the staves held in place by great iron hoops.

A spacious reception area next to the brewery is based in the original maltings. It houses a shop, a small museum dedicated to the brewery and the village, and a bar where visitors can sample both regular and seasonal beers.

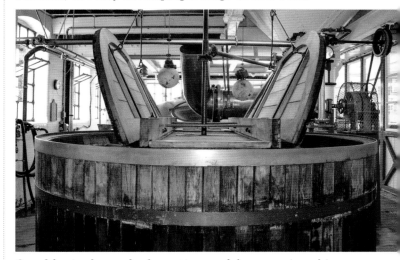

One of the circular wooden fermenting vessels knowns as 'rounds'

but also offering facilities for visitors to tour the site, eat in an elegant dining room called the Malthouse Kitchen and – if the fancy takes them – brew their own beer on a 3½ barrel pilot plant.

'We've spent £150,000 developing the restaurant with a fully fitted kitchen,' James says, 'and we're planning to get a licence for weddings to be held at the brewery. The visitor centre and tours are doing well – our provenance is important to the business. We're also investing in our pubs to improve the quality of both food and drink.'

Celebrating the diversity of beer

The biggest change is the beer range. For years, the brewery produced mild, bitter and the premium Old Hooky – both the brewery and its beers are known to its devotees as Hooky. But now James and his team are creating 50 to 60 different beers a year. They're not all regular brews. New beers are trialled on the pilot plant and if customers like them they become regular or seasonal members of the portfolio. Cotswold Pale is a case in point.

Hook Norton's production of 15,000 barrels a year is split 75 per cent draught and 25 per cent bottle. Keg now accounts for 5 per cent of draught and James says that will grow as a result of demand from publicans. It's the first time in its long history that the brewery has produced keg beer, but the world is changing. 'Cask beer is the best drink in the world when it's right,'

James says. 'But there are too many brands today and that leads to slower throughput, wrong temperatures and poor hygiene. The quality of cask beer needs focus and attention.'

To help with that focus, the recently created Barm Cellar holds regular training sessions to improve cellar and bar skills for publicans: barm is a brewers' term for yeast.

The demand for keg beer comes from Hook Norton's own pubs, which account for 15 per cent of sales, along with the free trade: the brewery delivers within a 50-mile radius. While most of the pubs are in rural settings, Hook Norton has a showplace outlet in Oxford, the Castle. It offers the brewery's cask and keg range along with guests from the likes of Tiny Rebel and XT, as well as the famous Czech lager Pilsner Urquell.

James smiles if you mention the big debate over the merits of cask and keg and what constitutes 'craft beer'. He thinks that's a metropolitan discussion among the chattering classes. 'The country is different to the town,' he says. 'People who go to our pubs won't sip a few halves – they will have several pints.'

James Clarke, managing director and former head brewer

Drinkers can choose from a permanent cask range of Hooky Mild, Hooky Bitter, Hooky Gold and Old Hooky, with the superb Double Stout among the monthly seasonal range. Keg beers include Cotswold Pale, Red Rye and a Black IPA.

James says he has noticed a growing interest in darker beers, which encourages him to stay true to Hooky Mild. It accounts for just five per cent of annual production, but he says it remains a core brand. 'At 2.8 per cent, it's a good lunchtime drink,' he points out.

The cask ales are brewed – as they have been for decades – with Maris Otter, the choicest and juiciest pale malt, and Challenger, Fuggles and Goldings hops in whole flower form. Coloured malts are added, according to individual recipes. They have been joined in recent years by 15 different malts and hops from Germany, New Zealand and the United States.

James is keen to build his relationship with beer drinkers. As well as brewery tours, members of the public can become brewers for a day and use the pilot plant to fashion their own beers. 'They get two nine-gallon firkins to take home when the beer is ready,' he says. They work hard for their beers, he adds, as they have to shovel the spent grain out of the mash tun when the brew is finished.

Hook Norton is well set for the future. As well as 50 staff, James employs his two sons at the brewery and one is going on the Brewers' Apprenticeship Scheme. The dynasty will endure and James is determined to produce beers for a wide and discriminating audience. 'We've got to celebrate the diversity of beer,' he says. 'We're 20 years behind the wine industry.'

It is catching up fast though, thanks to the efforts of breweries such as Hook Norton. As I drive back down Brewery Lane, I glance behind me. Already the old tower brewery is beginning to fade in the steam generated by the brewhouse. But I fancy, like Brigadoon, it will still be there in 100 years' time.

Hook Norton Brewery, Brewery Lane, Scotland End, Hook Norton, Oxon OX15 5NY
01608 737210
www.hooky.co.uk
Brewery tours available.

Regular cask beers:
Hooky Mild (2.8%)
Hooky Bitter (3.5%)
Hooky Gold (4.1%)
Old Hooky (4.6%)

Everards

EVERARDS is the beating heart of Leicestershire, deeply rooted in the county's history, life and sporting endeavour. The company dates from 1849: it has a long and proud heritage but it's vigorously facing the challenges of today's world.

It has had a peripatetic existence. It started life in Leicester city centre, opened a second brewery in Burton upon Trent in Staffordshire at the height of the pale ale frenzy of Victorian times, and moved to a new site at Castle Acres in Leicestershire in 1985.

William Everard, founder

The ultra-modern brewery, designed to produce a wide range of beer styles, was twice expanded. But the second decade of the 21st century forced chairman Richard Everard and his managing director Stephen Gould to face the commercial reality of the times. In common with all the family brewers, they found themselves squeezed by the global companies at one end and the burgeoning small 'craft' sector at the other. A brewery capable of producing 70,000 barrels a year was too big and a change of strategy, concentrating on its pub estate and disposing of its free trade business, has led to a carefully planned move to a purpose-built new site. Everards Meadows, still under construction in 2020 at a cost of £5.4 million, is due to open in spring 2021 and will house a new brewery with a capacity of 16,000 annual barrels, plus a beer hall and shop for visitors.

Great foresight

The family ancestors would be delighted that their brewery has maintained its links with Leicester and the wider county. The Everards are an ancient clan stretching back to the time of the Norman invasion in 1066. The name stems from 'ever', meaning a wild boar, once a common sight in the countryside, and suggests a pugnacious and determined character. The family became yeoman farmers, but in the 19th century William Everard witnessed the rapid changes taking place as a result of the Industrial Revolution, with thirsty mill and factory workers desperate for refreshment. With great foresight, William left his farm in Narborough in 1849 and went into partnership with a maltster, Thomas Hull, to buy the Wilmot Brewery on Southgate Street in Leicester.

To use a modern expression, William Everard chimed with the times. Leicester was expanding at a fast pace with new factories making hosiery and shoes, using canals and the railway to sell their products at home and abroad. William was the driving force at the brewery and within a few years he had established such a successful business that by 1875 demand outstripped the ability of the plant to produce sufficient beer. William commissioned his nephew John Everard, an architect, to design a new and bigger brewery, still on Southgate Street.

William died in 1892 aged 71 and he bequeathed an efficient brewery with 40 pubs to his descendants. The brewery utilised the new technologies heralded by the Industrial Revolution. In 1901 a magazine called *Modern Leicester* painted a vivid portrait of the new enterprise: 'The brewery is what is technically known as a 30-quarter plant brewery equipped with mash tuns, coppers, coolers and refrigerators while the fermenting vessels are provided with temperators, parachutes, and every appliance to facilitate the work and ensure it is being performed in a steady and reliable manner.' The report added that only the finest English malts and hops were used while pure water was drawn from a 300-feet (91m) deep artesian well. The range of beers included an India Pale Ale 'of a bright amber colour, particularly pleasing to the palate, and tasting well of the hops, and the famed Diamond Ale, a full-flavoured nutritious beverage.' Their Stout was also 'well spoken of by the medical profession for its purity and its nourishing qualities.'

Everards' brewery had adopted modern techniques with a zeal equal to that of the great pale ale breweries in Burton upon Trent. Brewing was now an all-year-round activity, with temperators – copper piping containing cold water – controlling the temperature of fermentation, while parachutes were devices that

Everards' brewery, Southgate Street, 1925

cropped excess yeast from the top of the fermenting vessels.

William Everard was succeeded by his son Thomas, who formed a new partnership with a local wine merchant, Charles Welldon. Once again, Everard was the leading figure and in 1899 the partnership was amicably dissolved. From then on, the brewery was known simply as Everards, with the family the sole owners. By now it had 70 pubs and was branching out of the city into the country areas of Leicestershire.

The success of Everards can be measured by Thomas's lavish lifestyle. He moved his family from one large estate to another, finally settling at Bradgate House, the seat of the Earls of Stamford and Warrington. The house required a large staff of servants, including a head coachman and groom who would drive Thomas to the brewery every day in a pony and trap even after the family bought its first car.

The rush to Burton

Before the partnership with Welldon ended, the decision was taken to open a second brewery in Burton upon Trent in 1892. This was not unprecedented. Burton, despite its small size, had become the world's leading brewing town as a result of the clamour for

India Pale Ale. Burton's domination of the pale ale trade was due to the remarkable qualities of the sulphate-rich waters of the Trent Valley. The sulphates acted as flavour enhancers and drew out the full malt and hops character of the world's first pale beers. Before water could be scientifically treated, brewers from London, Liverpool and Manchester hurried to Burton to establish plants there in order to produce pale ales with the required aromas and palates that drinkers, at home and abroad, expected. When Everards joined the rush to Burton, it took over a site that had been run by the Manchester brewer Henry Boddington. It was called the Bridge Brewery as it stood on an island in the River Trent adjacent to the bridge that carried travellers into the town: Everards could not have been closer to the source of Burton's watery success.

As Everards already brewed a popular IPA in Leicester, it may seem odd that the company was keen to produce another version of the style in Burton. But such was the acclaim for Burton-brewed beer that Everards would have been keen to brand its new products 'Burton Ales'. To be in the same town as the likes of Allsopp, Bass and Worthington gave the new brews a considerable cachet.

Everards flourished in Burton. The Bridge Brewery had a capacity of 10,000 barrels a year, but the company soon needed to expand to meet demand. Thomas

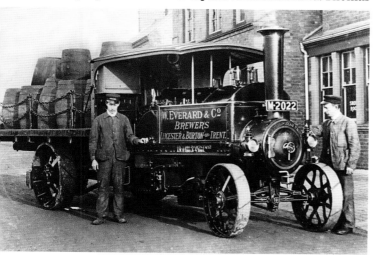

Everards' dray, early 20th century

Sykes was a Liverpool brewer who had built the Trent Brewery in Burton in 1881. When the brewery went into liquidation in 1896, Thomas Everard leased the buildings two years later and closed the Bridge site. The move was so successful that within three years Thomas bought the freehold of the Trent Brewery for £9,000. It was renamed the Tiger Brewery in 1970, cementing Everards' relationship with Leicester and its famous rugby club. Until the 1920s, when it switched to steam-driven lorries, the brewery transported beer from Burton to Leicester by train to supply its pubs in the city and the wider county.

A difficult period

As the Introduction shows, the First World War saw unprecedented increases in beer duty to help the war effort, along with restrictions on both pub opening hours and the strength of beer. The war was followed by an economic recession that led to brewery mergers and closures. Everards rode out the storm and in 1920–21 brewed more than 55,000 barrels of beer. That output wouldn't be exceeded for several decades as a further recession, with three million unemployed, took its toll in the two decades that preceded another world war.

Thomas Everard was succeeded at the brewery by his son William Lindsay Everard, who was later knighted and was elected as a Conservative Member of Parliament. He had to steer the brewery through the difficult period of the 1930s, with the threat of a new world war looming. The government, racked by the deep recession, raised excise duty by a penny a pint in 1931. This led to a serious fall in beer sales across the country. Everards was not immune, with its sales plummeting by a fifth. As a result, and with Southgate Street under threat from a new inner-city ring road, the decision was taken to end brewing in Leicester and concentrate production at Burton.

The Burton brewery's main products were Best Mild, Bitter and Best Bitter, with Mild the best seller and a firm favourite with industrial workers at the time. Sales of Everards' beers had started to pick up in the late 1930s, but the recovery was short-lived.

The Second World War, in common with the Great War, saw rationing of grain for brewers and hop production was restricted by both German bombing in the hop-growing region of Kent and land being commandeered for vegetable production. Beer was once again a convenient milch cow to help fund the war effort. Duty was doubled when war broke out and was increased in every year of the war.

Everards in one respect fared better than brewers in other parts of the country. Burton escaped being bombed and the breweries there emerged unscathed from the war. Others were less lucky: Boddingtons must have wished they had remained in Burton as their Manchester plant was destroyed. Six London breweries were put out of action and Ind Coope in Romford, Essex, not far from the East London docks, was attacked six times.

A major overhaul

The post-war world was a vastly different place to the first four decades of the century. When Sir Lindsay Everard died in 1949, he was succeeded by his son Tony who energetically threw himself into modernising all aspects of the brewery and its pubs. He believed that, as Everards was a family concern, all members of staff should be more actively involved in running the company. Social clubs were set up, including a Quarter Century Club for those who had worked at Everards for 25 years or more, while an annual dinner dance was held for all employees, with entertainment provided by the top bands of the day.

Society was changing. Young people had fresh ideas and no longer adopted their parents' attitudes to food and drink, while women increasingly challenged the 'men only' design of many pubs. Tony Everard responded with a major overhaul of the pub estate. Spit and sawdust went out and comfortable furnishings, warm decor and floral displays inside and out welcomed families. These Friendly Inns were complemented by several new pubs in Leicester that replaced those demolished to make way for the new ring road in the 1960s. By 1967, the company owned 125 pubs and hotels.

Beer was changing, too. In 1972 Everards bowed to the promotion of keg beer with its own version, Tiger Special, the name reflecting the fame of the Leicestershire Regiment and its long service in India before independence, and the equally acclaimed rugby club also known as the Tigers. Two years later Everards launched its own lager, Sabre, which soon accounted for a quarter of the brewery's production. But the dominance of brands and mass marketing led to Sabre being replaced by the Danish beer Tuborg.

In 1978, the pub estate grew to 150, boosted by the acquisition of more than 20 pubs from Ruddles. The arrival of CAMRA in the 1970s saw keg beer go into rapid decline and the brewery responded by launching a new traditional cask ale, Old Original. It was the first Everards' beer to be advertised on television, fronted by the actor and comedian Bill Maynard who lived in Sapcote in Leicestershire. In 1982, the quality of Old Original was recognised when it won two awards at the London Beer Festival: Gold in the strong ale class and then the supreme championship gold medal in competition with 70 beers entered by 49 breweries. The brewery's other beers – Mild, Beacon and Tiger – were also made available on handpump.

The return to Leicester

The success of Old Original was tinged with sadness for it was clear to the company that the Tiger Brewery in Burton, now more than 100 years old, needed a major and costly overhaul. In 1979 the company had bought 132 acres of land close to the M1 at Grove Farm in Leicester, with plans to build a new office and warehouse complex. Torn between updating the Burton plant and building a new brewery, the decision was taken to move some production to a new brewery at Grove Farm, which was renamed Castle Acres. In March 1985, the Chancellor of the Exchequer, Nigel Lawson, who was also a local MP, opened the first phase of the new brewhouse, which had the capacity to brew 12,500 barrels of Old Original a year. In Burton, a National Brewery Museum Trust was formed to run the Tiger Brewery as the country's

Castle Acres

PICK UP A PENGUIN

In sharp contrast to Castle Acres, Everards opened a tiny, 40-barrel brewery on the Falkland Islands in 1983 to mark the end of the conflict and to supply locally brewed beer to the islanders. It was the locals who decided, with a touch of irony, that it should be called the Penguin Brewery and they suggested, recalling a famous advertising jingle for a chocolate bar, that drinkers could 'Pick up a Penguin'.

The brewery was officially opened by the Governor of the Falklands, Sir Rex Hunt, in February 1983. The only beer was a cask-conditioned Penguin Ale. Unfortunately, as the army garrison on the islands was reduced, the brewery proved to be uneconomic and Everards closed the plant in 1986. Since then, a microbrewery, Beerworks, has opened, run by a local electrician.

only working brewery museum. Everards gave the trust a fixed-term contract to brew its other ales.

Over the ensuing five years, Castle Acres was expanded, and by 1990 it had an impressive capacity of 70,000 barrels. All the Everards' beers were not only under one roof but, equally important, were also back in Leicester.

Tony Everard had no children to follow him, but in 1977 his nephew Richard Everard joined the company after army service. Richard went on to become company chairman at a time of great challenges and upheavals in the brewing industry and pub trade following the Monopolies Commission Report and the government Beer Orders, which effectively ended the reign of the 'Big Six' national breweries. With the arrival of large non-brewing pub companies owning more than half the country's pubs, the remaining independent family brewers either improved their performance or ran the risk of going out of business.

A new philosophy

Richard Everard and his vastly experienced managing director Nick Lloyd developed what they called a new philosophy for the brewery, based on its strong family identity. A new corporate image was launched, featuring the image of William Everard and the founding year of 1849. In 1997, all preference shares were brought back and Everards became a fully private company again.

Richard Everard

In the late 1980s and early 90s the considerable sum of close to £20 million was invested in reinvigorating the pub estate with a greater emphasis on food and contemporary design, while several pubs were redeveloped to provide accommodation.

The beer range was also given new branding and their success was boosted by several significant awards in the 1990s. At the start of the decade, Beacon Bitter received trophies from both the Brewing Industry International Awards and CAMRA's Champion Beer of Britain competition. In 1998, Tiger Best Bitter won a gold medal in the BBI awards.

The year 1999 brought celebrations to mark 150 years of the company. The Duke of Edinburgh unveiled a plaque in the brewery's visitor centre to commemorate the anniversary and a special cask ale, Tiger Gold, was brewed for the year.

In the new century, Richard Everard formed a dynamic partnership with Stephen Gould, who joined

REACHING OUT TO BREWERS AND DRINKERS

Richard and Stephen say that in the fast-changing world of beer it's necessary to think like a microbrewery, be fast on your feet and plan 30 years ahead. With that in mind, in 2007 Everards launched one of the most innovative and unusual pub plans ever seen in the industry. It's called Project William in honour of the founder and enables the company to run a group of pubs in which other brewers can sell their beers.

'It raised a few eyebrows,' Stephen Gould says. 'People wondered why we would want to work with competitors and allow them to sell their beer in our pubs. But we view them as partners and collaborators and we're also keen to save as many pubs as possible from closure.'

'The partner brewers know pubs outside our trading area,' Richard Everard adds. 'We've had a close relationship with Titanic Brewery in Stoke-on-Trent for many years, which means we can sell our beer in the Potteries.'

Under the Project William scheme, Everards buys a pub and rents it to a partner brewer. Rent is based on capital invested and, in some cases, turnover and there's a supply agreement that means selected Everards' beers are on the bar alongside the partner's brews. The first pub in the scheme in 2007 was the Greyhound in Newcastle-under-Lyme, which had been closed for three years. It's surrounded by housing and Everards was convinced it had a good future. The pub cost £145,000

and a further £150,000 was spent on refurbishment. It reopened under the stewardship of Titanic and has been a roaring success since day one.

There are now 25 Project William pubs, the latest of which is Bod Trentham, more of a modern café bar than traditional pub, again run by Titanic (see also Titanic p.269). Project William is popular with CAMRA, not too surprising as around 63 per cent of beer sales in the pubs are accounted for by cask ale. Other breweries involved in Project William include Ashover, B&T, Lincoln Green, Rowton and Hop & Stagger.

To those who queried the viability of the scheme, Everards points to the hard, economic facts: in many cases, weekly takings in the pubs have grown from £3,500 to £14,000.

Stephen Gould

as trade director in 2003 and was promoted to managing director two years later. Stephen had worked with Bass and Punch Taverns and, as a native of Burton upon Trent, has a passion for beer and pubs. Richard and Stephen drove the company into the 21st century with a new focus. Cask ales remain the core of the business and their branding was updated, with a golden ale, Sunchaser, added to Beacon Hill, Tiger and Old Original. The brewery has increased its involvement with Leicester Tigers rugby club, signing a 10-year supply agreement that means home crowds of more than 20,000 can enjoy Tiger Bitter. The brewery also partners Leicester Riders basketball club, where again a captive audience can sample the ales.

In 2006, the company sold its core free trade business in order to focus on its pub estate. With cask ales central to its work, Everards is determined to offer beer in tip-top condition. As Stephen Gould says, you can monitor quality in your own pubs but it's more difficult if your beer is on sale in Exeter.

Cooperation and partnership are key words where the new brewery is concerned. As well as the Everards'

core range, the brewing team work with such breweries as Brunswick, Lincoln Green, Raw and Titanic to fashion a wide range of limited-edition beers: 18 new beers were produced in 2018. At the new site, there will be a pilot plant with a 4½-barrel brew length, which will enable short-run beers to be trialled. The flexibility of the main brewery will allow lager to be brewed, with a four-week maturation time. Keg beer can also be produced if the market demands, but Richard and Stephen believe cask ale will recover from the downturn of 2018 and will remain central to their business.

Everards Meadows is American and Australian in concept. The Beer Hall is a tap room where visitors can eat and drink and watch the brewing process.

Not only is the brewery fit for the future, but so is the family. Richard's son and daughter, Julian and Charlotte, are non-executive directors and Julian will eventually become chairman when his father retires.

Everards is back where it belongs in Leicestershire and looks with confidence to the future.

Charlotte, Richard and Julian Everard at the official ground breaking of the new brewery site, February 2019

Everards: office at Devana Avenue, Optimus Point, Glenfield, Leicester LE3 8JS · 0116 201 4100
www.everards.co.uk

Regular cask beers:
Beacon Hill (3.8%)
Sunchaser (4%)
Tiger Best Bitter (4.2%)
Old Original (5.2%)

KING COTTON AND BEER

THWAITES · JW LEES · ROBINSONS · JOSEPH HOLT · HYDES

THE RISE and success of family brewers in north-west England has powerful links to the Industrial Revolution and especially to the cotton trade in the region. Mills appeared at great speed in the early and mid-19th century to make textiles: Richard Arkwright opened the first mill to be driven by steam engines in 1781. The industry so dominated Manchester that it was nicknamed 'Cottonopolis' and was responsible for 32 per cent of global cotton production.

There were 100 mills operating by the 1850s and great warehouses were built to hold stocks of cotton and textiles. A cotton exchange was opened to deal with the trade and both financial and commercial areas developed to support the industry. The Bridgewater Canal was dug to allow goods to be transported to the docks and to bring in supplies of raw cotton from the West Indies and the southern states of America. When steam trains arrived, special lines were built to move cotton and textiles around at speed.

Many of the mills and warehouses were masterpieces of architecture, but working conditions for men, women and children were appalling. Writing in 1835, the French diplomat and historian Alexis de Tocqueville painted a vivid portrait of Manchester: 'A thick black smoke covers the city. The sun appears like a disc without rays. In this semi-daylight 300,000 people work ceaselessly. A thousand noises rise amidst this unending damp and dark labyrinth… the footsteps of a busy crowd, the crunching wheels of machines, the shriek of steam from the boilers, the regular beat of looms, the heavy rumble of carts… noise from which you can never escape in these dark half-lit streets.'

The astonishing growth in population – 70,000 in Manchester in 1801, 303,000 by 1850, for example – meant not only back-breaking work for the mass of the people but also squalid housing. These conditions created an insatiable demand for beer in the solace of the pub. Family brewers rushed to meet the demand and grew at a rapid pace. But it was never an easy business. Fluctuations in the cotton trade meant there were periods when workers were laid off and unable to afford the small pleasure of a tankard of ale. This was seen at its most dramatic during the American Civil War in the 1860s. When the northern troops blockaded the ports in the southern Confederacy no cotton could be exported and the mills of Lancashire fell silent.

Once trade resumed, the north-west boomed again. When the cotton trade eventually went into slow decline, new industries such as chemicals and engineering sprang up to replace King Cotton. Workers went on drinking good ale, family brewers prospered and continue to do so today.

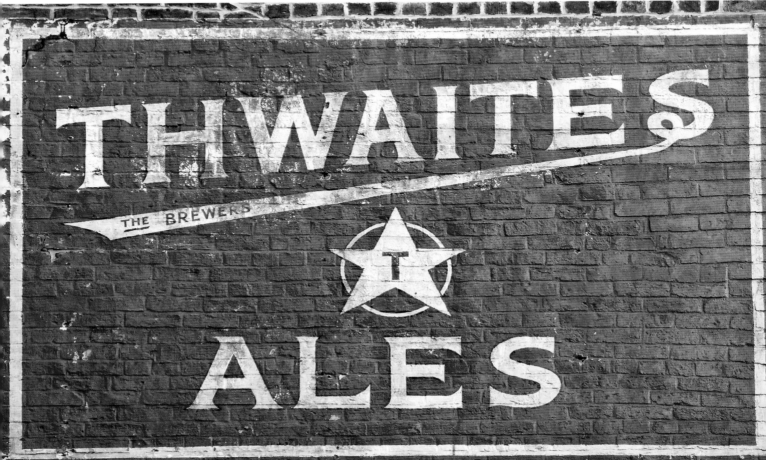

Thwaites

1807 · BLACKBURN

THWAITES is justifiably proud of its heritage as the biggest brewery in Lancashire and its major role in north-west England. Its success has been driven by that pride and also by the powerful entrepreneurial spirit of the Yerburgh family that runs the business. The Yerburghs are descended by marriage from the founder, Daniel Thwaites, and the sixth generation of the family is forging a new path to success in the future.

Working for Thwaites creates a powerful loyalty from the staff. In the brewhouse, members of the team have an impressive number of years on their CVs. Glyn Bennett can boast a remarkable 40 years with the brewery, followed by Harry Brunt and Pete Shepherd with 22 years each, and Mark O'Sullivan and Stuart Smith both notching up 16 years.

Thwaites historically has been linked, almost by an umbilical cord, to Blackburn and it's a shock to find the brewery has been operating since 2018 on a former farm site at Mellor Brook in the Ribble Valley. But it's clearly a good place to be as the Ribble Valley was named the happiest place to live in Britain in a survey in 2019 and happy places produce happy beer.

Chairman and chief executive Rick Bailey, the son-in-law of former chairman Ann Yerburgh, says the move from Blackburn was necessary as the old brewery, updated in the 1960s, was creaking at the seams and would have needed massive investment to make it fit for the future. The move was also driven by a sharp change of direction in how the company is run.

The free trade has been sold and Thwaites no longer deals with supermarkets or pub companies. 'We only sell to our own pubs,' Rick Bailey says. That is substantial business as Thwaites owns 230 tenanted pubs, 21 managed pubs plus 10 hotels and 12 'inns of character'. 'We could have become a pub and hotel company, but we wanted to keep the flame of brewing burning,' Rick adds. 'Brewing is an important part of the business and our heritage and will continue to be so.'

The move took seven years to plan. While Thwaites sold two of its leading brands, Wainwright's and Lancaster Bomber, to Marston's, it has launched a new core range of award-winning beers.

Rick Bailey, chairman of Thwaites and the IFBB

From farming to brewing

It's fitting that the new brewery has been built on former farmland for Daniel Thwaites, born in 1777, came from farming stock in the Lake District. He left home to train as an excise man or tax collector. When he passed his exams he was appointed as assistant officer in Preston in Lancashire. After several moves to other towns, Daniel arrived in Blackburn where he decided to leave the excise service and seek alternative employment. His marriage to Betty Duckworth, who came from a family of local grocers, enabled Daniel to become a partner with Edward Duckworth and William Clayton in a new brewery in the town in 1807. Daniel effectively ran the brewery while Duckworth and Clayton looked after their other businesses. The partnership deed spoke of the Art, Trade, Mystery and Benefits of a Brewery and at first brewing was indeed a mystery to Daniel, who had no experience. But he was quick to learn, which was as well because Blackburn was a booming mill town with thousands of parched throats to refresh.

Daniel became sole owner of the brewery when his two partners died or retired. The company became Daniel Thwaites & Co, Ale & Porter Brewers. Of the 14 breweries claimed to exist in Blackburn at that time only one other was a commercial brewer while the rest were publican brewers. Thwaites' only competitor supplied domestic homes in the main and Daniel was able to build a successful trade by supplying inns and pubs and his own estate as he bought tied outlets.

The inclusion of porter in the title of the brewery highlighted the success of Daniel's business. In his travels as an excise officer he had encountered porter being brewed in such major cities as Liverpool, Manchester and Sheffield. But smaller towns tended to concentrate on strong ale as they lacked the space to store porter in large vats for several months. Daniel bought additional land alongside the brewery and expanded his site in order to add porter. As porter was both weaker and cheaper than strong ale, Daniel was able to make a good living from selling substantial quantities of a style of beer that was just as refreshing for mill workers as it was for London porters.

Local people were not his only customers. The brewery, in the central Eanam district, was close to a major turnpike that brought visitors by stagecoach from Burnley, Halifax and Leeds to Blackburn where they stayed at nearby coaching inns. Daniel and his partners had also chosen Salford Bridge as a site for their brewery for another good reason – a constant supply of fresh water from nearby rivers, streams and ponds. The Eanam area flourished, with new housing springing up, providing additional customers for Thwaites's beers.

The poorer districts of Blackburn didn't fare as well. Fluctuations in the cotton trade led to repeated demonstrations and strikes by the town's mill workers, culminating in what were called the Blackburn Riots of 1878. Cotton workers, faced with a 10 per cent cut in their wages, attempted to form a trade union and they were attacked by the police when they marched through the town, recalling the Peterloo Massacre in Manchester in 1819. Thwaites in Eanam was largely unaffected by these events, but beerhouses and ale houses in working-class districts suffered when their regular customers were unable to afford beer.

Prosperity for the second generation

Daniel Thwaites's 36 years at the brewery ended when he died in 1843. His success in business can be measured by his will in which he granted his wife Betty an annuity of £240 a year, worth £12,000 today. He also placed in trust £3,000, worth £150,000 today, for each of his eight daughters. He left the brewery, equipment, stables, land and pubs to his sons. Daniel Jnr and Thomas Thwaites took over the business at a time of great tumult. There was continuing strife in the northern mill towns, demands for political reform with a widening of the franchise, and agitation over repeal of the Corn Laws. On the plus side for the brewery, the rapid increase in Blackburn's population, from 38,899 in 1811 to 71,711 by 1841, meant there were

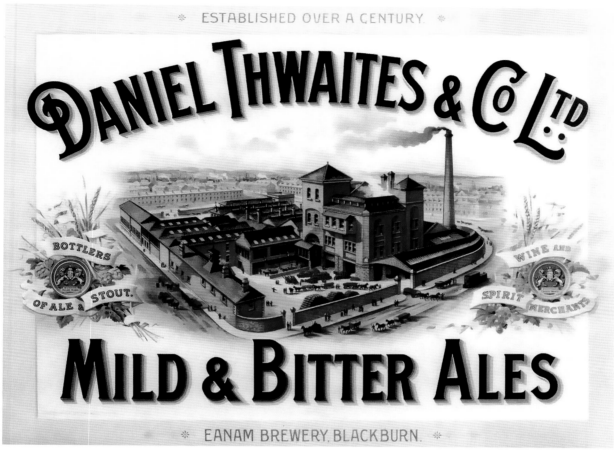

many more customers for Thwaites's ales. The arrival of the railway also boosted the brothers' fortunes. The Liverpool and Manchester Railway opened in 1831 and was followed by the West Lancashire Railway that linked Blackburn, Preston and Southport. Other lines sprang up with the result that not only could passengers visit Blackburn and its pubs in large numbers but also such essential materials as coal, malt and hops could be transported quickly and at a fraction of the price of horse-drawn vehicles.

Thomas Thwaites retired from the brewery in 1844 and Daniel was joined by his younger brother John and a new business partner, his cousin Joseph Yates. The three partners set about modernising the brewery by extending the premises and installing the latest model of steam engine to drive the brewing process. The business flourished thanks to an economic boom in the middle of the century, with wages rising and legislation that cut the working week and brought in half-day working on Saturday. The result was that many more people went to the main leisure attraction – the pub. In the 1860s and 70s consumption of beer increased per head from 31.6 gallons a year to 40.5 gallons and Daniel Jnr and his partners moved quickly to meet the growing demand for a new type of beer – pale ale. As a result of the rapid growth of the railway system, brewers could move out of the restrictions of their small towns and sell beer far and wide. The pale ale revolution that started in Burton upon Trent spread rapidly to other areas of the country and in Blackburn Thwaites responded with a new amber-coloured pale beer.

The partners became prosperous, so much so that John Thwaites preferred the life of a country gentleman and rarely appeared at the brewery. When Joseph Yates decided to retire, Daniel thought the time had come to dissolve the partnership and in 1859 the brewery was once again Daniel Thwaites & Company. The economic boom came to an abrupt end in the 1860s when the American Civil War led to a cotton famine in Lancashire, with mills closing and thousands thrown out of work. In spite of the shocking hardship in Blackburn, Thwaites continued to expand. Daniel bought the Snig Brook Brewery with an annual output of 10,000 barrels and he continued to build his tied estate with many more pubs. By 1878, Thwaites was producing an impressive 100,000 barrels a year. This level of production was in step with national sales: in 1869, 51 million barrels of beer were brewed, 4.6 million more than the previous year. By 1871 consumption had risen by a further 1.3 million barrels.

Daniel was active in public life. He became a magistrate and was briefly a Tory member of parliament: his election campaign was marked by the vociferous opposition of the temperance movement, which supported the Liberal Party. As well as homes in Lancashire, Daniel and his wife Eliza lived in some style in a townhouse in Kensington, London, where their daughter Elma planned to marry Robert Yerburgh, the MP for Chester. In September 1888 Daniel had a stroke and died. The extent of his success as a brewer was measured by the estate he left of £464,516, equivalent to £28 million today.

Honeymoon brewster

Elma Yerburgh was not the only woman to run a brewery, as this book shows, but she is surely the only woman to inherit one while she was on her honeymoon. It was expected that she would sell the brewery as it wasn't considered fit and proper in polite society for a rich young woman to work let alone run a large business making beer. At first she left the day-to-day running of the brewery to her general manager, William Ward, but by 1896 she became more closely involved as important decisions about the future role of Thwaites had to be taken.

The economy improved that year and with stricter control of licences and the collapse of many beerhouses there was a scramble by commercial brewers to extend their tied estates. With fierce competition from other brewers in the area, Thwaites had to defend and improve its market position. Elma, her husband and the brewery managers all agreed that the brewery should follow in the footsteps of a growing number of other brewers and become a public company that could attract income from shareholders. As a result, in March 1897, Daniel Thwaites & Co Ltd was formed and the issue of shares was soon fully subscribed.

Elma and her fellow directors set about the urgent task of buying new pubs and bringing existing ones up to date. They had to meet the needs of a new middle class looking for greater creature comforts in pubs that were divided into lounge bars offering pale ale and public bars serving cheaper mild to working-class drinkers.

Elma Yerburgh, 1864–1946

In 1897 Elma appointed a new general manager, John Thorpe. He brought considerable experience of the industry having worked at the major Birmingham brewer Mitchells & Butlers. He was given scope to update the brewery with an ice-making machine, a new hop store and new cold liquor tanks at the top of the building. Thorpe's innovations worked well. In the first quarter of 1898 the brewery sold 14,000 barrels compared to 10,000 for the same period the previous year. Further expansion took place when it was decided to increase the company's capital and the issue of further shares brought in £100,000.

Difficult trading conditions

Thwaites entered the 20th century with an improved brewery and an estate of 219 pubs. But the Edwardian age brought problems as governments attempted to curb the spread of public houses and the consumption of alcohol. A Licensing Bill in 1908 brought in by a Liberal government sought severe restrictions on the issue of pub licences and wanted to ban the employment of women in pubs. The latter proposal led to 100,000 barmaids demonstrating in London and the Bill was defeated in the Lords. The Liberal chancellor, David Lloyd George, got his revenge when his budgets in 1908 and 1909 massively increased the duty on beer in order to help pay for the introduction of the first old-age pensions. Lloyd George's attacks on the brewing industry were given full throttle during the First World War with ever-increasing duty rates, restrictions on pub opening hours and cuts in the supply of raw materials to breweries.

Despite the difficult trading conditions in the 1920s, Thwaites launched a new beer that was to become its best-selling brand. The name – East Lancashire Pale Ale – marked a rebranding of the brewery's beers to underscore its proud position in the county. The beer was a mouthful in every sense and drinkers simply asked for 'an East Lancs'. At the same time, Thwaites added East Lancashire Cream Stout, but this was discontinued after the Second World War

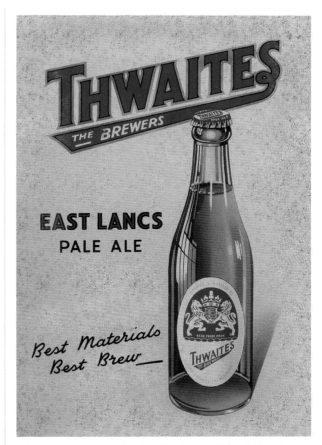

when, at a time of food rationing and food shortages, the government banned misleading advertising and branding. The famous beer Mackeson Milk Stout became just Mackeson Stout. In fact neither of the beers used milk or cream but added lactose, a bi-product of cheese making.

There were many mergers during the hard trading times of the 1920s and, in 1922, Thwaites's directors increased the company's capital to £1 million to enable them to buy Henry Shaw's New Salford Brewery, which added 87 pubs to the estate. In 1927 Thwaites bought the Fountain Free Brewery, which came with 11 pubs. In due course, Shaw's site was sold to Duttons and Fountain Free closed. Thwaites saw the acquisition as vital to defend its share of the Lancashire market, especially when the major brewer Matthew Brown moved its operations from Preston to Blackburn.

ELMA YERBURGH: PoW

A curious incident in 1914 saw Elma and Robert Yerburgh held as prisoners of war in Germany. Robert's health was poor and in June that year Elma went with him to the spa town of Bad Nauheim in Bavaria. War was declared between Germany and Russia while they were 'taking the waters'. Every train was filled with troops and Elma and Robert were placed under curfew as they were unable to leave. When Britain entered the war, the Yerburghs were held as prisoners of war. Nine weeks later they were told they could leave Germany on condition that they travelled through Switzerland where they had to stay for three weeks. Robert joked that they could have continued their journey without staying in neutral Switzerland 'but I had given my word as an Englishman and so we stayed for three weeks.' The adventure did little to improve Robert's health and he died in 1916 aged 63.

The 1930s were a difficult time for Thwaites. The economic depression led to mills closing, with thousands losing their jobs. Means testing of benefits forced many unemployed into the workhouse while others left the area and headed south in search of work. With plummeting beer sales, many of Thwaites's tenants failed to make a living and had to be replaced by managers on meagre salaries. As trade started to improve in the late 1930s, Thwaites began a programme of pub improvements, especially in such holiday resorts as Blackpool and Morecambe, which attracted those holidaymakers largely unaffected by the depression.

The brewery survived the privations of the Second World War and it was fortunate to have a large number of American servicemen stationed in the Blackburn area, with the result that pubs were often packed with GIs sampling English ale rather than American lager. When Boddingtons Brewery in Manchester was bombed, Thwaites, in common with Joseph Holt and Robinsons, supplied Boddingtons' pubs with beer.

Modernisation

Elma Yerburgh, after a long period at the helm, died in December 1946. She was succeeded by her grandson Captain John Yerburgh, who had enjoyed a privileged upbringing in London and had a distinguished war career as a tank commander. He had no experience of the brewing industry or the north of England when he arrived in Blackburn and he joined the board as a director before later taking over as chairman. Elma was aware of his inexperience and, rather like a football club that surrounds a new young coach with retired players, she had arranged for John to be shepherded by older directors. John was shocked by the Dickensian atmosphere of the brewery, with clerks sitting on high stools and every stage of brewing

The Star Brewery in the 1960s

carried out by hand. In 1948, the Eanam Brewery was given the more modern title of the Star Brewery and John Yerburgh and his fellow directors set out to modernise the business.

They needed more pubs and in 1949 bought the Bury Brewery for, at the time, the enormous sum of £1 million. While Bury was a small brewery, it had a substantial estate of 84 pubs and they gave Thwaites a presence into such areas as Manchester, Rochdale and Bury itself. The purchase was followed in 1956 by the Preston Brewery with 17 pubs.

Thwaites responded to the popularity of bottled beer in the 1950s by installing a new bottling plant that could fill 900 dozen bottles an hour. Bottled beers included a new strong ale called Old Dan that proved popular. When commercial television arrived with many expensive advertisements for national beer brands, Thwaites took the unusual step for a regional brewer of promoting its draught and bottled beers on Granada TV, which covered the north-west of England. Much use was made of the brewery's dray horses to highlight Thwaites's support for traditional values. The horses remain and are used to promote and market the brewery.

The 1960s was a decade of merger frenzy in the brewing industry. In the north of England, Tetley in Leeds merged with Peter Walker of Warrington to form Tetley Walker, which then joined forces with Ansells and Ind Coope as Allied Breweries. Duttons in Blackburn was sufficiently concerned by these developments to approach Thwaites with a proposal

to merge the two companies. John Yerburgh fiercely opposed such a deal and was determined to maintain his company's independence. It proved a wise decision as Duttons was bought for £8 million by the national brewer Whitbread, which closed the brewery. Blackburn's other brewer, Matthew Brown, was later bought by Scottish & Newcastle and eventually closed.

The security of the brewery lay in modernising all aspects of the business. The offices were computerised, but the major development was building a new brewhouse that came into operation in 1966. The new brewery tower dominated the skyline of Blackburn, with a neon sign proclaiming Thwaites in red letters: it became an icon of the town. Old, open square fermenters were replaced with enclosed conditioning tanks and there was a new bottling hall, followed in due course by a canning operation. The scale of the modernisation can be seen in the costs: £5.5 million for the brewhouse and fermenting rooms and £3 million for the bottling hall, considered to be one of the most modern and efficient in the industry.

John Yerburgh became chairman of the company in 1966 and was set on further expansion. He chose Northern Ireland and bought a small bottling plant in Belfast, which he turned into warehousing for the

John and Ann Yerburgh with the brewery dray, 1974

distribution of Thwaites's beer. Twenty-seven pubs were bought in the province and soon 300 kegs of beer were carried from Blackburn to Belfast every week. All seemed set fair for the future until the Troubles started. The warehouses were bombed, pubs were blown up and Thwaites started to lose money on the venture. After two years, John Yerburgh decided to pull the plug on the Northern Ireland business.

An attempt to enter the lager market in the 1970s was an object lesson in the power of the new national brewers and the marketing of their brands. Thwaites launched a lager called Stein that rapidly built excellent sales of 50–60,000 barrels a year and continued in production until 2010. The big brewers noticed the success and hit back with major advertising campaigns to promote their lagers. Carlsberg alone spent £2 million on one advertising campaign. The result was that a growing number of drinkers in Thwaites's pubs asked for Carling and Carlsberg, as they thought they were genuine foreign lagers – in fact they were brewed under licence in Britain. Reluctantly, Thwaites was forced to withdraw from the lager market. It sold Carlsberg in its pubs and signed an agreement with the Danish company to brew its Tuborg under licence in Blackburn.

Cask to the fore

Fortunately, the arrival of CAMRA turned the spotlight back onto ale and Thwaites came to national attention when it won a series of awards in the organisation's Champion Beer of Britain competition for both mild and bitter, including Supreme Champion for mild in 1986. The decade ended with the Monopolies and Mergers Commission investigation into the brewing industry, which led to the government's Beer Orders forcing the Big Six national producers to divest themselves of several thousand pubs. Thwaites was unaffected by the Beer Orders but it had taken the opportunity to buy Yates & Jackson of Lancaster in 1984, bringing 40 new pubs and the Lancaster Bomber brand. In 2005 Lancaster Bomber was

Freddie Flintoff promoting Lancaster Bomber

promoted by the England cricketer Freddie Flintoff, who had been instrumental in helping win the Ashes back from Australia. His participation helped the beer become a national brand, with a key link to Lancashire County Cricket Club and its Old Trafford ground.

In 2000 Ann Yerburgh, who had been on the board for many years, succeeded her husband John as chairman of the brewery. It was on her watch that the momentous decision was made to move from Blackburn to the new site at Mellor Brook.

Rick Bailey describes Mellor Brook as an artisan brewery with all the beers handcrafted by Mark O'Sullivan and his team. The site can produce 12,000 barrels a year and has the capacity to grow to 15,000 barrels. Within a short time of opening, two additional fermenting vessels have been installed to keep pace with demand. Unusually for this day and age, Thwaites now produces only cask beers and they are brewed with the finest raw materials – Maris Otter barley malt and Challenger and Goldings English hops, with some European hops for its popular Gold. Coloured malts, including amber, crystal, cara and black, are used in the beers. Against all the national trends, Rick says sales of mild are increasing. 'Customers are moving away from ubiquitous beers and want something special,' he says. The new plant is highly flexible and allows the brewery to produce a range of seasonal beers alongside the core brands.

Rick Bailey is the chairman of the Independent Family Brewers of Britain and he has seen at close hand how the 'squeezed middle' has been affected by Progressive Beer Duty, now called Small Brewers Relief (SBR). 'It was introduced for the best of intentions,' he says, 'but it had unforeseen consequences. It's created a structure that caused market distortion. It made life difficult for traditional family brewers who have seen their businesses decline … There's more choice but there are serious implications for overall profitability and SBR acts as a barrier to growth.'

'But brewing is in our DNA,' he adds. 'We have invested in the brewery and we plan to go on brewing far into the future.'

Sculpture at new head office

Daniel Thwaites, Myerscough Road, Mellor Brook, Lancashire BB2 7LB
01254 686868 · www.thwaites.co.uk

Regular cask beers:

Mild (3.3%)
Original (3.6%)
Gold (3.8%)
IPA (4%)
Amber (4.4%)

JW Lees

1828 · MANCHESTER

THE roll call of names at the Greengate Brewery in Middleton Junction makes it crystal clear it's firmly in family control for years to come: Richard and Christopher from the fifth generation and William, Simon, Christina, Anna and Michael Lees-Jones are now the sixth generation of the family to run the company. Michael, brimming with joie de vivre, is head brewer, so don't meddle with his mash tun, while managing director William Lees-Jones stresses the company is in for the long haul.

'When we're buying pubs,' he says, 'we always ask, "Will they be good for 50 years?".' New outlets will add to an estate of 150 pubs and hotels throughout northwest England. Despite intense competition from the array of new small breweries in the region, William says the company is thriving. Pubs and free trade are supplied by a brewery that produces around 60,000 barrels a year and has a capacity of 100,000.

There's also a 10-barrel micro plant where new beers can be tested. To prove Lees is not living in the past, the Boilerhouse range has included a rhubarb and custard lactose IPA, which sold out overnight. William says, 'These beers bring people into cask and the ones that sell well will become permanent members of the range.'

John Lees, the founder of the brewery, would have been no stranger to IPA but he would have balked at adding rhubarb and custard to his beer in conservative Victorian England. He came late to brewing as he had built a substantial trade and fortune as a mill owner

with plants in Oldham and Manchester. At the age of 50, he sold the business and bought a row of cottages in Middleton, then a leafy suburb outside Manchester, where he built his brewery.

Nobody knows why he abandoned the lucrative cotton trade, but he may have suspected it would go into decline as a result of cheap imports from the British Empire. Without doubt he witnessed at close hand Manchester turning into a mighty industrial metropolis. The cotton trade was followed by engineering and chemical works, while the Manchester

John Lees, founder

Ship Canal enabled the city to export to the world. When John Lees studied the brewing industry, he saw that porter was being replaced in popularity by the new pale ales that could be produced without the need for long periods of storage and therefore offered better and quicker profits. Middleton was a small but important area, linking the manufacturing towns of Oldham and Rochdale with the centre of Manchester and this link was boosted with the arrival of the Manchester & Leeds Railway in 1841. It turned Middleton into an important junction and enabled beer to be delivered at speed to free trade outlets.

John Willie

The brewery prospered and John brought his sons, John Junior and Thomas, into the business. It was when John William Lees, grandson of John Lees, took over at the brewery that it started to grow at a fast pace. John Willie, as he was known affectionately, was sent by the family to gain experience of the business world with the Lancashire & Yorkshire Railway, where he worked in every department and was finally given the prestigious post of station master at Wigan.

Mayor John William Lees

Then, aged just 23 and following the deaths of John Lees and John Junior, he took control at the brewery, changed the name to JW Lees and set about making it the biggest brewery in the area.

Success was rapid and in 1876 John Willie designed and built a new brewery to keep pace with the demand for his ales and stout. The Greengate Brewery was an impressive site. Alfred Barnard, who had visited some of the great breweries of London, Birmingham and Burton upon Trent and described them in his *Noted Breweries of Great Britain and Ireland,* was clearly impressed with the Greengate's 'lofty and handsome appearance and the magnitude of its building ... No expense was spared in its construction, and in fitting up the entire premises with a valuable plant and machinery of the newest description.' It had a 30-quarter cast iron mash tun, a 278-barrel copper and a fermenting room with 10 copper-lined vessels that held 100 barrels of beer each. The cellars could hold 2,000 barrels of beer.

John Willie became a pillar of the local establishment. He was twice mayor of Middleton and was chairman of the local Conservative Party. It's claimed that such was his power in the community that he could summon the local MP for dinner at Greengate House, the family home alongside the brewery, to discuss political issues. The MP in question was a certain Winston Churchill. There was, no doubt, lively debate around the dinner table about the influential temperance movement that was boosted by the Liberal Party's dislike of the brewing industry.

Following several years of expansion, Lees faced serious problems in the 20th century. As well as the difficulties faced by all brewers during the First World War, the Greengate brewery had earlier suffered the death of John Willie in 1906. As he had no children, he left the business to his wife Emma. For 28 years she engaged in 'good works'. She funded churches and founded court houses, and honourably set out to

improve the lives of working people. But little or no money was invested in the brewery, which was left to stagnate during the harsh years of unemployment and depression in the 1920s and 30s.

The start of the Lees-Jones dynasty

Emma Lees died in 1935 and control of the brewery passed to two trustees, Dick and John Jones. They were the sons of John Willie's sister Mary Matilda who had married a Manchester doctor, William Jones, from Anglesey in North Wales. When Emma died, Dick and John Jones changed their name to Lees-Jones and it's that family that has been in charge ever since.

The future of the brewery was put in jeopardy as a result of a rift between John and Dick Lees-Jones in the 1950s. This was a time when a series of mergers were creating large national brewers who were

hell-bent on buying smaller companies with pubs that could be used to sell heavily promoted new keg beers. John Lees-Jones was the chairman of the Greengate Brewery and he was tempted by an offer to buy the business from Hammonds United Breweries. Dick disagreed and bought his brother's shareholding. Dick was a keen philatelist and in order to fund the purchase he had to sell his valuable collection of stamps.

It was a noble gesture. Without it, Lees would have been sucked into what became the country's biggest brewing group, Bass Charrington, and the Greengate Brewery would almost certainly have closed. The driving force behind the mergers that created Bass Charrington was a Canadian, Eddie Taylor. He owned Carling Black Label lager and he came to Britain with the aim of converting drinkers to the joys of his fizzy brew. He ended up owning 20 per cent of the brewing industry with 11,000 pubs and an annual turnover of £900 million. It was a world away from life at Greengate, where mild ale and bitter were still the staple brews.

In the 1960s the brewery was driven forward by the brothers Richard and Christopher Lees-Jones who rapidly expanded the pub estate. They were helped by Manchester City Council, which provided sites for brewers in the region to open new pubs to replace ones

RAKING THE MOON

One of Lees best-known beers is Moonraker, a strong dark ale of 6.5%, available in cask and bottle. It was first brewed in 1950 and commemorated a local legend that told how a group of farmers, after a long night in the pub, had staggered home and fallen into a pond when they attempted to rake the reflection of the moon in the water, which they mistook for a truckle of cheese. The beer is brewed with Celeia hops from Slovenia and has a rich aroma and a palate of plums and dried fruit.

that had been bombed during the Second World War or closed by road widening schemes. By the end of the 1950s, Greengate had increased production fivefold to 100,000 barrels a year and the directors had taken the fateful decision to produce lager: Lees was one of the first regional brewers to go down the lager route. The new beers, Lees Tulip Lager, Edelbrau Lager and Edelbrau Lite, were a resounding success and enabled the brewery to build a foothold in the massive working men's club trade. Lees also established a good base in North Wales where there was a demand for chilled beer due to the presence of the Wrexham Lager Company.

Mild faith

Traditional cask beers nevertheless remained the bedrock of the brewery. But consumer tastes were changing. William Lees-Jones says in 1900 mild ale outsold bitter six to one but by the end of the century that figure had been reversed. Today only a tiny amount of mild is produced but the brewery keeps faith with the style and often produces a special mild to coincide with CAMRA's annual 'Make May a Mild Month' promotion.

The brewery has been overhauled in recent years, with new coppers and a copper whirlpool, as well as a mash mixer and lauter tun to brew lagers. Old open fermenters have been replaced with stainless steel covered vessels. Conical vessels in the brewery yard are used to store lager and keg beer. The 60,000 barrels annual production is evenly divided with one-third cask, one-third lager and one-third keg.

The 10-barrel Boilerhouse micro plant, installed in 2018, takes its name from a redundant boiler room and is described as a place to foster innovation and produce challenging new beers. There's one regular beer, Craft Pale, a 4.2 per cent IPA, brewed with pale malt and Citra, Mosaic and Pilgrim hops. One-off beers have included a Belgian-style Saison, Summer Session Ale, stout and the previously mentioned Rhubarb and Custard Lactose IPA. The brewery also has a mainstream range of six seasonal beers, ranging from a plum pudding ale for Christmas, a golden ale for Easter and a citrussy summer beer.

None of these beers, however, should disguise the fact that JW Lees remains true to its long-standing and best-selling cask beer, Bitter, followed by Manchester Pale Ale and Founder's premium bitter.

HARVESTING A FINE ALE

Lees 11.5% Vintage Harvest Ale is awaited by beer lovers with all the keenness of wine drinkers anticipating the year's new offerings from Bordeaux. The beer is sold only in bottle and is popular in the United States. It's brewed with pale malt and Goldings hops. When asked why a beer made with pale malt is ruby red in colour, head brewer Michael Lees-Jones says: 'Because we brew the bollocks off it'. This is not a term found in most brewers' manuals but means that during the long and vigorous boil with hops some of the malt sugars are caramelised. The beer, thanks to its strength, will change over time. In a tasting at the brewery, a young 2018 had sultanas, raisins and butterscotch on the aroma and a palate balanced by peppery hops. A 2014 vintage was darker in colour and had notes of Dundee cake, molasses and blood oranges, while the 2000 vintage was much darker with a rye bread and Christmas cake character. A sample of the very first vintage brewed in 1986 had notes of chocolate, Marmite and dark, burnt fruit.

William Lees-Jones

Managing director William Lees-Jones, who worked in advertising in London before taking the helm at the brewery, is bullish about the future. He says Lees campaigned vigorously against Small Brewers Relief, but the company is not suffering as it has built its pub estate and controls distribution of its beers rather than relying on pub companies with their demands for deep discounts on prices. The 150-strong pub estate includes 293 bedrooms and nearly all the pubs serve quality food.

William and his fellow family members have thoroughly modernised the company, but they will stay true to the beliefs in quality and rugged independence laid down by John Willie Lees.

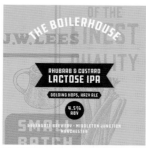

JW Lees, Greengate Brewery, Middleton Junction, Greater Manchester M24 2AX
0161 643 2487 · www.jwlees.co.uk

Regular cask beers:
Dark (3.5%)
Supernova (3.5%)
Manchester Pale Ale (3.7%)
Cosmic Brew (3.9%)
Bitter (4%)
Dragon's Fire (4%)
Craft Pale (4.2%)
Stout (4.2%)
Founder's (4.5%)
Gold (4.5%)
Moonraker (6.5%)

Michael Lees-Jones, head brewer

Robinsons

1838 · STOCKPORT

IT was the most unlikely fusion in the modern beer world: suited and booted family brewers joining forces with a heavy metal rock band to create a beer that took the world by storm. The beer, called Trooper, was brewed with Iron Maiden and is now consumed by vast crowds at their concerts from Latin America to Russia.

The success of Trooper also took Robinsons by storm. In 2012 the family installed a new brewhouse at a cost of £6 million. It has a capacity of 80,000 barrels a year and Oliver and William Robinson, the sixth generation of the family to run the Unicorn Brewery in Stockport, confidently thought that level of production would take several years to reach. But when sales of Trooper took off in 2013, the brewery was soon rocking to the tune of 60,000 barrels a year and full capacity was hovering on the horizon.

Oliver Robinson, who looks after the brewery side of the business while William oversees the tied estate of 256 pubs, is at pains to stress that Trooper hasn't sidelined his other main brands. Trooper chalks up the biggest volumes but Unicorn Bitter and Dizzy Blonde are the two major ale brands for the large tied estate.

Robinsons celebrated 180 years of brewing in November 2018 and can take pride in the fact that, despite sales of cask ale being in the doldrums for a few years, it accounts for 80 per cent of annual production at the Unicorn – that's 10 per cent higher than the national average for cask beer brewers. The success of Trooper has seen export sales quadruple,

with Unicorn and the legendary strong ale Old Tom available in foreign markets.

Trooper was the result of Robinsons being approached by Bury-based band Elbow. The band, who wrote the BBC theme tune for the 2012 Olympics, drank in the Castle, one of the brewery's Manchester pubs, and they asked Robinsons to make a beer for them. The interest aroused by the beer led to the brewery being contacted by the management team of Iron Maiden with a proposal to create a beer for the group. It turned out that lead singer Bruce Dickinson is a beer lover who lives in Chiswick, West London, where he regularly sups Fuller's and other local brews. His team approached several breweries and Bruce tasted the trial beers they produced for him. He chose

the Robinsons' version but asked for more hop character: the result was Trooper.

'The demand was enormous,' Oliver Robinson says. 'Iron Maiden has 16 million followers on social media and news of Trooper brought people to Stockport for brewery tours – they included a group who came all the way from Brazil. We're now exporting beers to 50 countries. We never were a sleeping giant – we just got on with things quietly – but now we have an international reputation.'

Brewery tours include a new, spacious visitor centre that traces the history of the family brewery from the early 19th century. Among ancient delivery vehicles and sepia prints of old taverns and bewhiskered Stockport gentry there's a very modern image of Trooper and Iron Maiden, depicting a snarling, skull-like figure brandishing a Union flag.

Early success at the Unicorn

Heavy metal rock groups are a long way removed from the quiet and almost bucolic origins of the brewery. The Unicorn was an inn built around 1722 on Lower Hillgate, one of the major roads in a market town that, courtesy of the cotton trade, had expanded rapidly from a population of 5,000 in the 1770s to 21,000 by the 1820s. The Unicorn inn was built on land owned by the church, which meant for some time it wasn't allowed to sell beer on Sundays. The inn had a succession of innkeepers, including Sarah Patterson who claimed to have a horn in the bar that had come from the mythical beast. Mrs Patterson was followed by William Robinson in 1826 and he began the family's association with the inn. William was born near Sale and worked in the cotton trade. It's not known why he left his job to run the inn but the move may have been prompted by unrest in the cotton industry, which led to the Peterloo Massacre in Manchester in 1819, followed by riots by Lancashire weavers in 1826.

William had no experience as a brewer and bought beer from other pubs in the area that brewed on their premises. Despite intense competition in Stockport,

with 165 inns and taverns in the town, plus 121 beerhouses, William had great success at the Unicorn. When he retired, he left the inn to his son George and his wife Clarissa, who ran the inn until 1859 and may have started to brew ale in a small way: the records are unclear. It was when George's younger brother Frederic took over that brewing developed on a larger scale. It was Frederic who effectively launched the brewing dynasty and for many years the company was known as Frederic Robinson Ltd before becoming simply Robinsons.

Frederic had an eye for business and he saw the potential of increasing his income by meeting the growing demand for beer. By 1859 an average of 22 gallons of beer per person was drunk every year – that's almost half a pint a day for every man, woman and child. After the years of unrest earlier in the century, wages were rising and, with few other outlets for recreation, going to the pub was a popular pastime.

The Unicorn expanded production when Frederic bought a warehouse behind the inn and adapted it for brewing. He started to sell beer beyond his locality

Frederic and Emma Robinson with children Emma, Eleanor, Mary and William

and by the 1870s he had a small fleet of horse-drawn drays to carry his ales further afield. But the last quarter of the 19th century brought problems for the brewery. The arrival of the railway meant that bigger brewers, especially those based in Burton upon Trent, Liverpool and Manchester, could move their beers around quickly and cheaply, undercutting smaller producers. Frederic Robinson responded by building a small estate of tied houses where only his beers were on sale, effectively keeping out his competitors. His first pub was the Railway Inn – a name that commemorated the arrival of the iron way – at Marple Bridge, four miles east of Stockport. The pub is still a Robinsons' house but was renamed the Royal Scot in 1975.

Frederic energetically improved the quality of his brewing vessels and bought land adjacent to the Unicorn to allow for extensions to the plant. He had the good fortune to become the local distributor for Guinness stout from Dublin: as many people of Irish descent lived in the Stockport area, sales of Guinness became an important source of income for the brewery.

By the 1880s Frederic had become a wealthy and eminent Stockport citizen. The wedding in 1889 of his son William to Priscilla Needham, daughter of a leading industrialist, was one of the high fashion events of the year. But just four months after the wedding, Frederic died suddenly, aged just 54. The local newspaper, the *Stockport Advertiser*, in an obituary, praised him for 'steadily extending his business. Very recently important alterations have been carried out at the brewery, the structure having been considerably enlarged, the brewing plant thoroughly modernised, and the fittings of a first-class brewery having been put in so as to enable the firm to cope with their large and increasing trade.' The funeral cortege went from Frederic's home to the borough cemetery, passing Hillgate en route, and the newspaper reported that 'along the route there was noticeable every mark of

esteem for the deceased gentleman, blinds and shutters being drawn on every side.'

Frederic's widow Emma took over the brewery with her sons Herbert and William. William became the driving force of the company. Despite fierce competition from other brewers, he expanded the brewery but was careful not to over-indulge in buying property. This was a wise move as a decline in beer consumption early in the 20th century led to several breweries with large property portfolios running into financial difficulties.

Old Tom

In 1893 William's eldest sister Emma married Robinsons' head brewer Alfred Munton, who was to play a major role in the development and success of the company. Munton helped oversee the expansion of the brewery and its ales, and added new equipment, such as a microscope, which improved the keeping qualities of the beer. In 1899, he launched a new beer that became a Robinsons' legend.

Old Tom is a barley wine with an original gravity of 1080 degrees – 8.5 per cent in modern terms. The beer was so strong that when it was first brewed Customs & Excise queried the strength, on which the

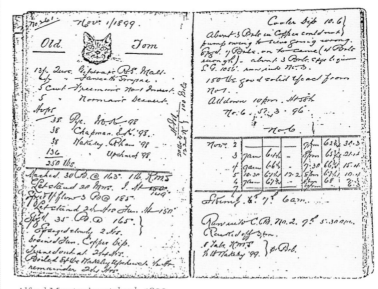

Alfred Munton's notebook, 1899

Bitter Beer, Stout, Extra Stout and Harvest Ale. Despite being the agent for Guinness, Robinsons brewed two of its own stouts. Harvest Ale probably referred to a beer produced with the first malts and hops of the annual harvest and may not have been a regular product.

As the new century progressed, beers were given more familiar names rather than obscure Ks and Xs. They included Best Mild, Best Bitter, Light Dinner Ale and Light Bitter Ale. Best Mild was a light mild (as the recipe shows), in contrast to the more familiar dark versions. Until the 1960s, it was Robinsons' best-selling beer and it was eventually renamed Hatters Mild to celebrate Stockport's hat-making industry, which was more than 200 years old. But as sales of mild declined, the decision was taken in the 21st century to stop production, much to the anguish of the local branch of CAMRA.

AN XX RECIPE

Alfred Munton's record books include the recipe for XX Mild Ale from 1899. The grains are Plumage Archer, Maris and Chevalier pale ale malts, with Irish ale malt, Barrett's/Joe White Pale Ale Malt, flaked maize, invert sugar, candy cane and malt extract. Hops, added in three stages in the copper, were Fuggles, followed by French Fuggles and Keyworth Mid Season, and finally Brewer's Gold, French Fuggles and Goldings. Goldings and French Fuggles were added in the conditioning vessel.

The house yeast strain was pitched in the fermenting vessels at a rate of one pound per barrel. After 24 hours, the beer was dropped to a secondary fermenting vessel, which suggests the brewery was using a 'double drop' system of fermentation (see p.47). Following fermentation, the beer was racked into casks and left to condition in the brewery for four to five days before being released to trade. The beer had an original gravity of 1052 degrees or 5.2 per cent ABV in modern terms. This shows that mild ales were considerably stronger in Victorian times than in the 21st century. It's interesting to note that the quintessentially English hop variety, the Fuggle, was being grown in France at the time.

brewery had to pay duty. It's brewed with pale and crystal malts, and a small touch of chocolate malt with caramel for colour. The hops are East Kent Goldings. The beer has a rich vinous character, with the fruit balanced by peppery hops. Munton himself drew the face of a cat on the label, an image that has survived today. It's not known why he chose a cat, but it may have been the brewery feline, which kept the malt store free from rodents. Today, thanks to the success of Trooper, more Old Tom is sold in export markets than at home. Two versions used to be produced: Gold Crown was bottled straight from a hogshead – a giant oak cask that holds 54 gallons – while Silver Crown was conditioned in tanks. Only the tank version is produced today. In 2019 Robinsons added a chilled keg version of the beer.

Other beers of the period, shown in a price list from the early 20th century, included AK Ale, thought to stand for light bitter or pale ale, XX strong mild,

On the takeover trail

Despite difficult times at the start of the 20th century, with a vociferous temperance movement and the threat of war, William Robinson was able to expand both production and his pub estate. By 1910 he owned more than 30 pubs, a considerable achievement when many pubs were closing. Following the Licensing Act of 1904 – the result of noisy campaigning by the temperance lobby – almost 10 per cent of pubs that were open in 1906 had closed by 1914.

In order to meet the demand from his pubs, William's production grew from 23,251 barrels in 1907 to 34,693 by 1912, a 49 per cent increase. With other breweries facing collapse, William went on the takeover trail and bought the Heginbotham brewery in Stalybridge. It was founded in 1851 as a wine and spirit merchants, expanded into brewing and owned a few pubs in Stalybridge, including the King's Arms, a major coaching inn. The brewery foundered, not as a result of the hard economic times of the early 20th century but from a family tragedy. John Heginbotham, who ran the company, died suddenly in 1912 from ptomaine poisoning, a rare form of food poisoning thought to be caused by eating decayed meat. All six members of the family present at the meal were taken ill and were unable to continue running the company, which went into voluntary liquidation in 1914. William Robinson bought the assets for £11,899 in

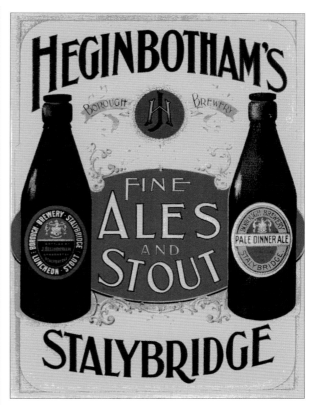

1915 and they included not only the brewery but five pubs and two off-licences. The Heginbotham brewery closed: as beer consumption declined during the First World War due to both rising prices and the absence of many thousands of potential drinkers who had joined the armed forces, William didn't need the additional capacity available in Stalybridge.

Alfred Munton died in 1918 following 28 years with the brewery, during which time he had developed a fine range of beers and left Old Tom as his legacy. By 1918 William's three sons had joined the business. Frederic, the eldest son, had won a BSc with Honours from UMIST, the University of Manchester Institute of Science and Technology. In common with Munton, he was to leave a lasting legacy at Robinsons. He went on to gain a master's degree in science, taking yeast as the subject of his thesis. He built the brewery's first laboratory to ensure his beers were free from infection and he designed a new brewhouse in the 1920s that

Women workers at the brewery during the First World War

would see service until the second decade of the 21st century.

Robinsons didn't follow the route of many other breweries that became public companies, enabling them to raise money from the stock market. But the family felt the need to safeguard the company's assets and in 1920 it became a private limited company with capital of £300,000. William Robinson became chairman and managing director and he celebrated the brewery's new status by buying seven pubs. William and his three sons, who all became directors, spent the 1920s carefully expanding the pub estate and improving many of their outlets. Pubs faced competition from cinema, radio and sport, and they had to meet the demands of a more sophisticated population that was not impressed with old-fashioned 'drinking dens'. Pubs needed to be more attractive as beer was expensive as a result of heavy increases in beer duty. Beer consumption in the 1920s was more than a third lower than before the First World War.

Robinsons bought its second brewery in 1926, Scholfield's Portland Street Brewery in Ashton-under-Lyne, which had both a fascinating history and a celebrated beer style. It was founded around 1824 at the Friendship Inn in Ashton by Thomas Scholfield who brewed on the premises and launched a friendly society there called the Society of Ancient Shepherds. There must have been many venerable shepherds at the time as the organisation grew into a national movement with more than 80,000 members.

Robinsons' fleet, c.1910–20

The brewery moved several times to meet the demand for its beers. As well as such staples as mild and bitter, Scholfield's became famous in the area for its milk stout, which was launched in 1908 when ownership had passed to a nephew of the family called Jeffrey Grime. Milk stout was promoted somewhat disingenuously as 'each pint bottle containing the energising carbohydrates of a half-pint of pure milk'. In fact, most milk stouts, including the famous Mackeson, are made with the addition of lactose, a by-product of cheese making, rather than whole milk.

Jeffrey Grime had no male heirs and when he reached the age of 65, he decided to sell the business. William Robinson paid £137,000 for Scholfield's, which came with a healthy estate of 42 pubs and a wine and spirits division. The new pubs enabled Robinsons to expand its business into an area of the north-west where it had not featured before.

The new brewery in Stockport designed by Frederic Robinson was built between 1925 and 1929. It was a seven-storey tower plant topped by ornamental stonework, including four imposing unicorns that became a major landmark in the town. The new plant enabled the family to greatly increase beer production. They needed more pubs and in 1929 bought Kay's Atlas Brewery in Manchester, which came with a substantial tied estate of 86 pubs and gave Robinsons entry into the major city of the north-west.

New pastures

William Robinson died in 1933 after devoting 55 years to the brewery. He was succeeded by his son John, whose three sons joined him in the 1950s and 60s to ensure the brewery would remain in family hands.

Robinsons remained successful and profitable in the difficult period of the 1930s, with economic depression at home and a new world war looming. While other brewers concentrated on urban pubs, John Robinson developed a strategy of buying pubs in country areas, including rural Cheshire and the Derbyshire Peak District. He saw that while high

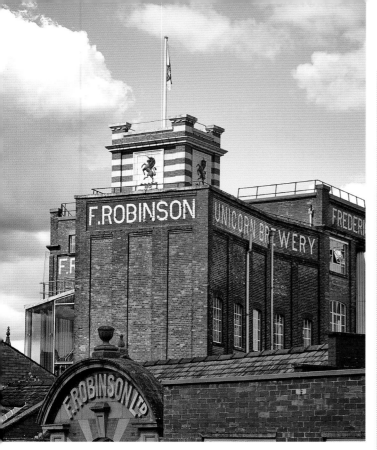

unemployment was depressing beer sales in towns and cities, the affluent middle class had access to motor cars and enjoyed days out in the country. They expected pubs to offer comfort and good food and wine as well as beer, and John Robinson and his team invested heavily in refitting and improving their rural estate. Rural pubs were also cheaper to buy than ones in towns and cities.

One pub that didn't survive the 1930s was the original Unicorn inn. Though still operating as a pub, it was demolished in 1936 to allow for brewery expansion. It was a sad end for an ancient hostelry that had given its name to the brewery and its beers.

Robinsons survived the Second World War intact, but was affected by substantial increases in duty to help the war effort and a shortage of raw materials. The brewery came to the rescue of Boddingtons in Manchester when the Strangeways Brewery was destroyed by enemy bombs in 1940. While the brewery was rebuilt, Robinsons filled casks with its own beer

that went to Boddingtons' pubs. The Unicorn suffered a serious fire in 1943 – it took three hours to bring it under control – but this wasn't due to enemy action. Fortunately, the brewhouse escaped unscathed, as did the malt store. The brewery cat, which was called Ginger, not Old Tom, was rescued by the fire brigade.

Despite the deprivations of war, John Robinson's drive to expand the pub estate led to the acquisition of an outlet in Wales, the Black Lion in Llanfair Talhaiarn, near Abergele. Recognising that Wales is a popular holiday destination for the people of the Manchester area, Robinsons invested further and now has 31 pubs in the country.

As Britain slowly recovered from the war and restrictions on brewing and ingredients were eased, Robinsons continued to expand both its pub and brewing operations. In 1949 it bought its main competitor in Stockport, Bell & Co. It began brewing in 1836 and built a strong local following for its ale and porter. The brewhouse was expanded to meet demand at a cost of £4,000 and it became the biggest brewery in the region outside Manchester. In 1850 the brewery came under the control of two Yorkshiremen, Henry Bell and Joseph Smith. They prospered and in 1872 they moved the brewing operations to a former tannery. When Smith retired, the company was owned by Henry Bell and his successors. By 1892 it owned 44 pubs in Stockport with a further 32 in Manchester and Derbyshire. A new brewery was built in 1930, but the company struggled during the depression. Output fell alarmingly and plans to modernise pubs were shelved. Talks of a merger with the Reddish Brewery were abandoned, but when the chairman, Henry Bell, died Robinsons stepped in and after protracted negotiations bought its rival in 1949, making it the biggest brewer in Cheshire.

In 1958 John Robinson was knighted for his services to public life in Cheshire. He oversaw the business at a time of major upheaval in the brewing industry. A series of mergers created five – later six – national brewing groups that accounted for half the industry's output. The national giants went on the acquisition trail and no regional brewer was safe, with two in Manchester, Boddingtons and Wilsons, falling to Whitbread and Watney Mann & Truman respectively. In order to compete and meet the demands of modern drinkers, Robinsons moved in a radically new direction. It added keg beer to its draught portfolio and stepped up bottled beer production. The brewery built a new packaging centre at Bredbury, which opened in 1976; it was one of the biggest initiatives ever undertaken by the family.

A RADICAL REOPENING

In January 2020 Robinsons reopened the historic Bull's Head in Market Place, Stockport. The Grade II-listed pub, built in 1733, had been closed for eight years and the brewery invested £400,000 restoring it to its former glory. The inn has a long association with radical causes in the area and in the 19th century large crowds were addressed from the balcony by such famous orators as Henry Hunt, Fergus O'Connor and Richard Cobden. A large group from Stockport went to Manchester in 1819 to join a vast demonstration of around 800,000 people demanding the vote for working people and reform of parliament. The meeting was held at St Peter's Field where the demonstrators were attacked by armed yeomanry and hussars who killed 18 people and injured several hundred. The event became known as the Peterloo Massacre.

Sir John Robinson died, fittingly, at his desk in the brewery in 1978. He had been chairman for 45 years and he bequeathed to his family a business that was fighting fit and strong enough to see off the national giants. By the end of the 1970s, only 142 breweries were still in operation and the nationals, dubbed the Big Six by CAMRA, now accounted for three-quarters of all the beer brewed in Britain. With a new chairman, Peter Robinson, the brewery continued to invest in its pubs while new fermenting vessels were installed to meet the revived interest in cask beer created by CAMRA.

A controversial takeover in 1982 created a degree of bad feeling for a while between Robinsons and CAMRA. The brewery in question was Hartley's in Ulverston in Cumbria, a town best known as the birthplace of Stan Laurel. Known originally as the Old Brewery, it opened in 1755 and grew to a large and successful business. By 1980 it had 56 pubs covering an area from Whitehaven to Lancaster. Robinsons bought Hartley's in 1982 and eventually closed the brewery in 1991 on the grounds that production had dropped considerably at Ulverston, which critics blamed on the heavy presence of Robinsons' beers in Hartley's pubs. The old brewery was retained as a distribution depot for several years but is now housing.

In the 1990s Robinsons was able to add to its pub estate as a result of the Monopolies Commission investigation of the brewing industry and the government's subsequent Beer Orders, which forced the national brewers to sell large parcels of pubs. Robinsons bought 56 pubs in Cumbria and nine from Bass, the latter ranging from Ulverston to Stockport. The brewery strengthened its local roots in 1992 by sponsoring Stockport County Football Club.

The company entered the new century in fine fettle with Oliver and William, the sixth generation, in charge. New beers were added, some of which are produced with a device called the Hopnik in the new

The Robinson family at the Bakers Vault, Stockport

brewhouse. This allows beer to circulate over a bed of hops to pick up additional aroma.

One new beer caused some controversy. The original labels and pumpclips for Dizzy Blonde, a golden ale, showed a young woman in a skimpy negligee, which led to vociferous criticism. The image has been radically changed and now shows a woman's face on an aeroplane fuselage in the style of American fighter planes in the Second World War.

Despite a few hiccups, relations with CAMRA are sound, exemplified by Old Tom winning the Strong Ale category in the Champion Beer of Britain competition in 1990.

The strength of family control is undiminished. As well as Oliver and William, Neil, Paul and Veronica Robinson joined the board in 2003, followed by Sara, who is now company secretary, and John Robinson, the latest addition to the board in 2009.

With the new brewhouse installed, Oliver, William and their relatives looked forward to increasing production over the following 20 years.

And then came Trooper…

Robinsons, Unicorn Brewery, Lower Hillgate, Stockport SK1 1JJ · 0161 612 4061
www.robinsonsbrewery.com
Tours by arrangement

Regular cask beers:
Wizard (3.7%)
Dizzy Blonde (3.8%)
Cumbria Way (4.1%, brewed for former Hartley's pubs)
Cwrw'r Ddraig Aur (4.1%, brewed for Welsh pubs)
Unicorn (4.2%)
Trooper (4.7%)
Cascade (4.8%)
Old Tom (8.5%)

Joseph Holt

THE address of the brewery founded by Joseph Holt in the middle of the 19th century underscores all the pomp and circumstance of the time: Empire Street, Cheetham. But it's not a brewery living off its past and it has a very modern image today.

In 2019 head brewer Jane Kershaw, aged 32, and the great-great-great granddaughter of Joseph Holt, was named Brewer of the Year by the Parliamentary Beer Club at a glittering ceremony in Westminster. Proudly holding her trophy, Jane declared: 'It's vital we make beer the number one drink of choice again and support our pubs, which are a significant part of our culture and identity.' You couldn't wish for a better call to arms from one family brewer to the others as they face the challenges of the 21st century.

Jane Kershaw, named Brewer of the Year by the All-Party Parliamentary Beer Group in 2019

Today, Joseph Holt not only welcomes visitors to its beautifully appointed Victorian offices, with wood panelling, engraved glass windows and portraits of family members adorning the walls, but it also has a very modern attitude to the beers it produces. As well as its uncompromisingly hoppy Mild and Bitter, it has a fashionable IPA and a citrus/fruity golden ale called Two Hoots. It was an early starter in lager production and its Diamond has won several awards, including Best in the World in the prestigious International Brewing Awards in both 2013 and 2017. The awards, held in Burton upon Trent, are judged by brewers from around the world. To be called the best on the planet when competing with beers from Germany and other Central European countries is a remarkable achievement. Between 2011 and 2017, Joseph Holt won a gold medal at each bi-annual event, a feat achieved by only three other brewers in the world.

Managing director Richard Kershaw underscores the family's commitment to brewing and retailing. 'Our pubs suffered when the smoking ban came in, but we've got over that and we've had three years of growth,' he says. The pub estate, which stretches from Manchester to Cheshire, Lancashire, Merseyside and Derbyshire, numbers 127 with 40 of them serving quality food. 'Food is a quarter of our business,' Richard says, and adds that he's buying top-of-the-range pubs and is investing heavily in modernising many older outlets, spending half a million pounds on each one. The free trade accounts for around one third of the brewery's income and Richard's son Andrew, who learned the ropes with a stint at St Austell Brewery, has joined Joseph Holt to expand that side of the business.

The company produces keg beers that include Northern Hop and American IPA, and owns a micro plant at the Horse and Jockey pub in Chorlton. The 500-year-old pub, bought in 2012, came with its own Bootleg microbrewery and the name is used for some additional brands. 'It's an extra arm and a great name,' Andrew Kershaw says.

One beer that is in steep decline is Mild. Richard says at one time Joseph Holt brewed three times as much Mild as Bitter. In 1979, 22,000 barrels of Mild were brewed but today that figure is down to just 300 barrels. However, a keg version of the beer, called Black, is doing well. 40 per cent of Holt's annual production of between 50,000 and 60,000 barrels is cask beer, with keg and bottles in the ascendancy.

The journey to Empire Street

Lager, keg beer and food-led pubs were a long way removed from brewery life when Joseph Holt started in business. The middle of the 19th century was a propitious time to open a brewery as Manchester was expanding at a furious pace. Driven by the cotton industry and the trades that fuelled it, new residential areas were springing up, most with rudimentary housing whose inhabitants were keen to visit pubs, drink beer and forget about the hard grind of their working lives for a few hours.

Joseph, who came from the textile village of Unsworth where his father was a handloom weaver, moved to Manchester in the 1840s and worked as a carter at the Strangeways Brewery. In 1849 he had the good fortune to marry Catherine Parry who used her energy, good income and sound business sense to set him up as a brewer. Catherine came from a family of well-to-do farmers in North Wales and she worked first as a governess and then ran her own school in Manchester. Catherine used the income she had made from her work to lease a plot of land, in 1848, in Cheetham where she built two houses. She raised £600 by mortgaging the houses and Joseph started work as a small brewer on the site. This was a time when the 1830 Beer Act allowed anyone to open a small pub with brewery attached for a fee of two guineas a year. There are no records in existence but it's thought Joseph had a modest trade at first, supplying his own pub, a few surrounding taverns and beerhouses, as well as local families for home consumption, delivering beer door-to-door rather like a milkman.

He clearly prospered for in 1855 he bought the Ducie Bridge Brewery and his family, which included his only child Edward, moved to a cottage in the grounds. He produced ale and porter on kit that included, according to an inventory, a 12-barrel pan, mash tun and two coolers.

Joseph Holt, founder

Joseph assiduously built his trade, offering loans at 5 per cent interest to people who wished to open pubs and beerhouses. By 1860, clearly doing well as a brewer with a good free trade, he was on the move again, this time to land owned by the Earl of Derby. He built a new brewery on what was to become Empire Street and he and his family and their successors have remained there ever since.

An indelible mark

Joseph faced difficult times in his first few years at the Derby Brewery. The Civil War in the United States and the blockade of the Confederate ports in the south meant the supply of raw cotton to Manchester's textile industry came to a shuddering stop. Economic depression gripped the region for several years and Joseph Holt, in common with all the Manchester brewers, saw sales plummet. When the Civil War ended, trade started to pick up and Joseph decided to row back from offering loans to beerhouses and to

build his own tied estate. By the time he died, in 1886, he owned 20 tenanted outlets. It was a wise move as two pieces of legislation – the 1869 Beer Act and 1872 Licensing Act – ended the free-for-all in brewing and selling beer. Justices now had the power to refuse new licences and withdraw them from premises on the grounds of bad behaviour. Beerhouses went into rapid decline and it was only those brewers who could afford to buy and tie pubs who remained in business. Joseph Holt was one of the survivors.

The 1870s was a time of economic recovery and the consumption of beer reached unprecedented levels. Joseph Holt installed stabling for dray horses, and blacksmith's and cooper's shops at the brewery, but as his health started to fail, he handed control of the business to his son Edward, who had worked with his father since 1875. Joseph died in his home at the brewery in 1886, aged 73, and Catherine followed six years later, aged 82. Both had left an indelible mark on Manchester.

After working alongside his father for 11 years, Edward Holt set about expanding the business with

Edward Holt

amazing zeal. He survived economic downturns and not only brewed more beer but also dramatically increased the number of tied houses. Between 1886 and 1892 he bought 27 new pubs, mainly on the north side of Manchester and in Salford. A further 12 new outlets were added in the following few years and between 1896 and the close of the century he added an additional 42 new tied houses in Manchester and Salford. In 1897 he bought the Bentley Brewery in Prestwich and the Crumpsall Brewery in Cheetham Hill; both breweries closed and their pubs were added to Holt's estate.

The large tied estate needed more beer and in the final decade of the 19th century annual production soared from 16,068 barrels to 40,350. This boom, however, was short-lived. A royal commission on licensing laws led to government legislation in 1904 to reduce the number of licensed premises in the country and justices were given greater powers to refuse new licences. On top of this, alcohol duties were increased to help pay for the cost of the Boer War, a trend that would continue throughout the First World War. As a result of these measures, production at Joseph Holt fell for the first time in a decade and several of the company's pubs closed after being refused new licences.

As pubs shut – and Joseph Holt lost a total of 29 – off-licences grew in popularity and Edward Holt responded by building a bottling line at the Derby Brewery. Three beers were bottled: Holt's Bitter, Burton Ale supplied by a Burton brewer and Guinness stout. The initiative was an immediate success and bottling accounted for more than 2,000 barrels in the first full year of production. By 1920 the amount had almost trebled and packaged beer formed more than 10 per cent of annual sales.

Edward Holt, later Sir Edward, ran the Derby Brewery for 46 years until his death in 1928. As well

SPEARHEADING THE FIGHT AGAINST CANCER

Sir Edward Holt and the successive family generations are known and respected in Manchester for their long support for the Christie Hospital along with the Holt Radium Institute that bears their name. The Christie Hospital was founded in the 1890s to tackle the rising problem of cancer, caused in no small part by the number of people working in unhealthy mills and factories. The pioneering work at the Christie led to research

into the potential use of radium, a radioactive material discovered by Marie Curie. Radium was astonishingly expensive – 60,000 times greater than the price of gold – and the hospital appealed to the business community in Manchester for support.

Sir Edward Holt responded by creating a fund to deepen research into cancer and the use of radium. He personally donated £2,000 and in total raised £20,000, worth £3 million in today's money. The research was successful and Sir Edward and his wife, Lady Elizabeth, provided additional funding for the new Holt Radium Institute in Nelson Street. In the 1930s both the institute and the Christie Hospital amalgamated in a new and bigger

site in Withington. Research there led to the introduction of radiotherapy and chemotherapy, which replaced radium as more modern ways of treating cancer.

The Holt family, including Sir Edward's son, who was also named Edward, continued support for the hospital, followed by the Kershaws who organised fund-raising campaigns for the hospital to mark the company's 150th anniversary in 1999. £301,000 was raised and in 2014, which marked 100 years since the launch of the Holt Radium Institute, a further £402,000 was raised. In 1996 Lady Margaret Holt, widow of the second Sir Edward, died and left £7.5 million in Holt's shares to the hospital – the biggest legacy ever made to a hospital in north-west England.

as brewing, he had a full civic life. He was a Conservative councillor from 1890 and was twice elected Lord Mayor of Manchester despite vociferous opposition from the temperance movement. He was the main driving force behind a scheme to enhance the water supply brought to the city from the lakes in Cumbria and was knighted in recognition of this work.

Trying times

Joseph Holt suffered along with all brewers the harsh and ever-rising duty rates during the 1914–18 war. Restrictions on output meant that the Derby Brewery in 1917 brewed just 27,959 barrels, around half the pre-war levels. Many members of staff and pub tenants were called to the armed forces and several failed to return. They included Captain Joseph Holt, Sir Edward's son, who had been groomed to take over the business but was killed at Gallipoli in 1915, aged just 33.

Brewing boomed once wartime restrictions were lifted and servicemen returned home. For a few years in the early 1920s, men worked shifts to keep the brewery operating 24 hours a day. At this time, Sir Edward's health began to fail and as the family was faced by the imposition of death duties the business was reorganised to become a private limited company, with all the shares owned by the family. Sir Edward became chairman and his brother-in-law Buckley Brooks joined the board, with Brooks as manager. Sir Edward also invited Harold Slaney Kershaw and

Charles Dempster to join the board. Both were family members through marriage and the Kershaw family became central to the success of the brewery from then on.

Joseph Holt Ltd faced difficult times in the 1920s and 30s. The early boom in brewing came to an end. Crippling levels of unemployment hit the north of England especially hard, accompanied by lengthy strikes in the mines and the General Strike of 1926. Production at Joseph Holt fell by more than 10,000 barrels a year with bottled beer declining by close to 20 per cent.

Sir Edward died in 1928 and the second Edward took over as chairman, with the baronetcy passing to him. The new board faced major problems for most of the 1930s with continuing unemployment reducing beer drinking, and in some cases pub tenants' rents had to be reduced to help them survive. The shocking impact of unemployment in Manchester was highlighted by the occasion when Joseph Holt advertised for a new joiner: the queue of applicants stretched down Empire Street, round the corner and up Cheetham Hill Road.

The economy and beer sales picked up towards the end of the decade, but the recovery was short-lived with the start of the Second World War. Manchester was targeted by the German air force, but the Derby Brewery escaped almost unscathed, save for a bomb being dropped on the joiners' shop. The neighbouring Boddingtons Brewery was badly damaged and production stopped. In common with Robinsons in Stockport, Joseph Holt came to Boddington's aid and supplied the brewery's pubs with beer until production at the Strangeways plant could start again.

Following the return to peace, Holt's directors decided to float the brewery and its pubs as a public company. It became Joseph Holt PLC in 1951 with the brewery valued at £19,343 and the pub estate worth £675,532. The figures were in stark contrast to the modest figure of £6,000 recorded for the brewery in the 1890s.

HOLT'S PUB BECOMES A TV STAR

In 1960 the King William IV pub in Salford was closed due to a compulsory purchase order. The pub was demolished but part of it lives on as a TV legend. Before demolition, Granada Television took out the bar and it has been used ever since as the bar of the Rover's Return in *Coronation Street*.

Sir Edward Holt died in 1968, aged 85, and with 64 years' service to the brewery. He was succeeded by his nephew Peter Kershaw, who steered the company through the difficult years of the 1960s and 70s, which saw the rise of giant national brewers and their keg beers and lager. While Joseph Holt entered the lager market with its own brands, it remained committed to draught ale. The arrival of CAMRA in 1971 saw interest in cask beer increase. By 1979 brewery volumes had risen substantially and half a million pounds were invested in expanding and renewing equipment at the brewery so capacity could increase by 50 per cent.

By the early 1990s increasing demand for Holt's beer led to further expansion. Additional fermenting capacity and kegging equipment were installed, and new buildings erected on the site of the old stables enabled production to again grow by 50 per cent. At the same time, several old regional breweries were being taken over and closed by national companies. The disappearance of the Oldham Brewery and then Boddingtons gave a further boost to sales of Holt's beer – though no one at the Derby Brewery expressed any pleasure at the demise of companies with whom they had enjoyed good neighbourly relations for many years, not least during the Second World War.

Investment and a community focus

Today, brewers Phil Parkinson and Lloyd Rees start a tour in the brewery yard where a new bore hole has been sunk for a supply of 'liquor' or brewing water: water from an old, deeper bore hole is no longer of sufficient quality for brewing. Inside the brewery, the expanded capacity can be seen by not one but two mash tuns and two coppers that can cope with brew lengths of up to 150 barrels. Thirty fermenting vessels cope with ale and lager, with conical lager tanks outside the brewhouse. Lager is hopped with the Celeia variety from Slovenia, while ales use two English varieties, Admiral and Whitbread Goldings.

Holt's Bitter is brewed with pale and black malts while Mild is made with pale, crystal and black malts

Jane, Andrew and Richard Kershaw

and brewing sugar. Two Hoots is brewed with a blend of pale and lager malts and hopped with an English version of American Cascade while IPA is made with just pale malt and Cascade.

In 2000, the family launched a successful bid to return the company to private ownership. Brewery and pubs are now back in family hands, keeping them safe from marauders in the global brewing industry.

Richard Kershaw says: 'We can take long-term decisions,' vital at a time when family brewers are being squeezed by micros and global producers. He is sanguine about Small Brewers Relief: 'It encouraged drinkers to try different brands and it made a lot of noise in the industry, but it has distorted the market.'

He stresses that Joseph Holt is about more than just making and selling beer, and retains its strong links to the community. Pubs stage events to raise money for local charities: in 2018, 46 pubs raised funds to donate to a total of £114,000 for Maggie's Manchester – centres that offer counselling for people with cancer – with a further £160,000 raised for the Christie in 2019. As Richard says, 'Raising those sums

of money in some of the most deprived areas of the country is remarkable and is a great tribute to our staff and customers.' As a result of these initiatives, Joseph Holt won the Community Company of the Year award three years running from the British Beer and Pub Association.

The Christie remains top of the list for Joseph Holt. In 2014, to celebrate the 100 years' partnership with the Christie Hospital and Holt Radium Institute, Richard and Andrew Kershaw cycled through northern France, Belgium, Germany and northern Denmark, clocking up 1,134 miles in a fortnight.

They deserved a beer at the end of the journey.

Joseph Holt, Derby Brewery, Empire Street, Cheetham, Manchester M3 1JD · 0161 834 3285 www.joseph-holt.com · Brewery shop

Regular cask beers:
Mild (3.2%)
IPA (3.8%)
Bitter (4%)
Two Hoots (4.2%)

Hydes

1863 · SALFORD

HYDES represents both the old and the modern faces of brewing. In 2012 it moved to a new site, the Beer Studio, in the buzzing Media City in Salford, with bright glitzy buildings that include the BBC complex. With modernity all around, the company remains committed to traditional cask beer. There's no keg beer or lager at the new Hydes but it has embraced golden and hoppy beers with some success.

The old Manchester and Salford, however, are not forgotten. Hydes is close to the Lowry Museum and has been given permission by the Lowry Foundation to use some of the artist's paintings on pumpclips and labels for six beers. They include Lowry, first brewed in 2015 and now a member of the core range of beers.

Quite what those iconic matchstick figures in Lowry's paintings would make of such a citrus/hoppy beer will never be known but they would almost certainly have preferred a pint of good old mild.

The new brewery is on a site with brewing roots. It's a former distribution centre for Greenalls of Warrington, which closed in 1990. The smart new brewing kit, which is mainly German built, enables Hydes to produce 10–12,000 barrels a year. That's a sharp drop on the capacity of the old brewery in Moss Side, which could make 140 barrels per brew, while the new plant is restricted to brews of 40 barrels, with the flexibility to go down to just 10 barrels.

Managing director Chris Hopkins says the decision to move to a new brewery was driven by a desire to produce many more craft beers as the market required rather than to qualify for lower duty rates enshrined in Small Brewers Relief. He says the Grade II-listed brewery in Moss Side was 170 years old, straddled five storeys and needed a lot of work to keep it fit for purpose. Sixty per cent of production was contract brewing, including a seven-year deal to brew Boddingtons Bitter, a famous Manchester beer now owned by AB InBev. When that contract came to an end, Moss Side would have had a large hole to fill. Other contracts included Harp Lager, Bass XXXX, Whitbread Trophy and Mackeson Milk Stout. The company had sold its free trade to Thwaites of Blackburn in order to concentrate on its 54 pubs and it was necessary to slim down the brewing side.

The Anvil

It's a different world to the one in which Alfred and Ralph Hyde opened their brewery in 1863. They had inherited a small brewery from their grandfather Thomas Shaw, but this must have been a tiny plant as the brothers led a peripatetic existence for more than 30 years, brewing at the Crown Brewery in Audenshaw before moving – as the quality of the water was poor – to the Mayfield Street Brewery in Ardwick. As the business expanded Hydes moved again, to the Fairfield Street Brewery, Ancoats, and finally to the Rusholme Brewery.

The wanderlust ended in 1899 when William Hyde bought the Queen's Brewery in Moss Side and renamed it Hydes Queen's Brewery. Much later, in 1944, it was renamed Hydes Anvil Brewery to incorporate the company's trademark, the Anvil, which implied strength. Part of the Anvil Brewery was used on one occasion as a film set for an edition of *Coronation Street*. A plaque was later placed on the loading bay with the words 'Jack Duckworth Drank Here', commemorating one of the characters in the soap opera.

Annie Hyde

When William Hyde died in 1916 the brewery was run for a remarkable 56 years by his sister, Annie, another example of a family brewery being run by a strong and determined woman in a business largely dominated by men. It was a baptism of fire for the young Annie. William had left debts of £4,390 and the family had to pay their creditors nine pence in the pound in order to save the brewery.

Annie is remembered by her great-nephew Neal Hyde as 'a tough and unyielding character who ran the financial side of the business to strict standards and with a rod of iron,' but who also 'could be extremely generous to people in trouble'. On one occasion in the 1920s, her nephew was driving to Buxton in Derbyshire when it started to snow. He realised that the car coming towards him was Annie's large chauffeur-driven Daimler. As it swept past him, he noticed that the rear hood was down and that Annie's 'only concession to the inclement weather was to sit bolt upright with a raised umbrella to ward off the snow'.

Alfred Hyde

The iconic, 140ft-high Anvil chimney was demolished in 1973

Annie and her brother William built a substantial tied estate, a necessary requirement in a city with many large breweries and fierce competition. Hydes's beers included Pale Ale, Extra Stout and Brown Ale. At one stage it also had a golden ale, Anvil Gold, which may have been prompted by the success of Boddingtons Bitter, which was exceptionally pale at a time when most bitters were brown or copper coloured. Hydes was also well known for its mild ales: at one time it brewed three different versions of the style.

An expansive range

The family is still firmly in control, with Adam Hyde working as company secretary and his niece Hattie Shotton as marketing executive at the Beer Studio.

The core range today is 1863 and Old Indie, both 3.5 per cent and examples of pale and dark mild, Hydes Original (3.8 per cent), the brewery's main bitter, and Lowry (4.7 per cent). But head brewer, the vastly experienced Paul Jefferies, has a sweet shop to play with on his new brewing kit and can produce as many as 55 beers a year. He uses 50 different hops, including varieties from the United States and Slovenia. As well as essential pale malt, supplied by Crisp in Norfolk, Paul uses 20 coloured malts and has also experimented with rice, maize and rye along with a lager yeast culture. The original Moss Side yeast strain is still used for the core range. Eighty per cent of the hops are English varieties, with Challenger and Fuggles used for Hydes Original, while Lowry has two American hops, Chinook and Citra.

Two new special beer ranges are called Beer Studio and Provenance and reach out to younger drinkers. The Beer Studio banner includes Venetian Red, Cara Bronze, Burnt Sienna and Moroccan Gold, while Provenance, which offers 12 beers a year, includes Bruges, Paddock Wood, Prague, Alsace, Yakima IPA, Yankee Pumpkin Ale, West Coast Wheat Ale and Apache APA. As the name Provenance suggests, the beers pay homage to the styles of such great brewing cities as Bruges and Prague as well as important American hop-growing regions like the Yakima Valley in Washington State. Paddock Wood is a hop centre in Kent created by the former brewer Whitbread and includes a museum tracing the history of hop growing and harvesting in the county.

Beer Studio and Provenance don't use the Hydes name but seasonal and occasional beers under the family banner include Ghostly Coyote, which blends

Adam Hyde with niece Hattie Shotton

some rice with malt and seven American hops, and Yucatan, which has rice and maize blended with malt and is fermented with lager yeast.

The brewing equipment is a hybrid of British and continental systems. The mash tun doubles as a lauter tun or filtration vessel where the used grain is filtered to wash out any remaining fermentable sugar. The sweet extract is boiled in a combined kettle and whirlpool where hop pellets are used. Fermentation is carried out in five 40-barrel vessels that are flexible and can be tuned to produce just 10 barrels.

Chris Hopkins believes the big range of beers has helped boost sales and cask ale is doing well in the brewery's pubs. The new plant underscores the family's commitment to brewing; Adam Hyde and other family members were determined the business

would not become a pub company. But pubs are not ignored and the estate has been strengthened by new outlets on the Wirral, in Chester, Wilmslow, Hyde, Didsbury and Nantwich. In 2015 Hydes opened a boutique hotel with a pub and 15 guest rooms in the Northern Quarter of Manchester. It's called the Abel Heywood and is named after a 19th-century publisher. He was mayor of Manchester and went to prison as part of his campaign to make newsprint available to produce popular papers for the working class.

Chris Hopkins says Hydes qualifies for Small Brewers Relief, but he thinks there should be a review of the system so that all brewers receive some benefit, and to remove what he calls the 'cliff edge' where relief ends. Both he and Paul Jefferies believe cask beer will survive but will be squeezed by keg.

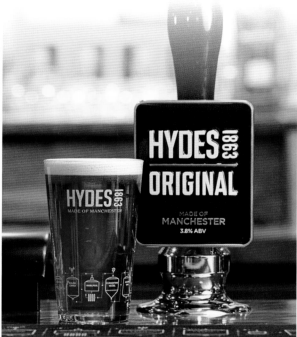

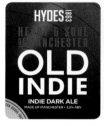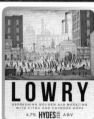

They may install a keg plant at some point but cask ale will always be their priority.

'Pubs are a profitable part of our business and we supply them with a fantastic range of high quality beers,' Chris says. Of those beers, Lowry, in cask and bottle, is a major success and points the way to the future.

Hydes, The Beer Studio, 30 Kansas Avenue, Salford M50 2GL · 0161 226 1317
www.hydesbrewery.com · Tours by arrangement

Regular cask beers:
1863 (3.5%)
Old Indie (3.5%)
Hydes Original (3.8%)
Lowry (4.7%)

The Abel Heywood, Hydes' boutique hotel in Manchester's Northern Quarter

143

THE
GOLDEN AGE

ARKELL'S · DONNINGTON · ST AUSTELL · TIMOTHY TAYLOR'S · CAMERONS
ADNAMS · BATEMANS · WADWORTH · CHARLES WELLS

THE second half of the 19th century marked a golden age for family brewers. As this section shows, a host of new family brewers opened for business, with the year 1875 marking the high tide for new companies. The rush to start breweries coincided with rapid changes in society. The population continued to grow and brewers raced to meet the increasing demand for beer. The rise of the new middle class widened the gap between those who drank dark ales and those who preferred the 'refined' character of new, paler beers. Pubs reflected this change, with clear divisions between the lounge bar for the better off and the public bar or vault for people on lower incomes. In the most extreme cases, the bars were divided by 'snob screens' to give the middle and upper classes privacy from the 'lower orders'.

Pale ale was not cheap. It cost between seven and eight pence a quart (two pints) while mild and porter cost four or five pence. In *The British Brewing Industry 1830–1980*, Richard Wilson says:

> Quality and cost made it [Burton pale ale]
> a status drink for the expanding lower middle
> class of clerks and shopkeepers, the armies of
> rail travellers and those "aristocrats of labour"
> [highly-skilled workers] whose standards of living
> rose appreciably after 1850. The other factor in its
> impact on beer tastes was the ease with which

a generation of country brewers succeeded in imitating, usually more cheaply, its light, sparkling, bitter qualities. Making a good Burton-type ale was the *sine qua non* for that generation of brewers who reaped the rewards of the great increase in consumption in the 1860s and 1870s.

In order to meet the increased demand, brewers expanded their range of beers. Family Ale, a low-strength pale beer, became popular for home consumption. As early as 1855, the Stafford Brewery's price list included X Ale, XX Ale, XXX Ale, XXXX Ale, Stafford Imperial, AK Ale, IPA, Porter, Single Stout and Double Stout – a range that appealed to all sectors of society. Many brewers also produced their version of Burton Ale, the strong, slightly sweet brown beer that preceded pale ale. Young's in south-west London brewed Burton Ale, which was later renamed Winter Warmer and was a rare example of the breed in the late 20th century.

In Victorian times, the pace of change in the industry was dramatic. Brewing was becoming a science. Louis Pasteur produced his seminal work *Études sur la Bière* in 1876, in which he analysed yeast and how it became infected. He visited several British breweries and encouraged them to install microscopes in order to avoid infections. At the Carlsberg Laboratories in Copenhagen, the brewing scientist

Emil Christian Hansen had painstakingly worked to produce a pure strain of yeast. As a result, British breweries started to employ head brewers who were also scientists and were able to improve beer quality out of all recognition.

The technology of brewing changed too. Cast-iron mash tuns, offering better heat retention, replaced wooden ones. The mash was stirred by steam-driven rakes and at the end of the mash it was 'sparged' by rotating arms in the roof: i.e., sprayed with hot water to rinse out any remaining sugars. Instead of producing several beers from one mash of grain, with decreasing levels of alcohol, the mash tun was used more efficiently to push through a new brew every few hours. Coppers, fired by coal or coke, turned from open pans into enclosed domed vessels that avoided heat loss and retained the essential aromas of the hops.

Beer was no longer cooled prior to fermentation in coolships or open pans that were open to attack by wild yeasts. Instead, the hopped wort was cooled in heat exchange units where the liquid was pumped through pipes or plates that alternated with pipes holding running cold water. When ice-making machines were invented in Germany, they were embraced with as much enthusiasm in Britain as they were by European lager brewers.

Fermentation was greatly improved. Drinkers demanded clearer beer, especially when commercial glass-blowing meant that glass replaced pewter in pubs and people were able to see the clarity of their brew. In order to cleanse beer of yeast, brewers in Burton developed the 'union system' of fermentation, using giant oak casks. As the beer fermented, yeast drove some of the liquid out of the casks and into troughs above where the yeast was retained. Unions can still be seen at Marston's brewery in Burton. Further north, the Yorkshire square method acted in a similar fashion, separating the yeast from the beer in two chambers (see Samuel Smith and Black Sheep).

To make use of the magical waters of the Trent Valley, some family brewers from London and Manchester opened second plants in Burton upon Trent in order to make pale ale. But by the end of the century scientists had learnt how to 'Burtonise' water by the addition of sulphates and second plants in Burton became redundant. While pale ale and IPA could now be brewed anywhere in the country, Burton remained a citadel of brewing and by the end of the century Bass was producing one million barrels a year, and was for a period the biggest brewer in the world.

In the pub trade, legislation curtailed the wild excesses brought about by the 1830 Beer Act and pubs were brought under the control of licensed magistrates. Many of the rough and ready beerhouses went out of business and were bought by commercial brewers. They invested in them to make them more comfortable for modern drinkers, and devised variations on existing beer styles that would be quick to make and more profitable. Tying up capital by ageing or vatting beer for long periods was no longer acceptable. With porter in decline and many consumers rejecting IPA as too strong and hoppy, brewers developed what they called 'running beers'. These were versions of pale ale and mild that were delivered to pubs and served within a few days once they had settled in their casks. They were the forerunners of today's real ales. Drinkers not only enjoyed running beers but dubbed the pale version 'bitter'. It was a type of beer that would become the hallmark of the family brewers as they entered the 20th century.

Arkell's

THE passion and commitment of brewing at Arkell's in Swindon was summed up by former chairman Peter Arkell: 'My initials are PA – Pale Ale. I was born in the brewery and I married a brewer's daughter. I'm in it up to my neck.'

His work clearly did him no harm: Peter Arkell died in 2010 at the robust age of 87. His family are still firmly in control: his son James followed him as chairman and helped oversee the celebrations for the brewery's 175th anniversary in 2018. This laudable milestone was marked with open days and brewery tours. But while there's an understandable pride in the brewery's past, the sixth generation of the family is also facing up to the challenges of the 21st century.

Head brewer Alex Arkell is expanding the beer range and has added an impressive new visitor centre, the Grape & Grain. The two-storey building with exposed rafters, opened by the Duchess of Cornwall in 2018, sells beer and branded clothing, and is decked out with fascinating memorabilia that traces the company's long history. Alex's brother George, in charge of close to 100 pubs, is upgrading them to meet modern consumer demands.

But as you tour the Grade II-listed brewery buildings, with narrow wooden stairs, iron gangways and ancient beer-making vessels, you can't escape the past. It's a story worth telling for it recounts how the founder, John Arkell, from a farming family in Kempsford, Gloucestershire, had the good fortune to latch on to the arrival of the railway in Swindon in the 19th century and brewed beer for pubs packed with workers building the new iron way.

Beer-making in the DNA

John Arkell was a well-travelled man for his time. Before launching his brewery, he emigrated to Canada, taking with him a group of impoverished farm labourers anxious to escape the harsh conditions and low wages in England. They established a small community in Ontario and called it Arkell in his honour. It has survived to this day and the Wellington Brewery in Guelph produces Arkell Best Bitter to commemorate it.

Founder, John Arkell, 1801–1881

Built behind the Kingsdown Inn, it had a steam engine as the motive force driving the brewing process and was a tower brewery, with the stages of brewing flowing from floor to floor.

Visitors today can see grain and milling at the top feeding the mash tun and copper one floor down, which in turn supply hopped wort – the sugary extract boiled with hops – to fermenters below. Cask beer is fermented in traditional square vessels, with modern conicals for keg beer and lager. On the ground floor, beer is racked into casks for onward delivery to pubs. In Victorian times, the casks would have been made of oak, with coopers building and repairing them before horse-drawn drays transported them to local ale houses. Today the casks are made of metal and horse power has replaced the horses.

John's fiancée missed the old country and he returned home to marry her and grow barley on his farm in Stratton St Margaret near Swindon. In the mid-19th century, before the rise of big brewers owning estates of pubs, most beer was produced by publicans. John Arkell followed the trend. He opened his first pub, the Kingsdown Inn, on the outskirts of Swindon, and started to brew there in 1843, using grain from his farm and hops from Worcestershire.

John had 12 children, two of whom emigrated to New Zealand where they were involved in starting no fewer than five breweries. Making beer is clearly lodged in the Arkell DNA.

John's business thrived and in 1856 he opened a second pub in Swindon's Old Town. The brewery expanded to keep pace with demand, and he celebrated his success by inviting friends to dine with him inside a new fermenting vessel. The *Swindon Advertiser* reported: 'Mr John Arkell invited his friends to dine in his new 3,000-gallon barrel; this novel dining room was the scene of much mirth and gaiety.'

Expansion couldn't meet the clamour for Arkell's beer. In 1861 he built a new 'steam brewery', embracing the new technologies of the Industrial Revolution.

The pace of change in the latter half of the 19th century was dramatic. Swindon had turned from a small market town into a vibrant industrial hub largely due to the brilliant railway engineer Isambard Kingdom Brunel, who based his Great Western Railway there and created a small army of thirsty industrial workers.

John Arkell continued to buy pubs, adding 20 in a decade, with the majority in Swindon. The growth of the estate meant that, in 1867, he was forced to expand the brewery still further.

John Arkell, known locally as 'Honest John', died in 1881. The *Swindon Advertiser* reported that shops were closed and blinds drawn as the funeral cortege made its way to Stratton church. The paper added: 'He was open and above board and radical in all he said and did. The poor had lost a good friend, a plain and simple friend.' He had been a staunch Liberal all his life and was well known for views that often met with hostility from the local establishment. It came to light some years later that the local Tory magistrates refused him a licence for his first pub and he had to appeal to higher authority, the Quarter Sessions, to gain it.

His sons Thomas and James took over the business and by 1900 the brewery owned more than a quarter of the pubs in the Swindon area.

Traditional and modern

When visitors tour the brewery today, they can be forgiven for thinking they're entering a time warp. It is splendidly traditional, with the original wood-jacketed mash tun from the 19th century and the mill where the malt is ground dating from 1908. The copper, where the wort is boiled with hops, is relatively recent, installed in the 1950s.

The workforce shows that it's not only the Arkell family that has a strong commitment to the brewery.

Bob Mercer, in charge of the mash tun, has worked there for 30 years, while his colleague Jack Bridgman has not only spent his working life at the brewery but his father also works there. Further down the production line, Chris Dicks in the fermenting room has put in 20 years and he followed his father and grandfather.

But Alex Arkell, the young and dynamic head brewer, proves the company is not living in the past. He trained at the renowned Siebels Institute in Chicago with its Master Brewer Programme, where he 'got lots of ideas and drank some super hopped IPAs.' He also studied in Munich where they know how to make a decent beer. As a result, he is well versed in modern brewing practice and has added a properly brewed and aged lager that has won plaudits, including a Gold medal from SIBA in 2014 in its national awards.

Cask ale, however, remains the rock on which the brewery is built. It accounts for 75 per cent of production and 3B is far and away the biggest seller. It stands for Best Bitter Beer and was first brewed in 1910. Before that time, a leather-bound brewing book from 1905 reveals the beers were enigmatically labelled X, XX and XXX, thought to stand for mild, pale ale and stout. Later in the 20th century the brewery produced GWR Ale to celebrate the 150th anniversary of the Great Western Railway, and RAF Anniversary Ale which marked the 75th anniversary of the Royal Air Force and happily coincided with Arkell's 150th anniversary. Beers that have long since disappeared include Arkell's Stout and Brown Jack Brown Ale, named after a racehorse that won the Queen Alexandra Stakes at Ascot six times in the 1930s.

Alex Arkell grows a small number of hops, but his main varieties are traditional English Fuggles and Goldings, with some organic hops from New Zealand. He takes Propena malting barley from a local farmer but the main grain in his beers is Maris Otter from Norfolk. Brewing liquor or water comes from the public supply – an original well is no longer in use. The water is 'Burtonised', which means mineral salts are

added to make it suitable for pale ales. The brewery currently produces 7,000 barrels or 10,000 hectolitres a year.

Alex has added to the cask range: Wiltshire Gold, a fashionable golden ale; HOPeration, a well-hopped IPA with American Cascade hops; Bee's Organic, using organic honey; and Moonlight, an amber ale. The last-named was launched in 2003 to celebrate the 80th birthday of the chairman, Peter Arkell, and saluted his role as a Second World War pilot, flying night-time missions over Germany. Peter also saw service in Burma and spent a year in hospital after crashing behind enemy lines. After the war he gained valuable brewing experience at the Tadcaster Tower Brewery before joining the family in Swindon.

The premium Kingsdown Ale dates from 1969 and was first brewed to celebrate Swindon Town FC winning the Football League Cup. In 2016 it was named Champion Beer in the Taste of the West annual awards.

As well as the core range, Alex brews a new cask beer every eight weeks. Old John Arkell would scratch his head in disbelief if he knew his descendant was producing beers with the addition of strawberries and vanilla, along with a double-hopped IPA, but they go down well in Arkell's pubs.

With an eye to both tradition and modernity, George Arkell is carefully improving his pubs and

GOOD GRUB IN A COUNTRY PUB

One Arkell's pub where food stands shoulder-to-shoulder with beer is the Royal Oak in Bishopstone, a short distance from Swindon. It's best known today as Helen Browning's Royal Oak, as it's run by the leading organic farmer and campaigner.

Helen is chief executive of the Soil Association and has turned the 1,500-acre Eastbrook family farm on the Marlborough Downs into an estate where animals are raised without the use of agrichemicals.

'The farm is run for the benefit of the animals and wildlife,' Helen says. 'We also improve the landscape and the soil.'

The proof of the pudding, you might say, is the food at the attractive and heavily beamed Royal Oak, with dishes prepared with produce from the farm along with other organic food sourced locally such as seasonal vegetables, cheese and ice cream.

The Royal Oak has 12 bedrooms and meals in the pub are accompanied by the full range of Arkell's beer.

Helen Browning's Royal Oak, Cues Lane, Bishopstone, near Swindon, SN6 8PP · 01793 790481 www.helenbrowningsorganic.co.uk/royal-oak

Alex, Nick, George and James Arkell

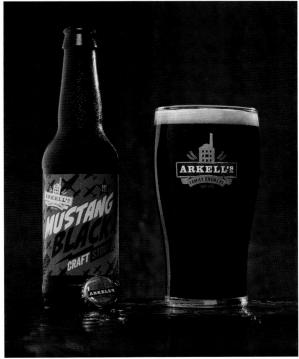

adding letting bedrooms where possible: the brewery now offers close to 500 rooms. The estate has expanded beyond Swindon and Wiltshire, with pubs in Berkshire, Gloucestershire, Hampshire and Oxfordshire. Arkell's snapped up several prize pubs in the 1990s from Whitbread, including outlets in Ascot, London, Newbury and Oxford.

More pubs were added early in the new century in Reading and Whitchurch. Quality food is available in a growing number of outlets, but George says his pubs are geared mainly to selling the brewery's beers. 'Pubs can get distracted by food – beer is what makes us tick,' he says. He adds that 'wet pubs', brewerspeak for outlets that lead on beer rather than food, are doing well.

If you want to see what makes Arkell's tick at first hand, visit the brewery and visitor centre. If you arrive by train – surely the only way to go to Swindon – cross the road at the station to the Great Western Hotel and raise a glass of 3B to the memory of both John Arkell and Isambard Kingdom Brunel. Their combined efforts ensured a brewery would go full steam ahead for more than 175 years.

Arkell's Brewery, Kingsdown, Swindon, Wilts SN2 7RU · 01793 823026 · www.arkells.com
Tours available; visitor centre

Regular cask beers:

Wiltshire Gold (3.7%)
3B (4%)
HOPeration (4.2%)
Bee's Organic (4.5%)
Moonlight (4.5%)

Donnington

1865 · STOW-ON-THE-WOLD · GLOUCESTERSHIRE

ONE word sums up Donnington: idyllic. Honey-coloured buildings with a water wheel are fronted by a large, tree-girt mill pond where black swans swim. The brewery stands in a valley of the Cotswolds, close to the historic market town of Stow-on-the-Wold, based on the ancient Roman Fosse Way.

The brewery buildings date from the 13th century when they formed a mill on the local manor. When the wool trade developed in the 16th century, a mill race was added – a water course that drives a water wheel – that enabled woollen goods to be made there. But in 1580 corn replaced wool and visitors today can see the ancient grinding stones, gears and cogs that once produced corn.

In 1827 the mill was bought by Thomas Arkell, and his grandson Richard transformed the buildings into a brewery in 1865. The Arkells of Donnington are cousins of the Swindon family and in modern times James Arkell, now the chairman of Arkell's of Swindon, learned his brewing skills at Donnington.

Cousins Peter and Claude Arkell in 2003

Richard Arkell had to pick up these skills as he went along, and existing ledgers show he had some problems at first: 'Too heavy... not right colour' say two of the entries. But he prospered, selling beer to the local gentry on their estates as well as to local taverns.

Richard's sons took over the business and eventually one son, Herbert, bought his brother out and ran the brewery alone. One of Herbert's sons, Claude, took over in 1951 after serving as an officer in the RAF during the Second World War. Claude grew his own barley and turned it into malt on a special malting floor that can be seen today. But eventually he bought Maris Otter from Norfolk farmers, which he milled at the brewery. Hops come from Hereford and Worcester while brewing water is supplied by a

spring beside the mill pond. The black swans on the pond first came from Australia and Claude took a keen interest in their welfare.

Over the years, the Arkells of Donnington built a small estate of 18 pubs, many in lovely rural locations in the Cotswolds, including Broadway, Lower Swell, Moreton-in-Marsh, Shipston on Stour and Stow itself.

When Claude Arkell died, he left no children and there were fears this much-loved brewery would close. But his cousins Peter and James Arkell came to the rescue and James has breathed new life into the enterprise. He has added a popular golden ale to the long-running BB and SBA and has opened a shop where visitors can buy branded clothes, calendars and beer for takeaway in draught polypins and bottles. But the brewery remains unchanged, with an internal water wheel providing the energy to drive belts for mashing and then pumping wort to the copper. The copper is a rare open vessel.

Donnington – 'The Fairest Brewery in All the Land' – lives on.

Donnington Brewery, Upper Swell, Stow-on-the-Wold, Gloucestershire GL54 1EP
01451 830603
www.donnington-brewery.com

Regular cask beers:

BB (3.6%)
Cotswold Gold (4%)
SBA (4.4%)
Double Donn (4.4%)

While visitors are welcome to tour the grounds and the shop, brewery tours are restricted to small groups and must be booked in advance.

St Austell

1851 · CORNWALL

IT's FITTING that Cornwall, that remote region of ancient legends and Celtic crosses, should have revived the fortunes of its leading brewery thanks to the summer solstice, a celebration dating from pagan times. It was a beer brewed for the total eclipse of the sun in August 1999 that enabled St Austell's beer sales and volumes to soar, with some of its products becoming leading national brands.

The beer was meant to be a one-off brew called Daylight Robbery. It was designed by Roger Ryman, who had joined St Austell as head brewer that year from Maclays in Scotland. He teamed up with a new managing director, James Staughton, who is the great-great grandson of Walter Hicks, founder of the brewery, and a member of the fifth generation to run the business. James's and Roger's task was to build sales at a time when many family brewers were struggling.

St Austell had a particular problem: Cornwall relies on tourism for a large proportion of its income and for the brewery it meant sales – to quote a former head brewer – 'fell off the cliff' at the end of the summer holidays. The brewery urgently needed to have more consistent sales all year round, which meant improving its profile beyond the West Country.

Daylight Robbery did the job. Roger Ryman said: 'It was the first new beer I'd brewed at St Austell. I was used to producing new beers every two months at Maclays. They were made, they sold and we moved on. With Daylight I thought that's a nice pint and then it just went ballistic. It had a great name and the timing was good, but a month after its launch it was the brewery's best-selling beer and sales carried on like that for the rest of the summer and into the autumn.'

In 2001, Daylight Robbery was renamed Tribute and became not just a core brand but the leading one, accounting for 70 per cent of annual production. To say Tribute revived St Austell's fortunes is a serious understatement. Before the beer arrived, brewing took place three times a week. To keep pace with demand, brewing was increased to three times a day and by 2010 production was running at 60,000 barrels a year, beating the previous record set in the 1970s.

A malty beginning

This feverish activity, along with enormous changes to the lifestyle, industries and culture of Cornwall, would have come as a considerable shock to Walter Hicks. Not that Cornwall was a quiet backwater in the middle of the 19th century. Tin, copper and china clay mining brought great wealth to the county, along with fishing. The arrival of the railway was due to the engineering genius of Isambard Kingdom Brunel, who linked Devon and Cornwall with the Royal Albert Bridge over the River Tamar and opened Cornwall to tourism. The miners, fishermen and visitors led to new pubs and hotels opening and with them a greater demand for beer.

Walter Hicks came from farming stock and in 1851 he launched his career by starting a malting business – a not unusual route into brewing, as this book shows. He supplied malt to many inns in the St Austell area that brewed their own beer and the success of this trade encouraged him to move into brewing. He may have brewed at the Seven Stars Inn when he acquired the lease in 1863, but what is certain is that he bought the London Inn on Market Square with a brewhouse and stables and added adjoining land.

Hicks was an innovator and aware of technical advances in brewing in other parts of the country. In 1869 he built a malt house and started work on what was called the Steam Brewery. Hicks used steam to heat the mash rather than direct heating

Walter Hicks

by coal fire, which could stew the grain. He also installed a refrigeration unit to cool the wort prior to fermentation. In a vivid description in 1870, the *West Briton* newspaper said the brewery was made up of:

> four storeys, the upper being fitted with three bins each capable of containing 100 bushels of malt, also two furnaces sufficiently large to hold 2,000 and 1,000 gallons. By a new and admirable apparatus, the mashing is most successfully carried on. The next floor has two large receivers. After the beer has been boiled it is poured into these vessels in which it passes to the next flat [storey] and immediately falls on a patent refrigerator. This ingenious and useful appliance is made of a number of copper tubes and perpendicularly set, through which cold water is constantly running; as soon as the beer drops off it is then passed at its required temperature into the [fermenting] vats.

The report added that the brewery was 'well supplied' with spring water pumped by a steam engine. When Hicks had the water analysed by chemists, he was encouraged to 'Burtonise' it by adding the mineral salts found in the waters of the Trent Valley, considered ideal for producing sparkling pale ales.

Walter Hicks was also a lucky brewer, who happened to be in the right place at the right time. Before the 19th century, St Austell had never been a major town and was described in 1842 as a poor place. But china clay – 'white gold' – transformed its fortunes. The decomposed granite had long been vital to making porcelain, but demand boomed when it was found it could also be used to manufacture paper, paint, cosmetics and medicines. In the 1850s the industry was producing 65,000 tons a year and employing some 7,000 men, women and children in the St Austell area, but by the end of the century output rose to 550,000 tons. As a result, the town became a key part of Cornish industry and the growing population needed the refreshment Walter Hicks's brewery could offer.

A new tower at Trevarthian Road

Hicks was joined at the brewery by his eldest son, also called Walter. In 1893 they searched for a site for a new and bigger brewery. They found the perfect place, two open fields off Tregonissey Lane, now Trevarthian Road, close to the train station. The land was measured at two acres and three roods: a rood was a quarter of an acre. Over the following years the site has expanded to some 14 acres, but the original mellow stone buildings are still the heart of the site.

In common with many Victorian breweries, the Hicks's new plant was built on the tower principle, with the brewing process flowing simply and logically from floor to floor. The two Walters were determined to have the best design money could buy and they commissioned the firm of Inskipp & Mackenzie to draw up the plans. Inskipp & Mackenzie had been involved in designing such major London breweries as Courage's Anchor Brewery at Tower Bridge and Taylor Walker's Barley Mow Brewery in Limehouse and they enjoyed a fine reputation.

As well as installing the best and most modern equipment in the brewery, the two Walters set out to build a pub estate to supply with beer. By 1910 the brewery owned 54 pubs and hotels along with several leaseholds and annual tenancies.

The brewery was registered as a limited company in 1910 and was known as Walter Hicks & Co Ltd. Walter senior was appointed governing director and was hoping for a quieter life leading to retirement. His hopes were dashed in 1911 when Walter junior, a keen motorcyclist, collided with a motor car in Helston and was killed.

Walter senior's younger son had no interest in joining the brewery and neither did most of his other children and grandchildren. The dynasty was saved by Walter senior's eldest daughter, Hester Parnall, who had to overcome the prejudice of rural Cornwall at the thought of a woman running a major business: the impact of the suffragette movement in London and other parts of the country had yet to be felt in the West Country.

Hester's rule

At the age of 82, Walter Hicks returned to run the brewery but for only a short period. The minutes of a directors' meeting in May 1911 record: 'I Walter Hicks do hereby appoint Hester Parnall, wife of Thomas Parnall of Belfield, St Austell, to be a Director of this Company in the place of Walter Hicks jnr now deceased.'

Walter Hicks died in 1916 at the venerable age of 87. Hester had just five years to learn the brewing business before she was in sole charge. In that short time, important changes were made that doubled capacity at the brewery. A new 100-barrel copper was installed and a new fermenting room was added. In fewer than 50 years, Hicks had quadrupled the potential capacity of his brewery but it would not be reached until the 1920s due to the problems of escalating beer duties, reductions in strength and the shortage of raw materials and workers that affected all breweries during the First World War. But by the 1920s output was close to 38,000 barrels, roughly twice that of the pre-war years.

Hester Parnall

Hester Parnall was aided by her solicitor, RG Barnes, and the general manager of the brewery, Alfred Ashton, but there was little doubt who was in charge at St Austell. When her husband died, Hester moved into the Hicks's family home and spent a good deal of time travelling. But she was in constant touch with the brewery. Thanks to the speed of the post and telegram services at the time, sometimes as many as three messages a day would pass between Hester, installed in Kent, London or Yorkshire, and Barnes and Ashton. She was a woman of few words as one telegram in 1925 suggests. It read: 'Yes. Parnall'.

Her presence in the brewery never went unnoticed. Clifford Hockin, who rose from office boy to company secretary, described her as: 'Ruling the company with the grace of a duchess combined with the aplomb of the successful businessman. All who came in to contact with her, and indeed those who did not, were on their best behaviour. Before the day-to-day

business was discussed, her pair of Pekingese dogs were carefully sited on the desk in the boardroom on pieces of white blotting paper laid out by the office boy.'

Tom Stephens, who worked at the brewery from 1924 to 1973, recalled: 'The first man to spot her chauffeur-driven Daimler arriving in the yard would tap out a message of warning on the water pipes, which could be heard throughout the brewery. She once sacked a chap she caught painting with a fag in his mouth, and she sacked one of the drivers for picking up a passenger. She was a proper dragon.'

1934 was a significant year for the brewery. The name of the business was changed from Walter Hicks to St Austell Brewery Co Ltd. The new name fitted well as it had long been informally called St Austell Brewery and it appeared on company livery. The Ellis & Sons Steam Brewery in Hayle, dating from 1815, was bought for £50,000 and the sale included 30 licensed premises. Ellis had suffered badly from the decline of

BROWN WILLY AND RED DUCHY

In the 1920s the brewery's stock draught beers were XX, XXX, XXXX, PA, BB and IPA. XXXX was known as Brown Willy after Cornwall's highest hill.

Head brewer Mr Smallwood was keen to develop a new and stronger bottled beer to compete with the popular pale ales produced by Bass and Worthington. He drew up a recipe for a beer he and Mrs

Parnall agreed should be called Duchy Ale. Smallwood, tongue in cheek, designed a label showing the outline of Cornwall in red.

He was fully aware that Bass used the red triangle as its trademark. It was the first registered trademark in Britain following the passing of trademark legislation in 1875. Bass rigorously protected

the trademark and was quick to take legal action against any infringement of its rights. But Duchy Ale with its red emblem escaped under the radar and it was used for many decades.

A new bottled version called Royal Duchy was introduced in 1954 and the emblem was also used for a keg beer called Extra. Duchy finally ceased to be made in 2009.

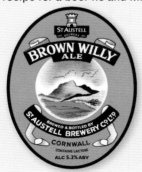

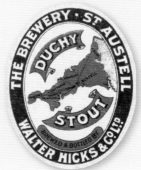

mines, shipyards and foundries in the area, but the sale proved a major boost for St Austell as it now had a strong presence in the west of the county.

Hester Parnall lived the life of a wealthy member of the local establishment. In 1927 she had moved to Tregrehan, the ancestral home of the aristocratic Carlyon family, where she indulged her passion for gardening. She entertained royally, her visitors including the Prince of Wales (later, and briefly, Edward VIII) and Wallis Simpson. Hester was a lifelong Conservative and when she welcomed the Tory prime minister Stanley Baldwin to Tregrehan in 1927 she closed the brewery for the day and invited all the staff to attend: it was not an invitation that could be refused, apparently. It was the first time a prime minister had visited Cornwall and an estimated crowd of 20,000 went to Tregrehan to greet Baldwin. The *Cornish Guardian* described the day as a 'gigantic picnic' with stalls, roundabouts, trick-cycling, wrestling, tug-of-war and clay shooting.

Hester Parnall died unexpectedly on 20 April 1939, aged 73, and her death came as a profound shock. As late as 7 April, with war looming, she had issued an order saying that new tanks should not be bought from Germany. The new chairman was Egbert Barnes who, like his father, Reginald, was a member of the ruling family as a result of Reginald marrying Hester's sister Mary Hicks. Egbert was 41 when he took over from Hester and was to stay in office for forty years.

Reform and Cornish smugglers

In sharp contrast to the patrician Hester, Egbert was a reformer. When he became chairman, he wrote a declaration of his intents for the brewery that said: 'Our first and constant aim must be directed to raising wages to a decent minimum.' He suggested that a brewery council be formed where all members of staff could voice their views about company policy and how to improve efficiency. He introduced a company pension scheme long before other businesses followed suit.

REMOVING THE SWASTIKA

Egbert Barnes's first task was to steer the brewery through the difficult times of the Second World War, with restricted supplies of raw materials and escalating duties. St Austell had a unique problem in Britain: it had to have the emblem of the swastika removed from bottle tops. The swastika had become infamous as the symbol of Hitler's Nazi Party, but it's an ancient sign with its origins in Sanskrit and originally was a good luck charm. Ancient forms showed the arms of the sign facing anticlockwise but the Nazis reversed it. Unfortunately, the St Austell version mirrored the Nazi one and was highly embarrassing, especially as Egbert Barnes had declared in 1939 that the first task of the brewery was to help defeat Hitler.

In 1948, with strict rationing in place as Britain recovered from the Second World War, St Austell managed to brew a strong beer with a gravity of 1060 degrees – approximately 6 per cent alcohol. This was increased to 1070 degrees in 1970. The beer was first produced in draught form and called Extra Strong Ale, but the draught was replaced by nip bottles and renamed Smugglers Ale, with a price of one shilling. It became a Cornish institution and there was uproar when it was discontinued in 1994 due to the planned closure of the bottling line.

One angry lover of the beer, known as DWE of Fowey, put pen to paper with a lament on hearing 'the ghastly news' and ended menacingly:

I'd like to find out who it was and meet him on the quay.
I doubt that I'd resist the urge
To shove him in the sea!

But you cannot keep Cornish smugglers down. The beer was revived in 2009 when a new bottling line was installed. The beer, 7.2 per cent, has a new recipe and is a blend of oak-aged barley wine and dark ale matured in oak whisky casks in the cellars deep below the brewery. It's brewed with Cornish spring water, Maris Otter pale malt, crystal and roasted malts, dark brewing sugar and hopped with First Gold,

Fuggles and Styrian Goldings hops with an addition of coriander. For the further delight of connoisseurs, there's a strong version called Smugglers Grand Cru, 11.5 per cent, which is bottled and then finished using the Méthode Champenoise at the Camel Valley Vineyard. It was named Champion Speciality Beer in the 2011 Quality Drinks Awards.

Smugglers in the late 1940s and 50s joined the mainstream beers of dark mild, bitter and Hicks Special. The main effort at the brewery in those hard times was to attempt to overhaul the pub estate, which had been neglected during the war. Egbert Barnes was joined in this endeavour by a new managing director, George Luck, who previously worked for Taylor Walker in London. With restrictions on building materials, improving buildings was slow work. But Barnes and Luck employed leading artists and architects of the day, such as Joy Cooper, Elisabeth Benjamin and Hans Feibusch to design and paint new signs and facades. Feibusch's mural at the Ship Inn in Fowey is especially striking. While Cornwall has long had strong artistic links, it's nevertheless remarkable to find pub signs and murals in the county inspired by Le Corbusier and Bauhaus.

Extra innovation

The brewery celebrated its centenary in style in 1951. The staff were taken on a weekend trip to London in four 'charabancs' or coaches where they toured the Festival of Britain. Society was changing and the brewery reflected this in 1954 when Tim Harvey, a director and Walter Hicks's great-grandson, started to develop a new wines and spirits division. At the same time, the brewery launched its first keg beer called Extra.

'It was a big innovation,' Tim Harvey said. 'We were one of the first breweries in the country to do it. Watney's Red Barrel was the leader in that field and Watney's had a large amount of trade in Cornwall and so we thought – let's do it too! It did not really involve new technology as such – essentially it was just bottled beer in much bigger bottles – but we needed ways of dispensing it and of course new tanks for chilling and filtering, these two processes being unheard of for draught beer.'

The cost of launching Extra came to £20,000, a considerable sum at the time. But there was a quick return on the investment as the beer proved a major success and was sold as far away as London. In 1976

The Ship Inn, Fowey, with the mural on the outside wall by Hans Feibusch (enlarged on the right)

160

it won a gold medal in a national beer competition staged by the *Sunday Mirror*, when it was up against 312 beers from 88 other breweries. In 1985 the name was changed to the old standby Duchy. As someone at the brewery said: 'People thought Extra sounded like a brand of petrol'. At the time, a popular petrol was Esso Extra which promised to Put a Tiger in Your Tank. St Austell made no such claims for its keg beer.

It did, however, suggest that a new traditional beer, Hicks Special Draught, 5 per cent, launched in 1975, could render the unwary drinker a few sheets to the wind. The beer, planned two years earlier by managing director Piers Thompson, George Luck and head brewer Alan Izat, had a faltering start but has since become a regular member of the portfolio and a legend in Cornwall. The beer is brewed with pale and darker malts and hopped with Goldings and Progress varieties. The rich malty, vinous beer, well hopped and with caramel and butterscotch notes, is stronger on the palate than its ABV suggests and explains why it's known to Cornish drinkers as Hicks's Sudden Death or High-Speed Diesel.

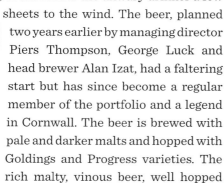

In 1992 the brewery opened a visitor centre and in 1999 launched the Celtic Beer Festival. The festival, which takes place at the brewery, features ales and lagers from Cornwall, Scotland, Ireland, Wales, the Isle of Man and Brittany, and raises more than £10,000 a year for the brewery's charitable trust.

The dynasty was consolidated early in the new century. James Staughton became managing director when Piers Thompson retired. James was joined on the board by his cousin, Piers Thompson junior, and another cousin, William Michelmore. The 21st century started with the brewery celebrating its 150th anniversary and the highlight of the year was a visit by Prince Charles, the Duke of Cornwall. Following a tour of the brewery, the prince went to the visitor centre where he agreed to be photographed pulling a pint behind the bar. Much to the embarrassment of the brewers present, the royal visitor filled the glass with foam but no beer. The fundamental error had been made of not pulling off the first pint to reduce excess carbonation. When one member of staff remarked that the prince would make a fine king, another replied: 'But a lousy barman!'

Proper Job

The brewery prepared itself for the challenges of a greatly changed beer market by a major overhaul of its range. Back in the 1990s it took steps to offer an improved range of beers to the free trade by buying Carlsberg-Tetley's wholesale business in Cornwall and the Scilly Isles. A decade later, Roger Ryman and his team prepared a root-and-branch overhaul of the beer range to make them suitable for the new century and for both the tied estate and national sales.

Tribute was not the only success. With the enormous interest in India Pale Ale, Roger Ryman went on an exchange visit to the Bridgeport Brewery in Oregon which produced an award-winning IPA. Fired with enthusiasm, Roger developed his own version known as Proper Job, which was first produced in

James Staughton, great-great grandson of Walter Hicks

A new beer was brewed to mark St Austell's 160th anniversary in 2011. Trelawny, 3.8 per cent, is named after the Cornish patriot Sir Jonathan Trelawny. It's a copper-coloured bitter hopped with English Goldings and Galaxy from Tasmania.

In order to get the maximum flavours from his beers, Roger Ryman worked with local farmers to grow a special strain of Maris Otter barley called Cornish Gold. It now accounts for three-quarters of the grain used at the brewery. Every year, Roger visited the Pacific Northwest of the United States to see the hop harvest and choose the finest varieties. They enable the likes of Proper Job and Big Job to burst with citrus aromas and flavours.

The range of beers has not gone unnoticed beyond Cornwall, and in 2008 Roger Ryman won the prestigious Brewer of the Year award from the All-Parliamentary Beer Group. The beer group is made up of MPs and Peers and enjoys the biggest membership of any group at Westminster, showing that honourable members have their priorities right.

The spread of St Austell's beers has grown as a result of building the tied estate beyond Cornwall. The brewery now has 15 pubs in Devon, backed by depots

cask for the Celtic Beer Festival in 2005 and bottled a year later. The name is Cornish dialect for something well done and refers to the proper job carried out by the 32nd Cornwall Regiment in defending the British residency in Lucknow during the Indian Mutiny of 1857. The beer is 5.5 per cent in bottle, 4.5 per cent in cask. It's brewed with pale malt and hopped with Brewer's Gold, Cascade, Chinook and Willamette varieties. It's considered to be one of the finest examples of new-wave IPAs and the brewery's second biggest cask beer after Tribute. It's also the undisputed best-selling bottle-conditioned IPA in the country. Its success has spawned a strong Double IPA called Big Job, 7.2 per cent in bottle, brewed with Centennial and Citra hops.

Piers Thompson senior

Roger Ryman, the head brewer who boosted St Austell's sales with Tribute

feeding the free trade in Ilfracombe and Newton Abbot. Brewing has been aided by a substantial overhaul of the brewery, with new mash tuns, coppers and grain silos. A new bottling line was installed in 2009 and the modern technology of the brewery enabled Roger Ryman to introduce Korev Cornish Lager, produced in the true European style with bottom fermentation.

Gem aids all-time record

Cask ale, however, remains the brewery's passion and commitment and between 2001 and 2011 it tripled annual sales with production running at 16.7 million pints a year. St Austell consolidated its position in the West Country in 2016 when it bought Bath Ales in Bristol, a microbrewery founded in 1995 and best known for its Gem best bitter. In 2018 St Austell invested £5 million in a new site at Warmley, near Bath, with a modern, flexible brewhouse that can produce cask, keg and lager. It's called the Hare Brewery, using the brewery's logo. Bath has moved out of the ranks of the micros and is brewing 23,000 barrels a year with a capacity of 50,000 barrels. The kit was designed by Roger Ryman and uses the modern Continental system of mash mixer, lauter (filtration vessel) and wort kettle. But the plant stays true to tradition with Maris Otter as the core grain. Hops are used in both whole flower and pellet form.

In 2019, following the sale of Fuller's brewery in London to Asahi, Fuller's head brewer Georgina Young moved to Bath Ales to work alongside Roger Ryman, offering a formidable team of expert beer makers. Cask ale accounts for 50 per cent of production, with keg 10 per cent and bottles 40 per cent. Alongside the ales, Bath has introduced a lager called Sulis, 4.4 per cent, named after Sulis Minerva, the Roman goddess of Bath. As well as the free trade, the beers can be enjoyed in the Hop Pole, Salamander and Swan in Bath and the Lamplighters and Wellington in Bristol. The brewery also runs the spacious Graze Bar at Bath Station. As well as a large restaurant, the bar has a one-barrel brewery that produces a house beer called Platform 3, indicating that Bath Ales and St Austell are going full steam ahead towards the Cornish brewery's 200th anniversary. As an important milestone leading to that anniversary, in 2019 St Austell and Bath Ales combined to produce 150,000 barrels of beer – an all-time record for the company.

In May 2020 Roger Ryman died, aged just 52, after a brave battle with cancer. His dedication helped to revive the fortunes of the brewery with such beers as Tribute and Proper Job, and he was a popular figure throughout the brewing industry and the wider beer-drinking community.

St Austell appointed Georgina Young as director of brewing in succession to Roger Ryman in July 2020. Georgina will oversee brewing operations at both Bath and St Austell.

Georgina Young, appointed brewing director of the St Austell Family Group in July 2020

St Austell Brewery, 63 Trevarthian Road, St Austell, Cornwall PL25 4BY · 01726 74444
www.staustellbrewery.co.uk
Visitor centre, tours available

St Austell regular cask beers:
Cornish Best Bitter (3.5%)
Trelawny (3.8%)
Tribute (4.2%)
Proper Job (4.5%)
Mena Dhu Cornish Stout (4.5%)
Hicks Strong Cornish Ale, previously HSD (5%)

Bottle-conditioned beers:
Proper Job
Big Job
Hicks Strong
Proper Black

Bath Ales' Hare Brewery at Warmley, between Bristol and Bath

Bath Ales, Hare Brewery, Southway Drive, Warmley, Bristol BS30 5LW · 0117 947 4797
www.bathales.com
Tap room for visitors, tours available

Bath Ales regular cask beers:
Prophecy (3.9%)
Gem (4.1%)
Platform 3 (4.5%)
Lansdown (5%)

Brewed under the Beerd name:
Monterey (3.9%)
Silver Tip (4.7%)

165

Timothy Taylor's

1858 · KEIGHLEY · WEST YORKSHIRE

THERE'S NO DOUBTING where Timothy Taylor's passion and commitment lie. I asked chief executive Tim Dewey what proportion of his annual production of 70,000 barrels was in cask form and he answered crisply: 'more than 80 per cent!' The brewery is powered by true Yorkshire grit. It's based in Brontë country, with small towns of cobbled streets and mellow stone buildings set against a backdrop of the encroaching moors brought vividly to life in Emily Brontë's *Wuthering Heights.*

Clearly cask beer is not a doomed love affair at Taylor's. Sales are growing, the site is expanding to cope with demand and the most famous brand, Landlord pale ale, accounts for an astonishing 80 per cent of output.

Tim Dewey, chief executive

Tim Dewey is an American, the first chief executive to come from outside the Taylor family at a company where only family members can own shares. There are currently 45 shareholders and they have handed day-to-day control to Tim, who has lived in Britain for 35 years. He has only a faint trace of an American accent but he stresses his origins with a mounted baseball on his desk. He came to the brewery in 2014 after a career in the spirits industry with companies such as Diageo and William Grant.

With no brewing experience, Tim admits he was amazed when he was chosen for the top job. The family was clearly impressed by his declared mission to boost sales, employ more sales staff, and to begin active marketing to take the good news of Taylor's beers to a wider audience.

'Research showed that 50 per cent of ale drinkers in the London area had never heard of Landlord,' he says – that's despite the fact it's won the Champion Beer of Britain award more times than any other beer. 'We had to get the message out.'

And the message has been heard. As well as making Taylor's beers available at CAMRA beer festivals, the brewery has taken them further afield to such events as CarFest North, and South, with Chris Evans and Craft Beer Rising in London. Tim Dewey says that while Taylor's made a new range of beers called Taylor Made, including Hopical Storm and Poulter's Porter, available for the London event, younger drinkers asked mainly for Landlord.

The tailor brewer

An American woman drinking strong Yorkshire ale (see below) would have astonished the founder of the brewery. Timothy Taylor came from Bingley and his family, in keeping with their name, were tailors. Timothy joined the firm when he left school and moved to Keighley – pronounced 'Keethley' – when a second branch of the business opened there.
He was an entrepreneur by nature and saw a move into brewing as a way to enlarge his income. While Keighley had nine beerhouses there was scope for more as a result of the rapid growth of the woollen trade and the town's rising population. Driven by the new technologies of the Industrial Revolution, the woollen trade expanded at a fast pace with steam-powered automation, while the arrival of the railway in Keighley in 1847 brought more thirsty workers to the town.

Timothy Taylor

Timothy's tailoring business had taken him to major towns in Yorkshire engaged in the wool trade and he saw the large number of ale houses and breweries that refreshed workers there. He decided he wanted more than a simple beerhouse in Keighley and aimed for a substantial commercial enterprise that would produce a high-quality product. Quality was vital as the railway was importing beers from Burton, Leeds and even London to Keighley and these ales, especially the new sparkling pale ales, met with consumer approval.

In 1858 Timothy and two partners took the tenancy of a barn and stable in Cook Lane and converted them into a brewery. In December of that year the local newspaper reported that the Cook Lane New Brewery was open for business and was producing 'Mild Ales, Bitter Ales and Porter'. The business clearly thrived for in less than a year it was able to buy its first two pubs. Timothy ended the partnership and forged ahead on his own. He soon needed bigger premises to brew beer and to make and supply malt to other breweries and ale houses. A golden opportunity arose in 1863 when the substantial Knowle Park Estate on the edge of town was put up for sale with a series of lots. The estate included farmland and had

LANDLORD WOWS POP DIVA

Tim Dewey isn't the first American to boost awareness and sales of Taylor's leading brand. In 2003, pop diva Madonna told Jonathan Ross on his television programme that she'd become a confirmed Anglophile thanks to her husband Guy Ritchie and as a result she enjoyed ale. Her favourite beer was Landlord: 'We go down to the Dog & Duck in Soho and with my flat cap drawn over my face I order a pint and a half of Landlord.'

Taylor's responded by changing the slogan for Landlord from 'For men of the North' to 'For men of the North… and Madonna'.

Two years later, Madonna once again sang the praises of Landlord when she appeared on the Michael Parkinson chat show and described the beer as 'the champagne of ales'.

As a result of this publicity, the phone rang off the hook at the Keighley brewery and Landlord became a national brand, available in Scotland, London and as far south as the West Country.

a supply of pure water from a spring. The soft water, filtered through layers of limestone and black rock, became a critical element in the taste and popularity of the beers.

The new site was an altogether different proposition to the one in cramped Cook Lane surrounded by insanitary housing and poor water. Knowle Park was a rural idyll with sweeping lawns and flower and vegetable beds. Timothy was able to farm there as well as brew and he built houses for his family and his wife's family.

The *Keighley News* in July 1885 carried an advertisement from T. Taylor & Co, brewers of Mild Ales, Bitter Beer and Porter 'from one shilling per gallon'. At a time when porter brewers in London had been accused of adulterating their beers with opium, tobacco and extract of poppies, Taylor was able to report that analysts had told the Anti-Adulteration Review that the Knowle Spring beers 'are, and deservedly so, classed with the best.'

When Timothy Taylor died in 1898, aged 71, he left £50,000 – a sizeable sum for the time and worth around £6 million today – with an estate of 24 pubs, a growing free trade with working men's clubs, and a malting business that supplied brewers throughout the West Riding of Yorkshire. He was succeeded by his sons Robert and Percy, who formed an unlikely

partnership as Robert was a keen sportsman who played rugby while Percy was a musician who played the flute and loved opera.

Nevertheless, the partnership worked well and in 1911 the brothers built a large extension to the brewery to cope with the demand for their beers. The new building housed a malt mill, a cast-iron mash tun, a coal-fired copper and a hop back. The vessels were clearly of the highest quality as the copper survived until the 1970s, while the other pieces of kit continued to operate until 2000.

In common with all family brewers, Timothy Taylor's endured the First World War with all the problems created by rising duties, reduced strength for beer and restricted licensing hours. The problems continued into the 1920s and in 1922 Robert and Percy Taylor uncharacteristically lost faith in the future of brewing and put the company up for sale. The major Burton brewer Samuel Allsopp made a bid of £112,000 for the Keighley business, but fortunately changed its mind and bought the Scottish brewer Archibald Arrol of Alloa instead.

High standards

In order to safeguard the independence of the brewery it became a private limited company in 1930, Timothy Taylor & Co Ltd, with all the shares held by family members. Five years later, Percy's son John Taylor joined the brewery – he said he was 'press ganged' –

following a pupillage at Bentley's in Rotherham. John remained at Taylor's for a remarkable 60 years and was chairman for most of that time. His work for the industry was recognised first by a knighthood and then elevation to the peerage as Lord Ingrow. For the brewery and for drinkers, John Taylor's lasting legacy was to insist that his beers should be made only from the finest raw materials. 'You can't make a silk purse out of a sow's ear,' he would say. If that meant paying more for malt and hops and charging a few pennies more for a pint than his competitors, he thought that was in the best interests of his customers. With his family, he steered the brewery through the difficult years of the Second World War and its aftermath and was then faced with the fresh challenges of a growing demand for bottled beer followed by the rise of keg production.

John Taylor also faced a crisis in the late 1940s that almost led to the sale of the brewery. The crisis was created when Robert Taylor's widow, Edith, died and her shares passed to her sons Philip and Sydney, who were faced with punitive demands for death duties. In 1953, when Philip Taylor died, a similar problem of death duties arose. Once again, some members of the family proposed selling the brewery, citing not just death duties but the problems of competing with bigger brewers and the high price of pubs if the company sought to expand its estate.

Percy Taylor, then the chairman, and John Taylor resisted the sale and the adroit switching of shares among family members, as well as an investment from the banker Sir Donald Horsfall, finally avoided the threat to the brewery's independence. The intervention by Horsfall, however, was not without controversy. Percy Taylor also died in 1953 and his widow, Gladys, 20 years his junior, promptly married Horsfall. It was said that she and Horsfall had had a relationship for some years and their rapid marriage was frowned on by polite society in Keighley.

Kegs and bottles were equally controversial. John Taylor, who became chairman and managing director in 1954, was determined to concentrate on cask ales and ensure quality was of the highest order. But he did develop a bigger bottled beer division and installed a new bottling line in the early 1950s. Special Pale Ale became a popular bottled beer along with Landlord Strong Pale Ale, Black Bess Stout, Blue Label Strong Ale and Northerner No 1 Dark Ale.

Taylor's team, c. 1952

COME LANDLORD FILL THE FLOWING BOWL

From humble beginnings as a filtered bottled beer, Landlord would go on to become a champion ale when it was sold in draught cask format. It was launched as a bottled pale ale in 1953 and was based on Taylor's BB that had been brewed in the 1930s. In 1953 it was called Competition Ale as the brewery ran a competition for customers to come up with the best name for the brand. It was won by a steward from the local Keighley Drill Hall Club who won £500 for suggesting Landlord.

The label for Landlord was designed by Philip Taylor's daughter Roberta who was an art student and devised the image of a jovial landlord.

When the beer was launched in cask form in the 1960s, it blazed a trail across the brewing industry, winning medals and prizes at an unprecedented rate from the 1970s. In 1999 and 2000 it won CAMRA's Champion Beer of Britain trophy and the Brewing Industry International Awards Supreme Champion simultaneously and it has won the CAMRA trophy four times, more than any other beer.

The unique character and flavour of Landlord comes from its malt and hops. Pale malt derives from Golden Promise barley, which is grown in the Moray Firth and Borders regions of Scotland: it's a grain that has its origins in the whisky industry. Golden Promise is low in nitrogen, which avoids a haze in the finished beer. Taylor's legendary head brewer Allan Hey, in post from 1966 to 1995, said the rain in Scotland produces 'a juicy barley, not those steel-tipped grains you sometimes get in England.'

The hops, used in whole flower form – Taylor's doesn't use pellets –

are Fuggles from Hereford and Worcester, Goldings and Whitbread Goldings from Kent, and Styrian Goldings from the shores of Lake Bled in Slovenia. The intense hop character of the beer is achieved at the end of the boil in the copper. The 'hopped wort' is then circulated over a deep bed of Styrian Goldings in the hop back, a receiving vessel that holds the liquid prior to fermentation.

Investment and expansion

A positive sign that Taylor's had returned to stability came in 1954 when John Taylor bought the Clarendon Brewery in Haworth. It wasn't a hostile takeover as there was an understanding that when Herbert Parker, the last surviving son of the founder, died his widow would sell the business to Taylor's. The Haworth plant closed and Taylor's added seven pubs to its estate, including the Fleece in Haworth. The atmospheric, beamed old coaching inn on a cobbled street remains one of Taylor's finest pubs, in the heart of Brontë country.

From the 1980s Taylor's has had to dig deep in order to keep up with the ever-increasing demand for

its beers. Charles Dent, who had married a Taylor daughter, became managing director in 1995. With head brewer Peter Eells (1994–2016) he forged ahead with a focus on quality combined with major improvements to the brewery. Lord Ingrow, the last of Timothy Taylor's direct descendants, died in 2002, aged 84. He had kept in close contact with the brewery as he said the pure spring water used for brewing was also ideal for mixing with his whisky at home.

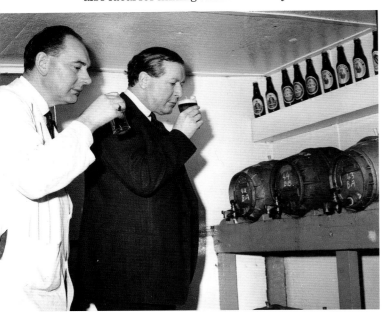

Head brewer Allan Hey with Lord Ingrow, sampling c. 1976

Between 1998 and 2003 a total of £3.5 million was spent on updating the brewery. New kit included vital additional fermenters, along with a boiler, hot liquor tanks, malt store and cask washer. A further £6 million went on improving pubs, with the estate extending from Fence in East Lancashire to Leeds, and from Halifax to Ripon. The current estate of 19 pubs ranges from community locals to ancient inns such as the Fleece in Haworth, or moorland taverns such as the Grouse in Oakworth.

The brewery expansion has continued under Tim Dewey's tutelage. Since he joined the business, £2.8 million has been spent on yet more fermenting vessels as production has grown from 60,000 barrels a year in 2007 to 70,000 in 2019. There's now a grand total of 26 fermenters, some open, where a 40-year-old yeast culture feeds greedily on the malt sugars in the hopped wort. The yeast came from the Oldham Brewery via John Smith's in Tadcaster. It's a two-strain culture and head brewer Andy Leman says, tongue in cheek, that the dominant strain is a Yorkshire one while the second strain comes from the West Pennines.

A 10-barrel pilot brewery has been installed where Andy Leman, second brewer Nick Berkovits and their team can try out fresh recipes and new varieties of malt and hops. In the main brewery, Taylor's could have rested on the laurels of the success of Landlord, but it continues to produce a full range of beers, including two mild ales, Dark Mild and Golden Best, the latter being the now-rare style of light mild. In spite of the nationwide success of Landlord, mild ale remains popular in the brewery's heartland. Sales of Best Bitter, renamed Boltmaker, were in decline

New brewery development, 2019

The current brewing team, Andy Leman seated

and its future was in doubt, but in 2014 it won the Champion Beer of Britain trophy at the Great British Beer Festival and sales have grown appreciably since then. A golden ale called Knowle Spring has been added to the range, while Ram Tam, which is Landlord with the addition of coloured malts, is a local popular 'winter warmer'. In 2019 the brewery launched Ram Tam outside Yorkshire as Landlord Dark.

The Taylor Made range of 330ml bottles has been introduced with an appeal to younger drinkers but with a strong link to the brewery's origins. The beers include a hoppy/fruity pale ale called Hopical Storm, 1858 Brown Ale, Poulter's Porter and Cook Lane IPA.

Cask ale, however, is and will remain the belt and braces of the Taylor range. Tim Dewey, a confirmed Anglophile, says succinctly: 'Cask beer is an important part of the British beer scene.'

Timothy Taylor's, Knowle Spring Brewery, Keighley, West Yorkshire BD21 1AW
01535 603139 · www.timothytaylor.co.uk
Trade tours only

Regular cask ales:
Dark Mild (3.5%)
Golden Best (3.5%)
Boltmaker (4%)
Knowle Spring (4.2%)
Landlord (4.3%)
Ram Tam/Landlord Dark (4.3%)

Camerons

1865 · HARTLEPOOL

THE lion roars in Hartlepool. The rampant red stone animals that greet visitors to Camerons' brewery, and also adorn pumpclips and labels, are a sign of strength and endurance. The brewery has survived changes of ownership – including a former heavyweight boxer turned property tycoon – but is once again firmly in family hands. Today the family is the Soleys who replaced the founding Camerons.

It will surprise even well-informed observers of the beer scene that Camerons is the eighth biggest brewery in Britain. It has a capacity of 600,000 barrels a year, and in order to fill their vast vessels, the Soleys have marked out a distinctive route to market. Camerons is a contract business, brewing beer for Carlsberg and Heineken and many other companies. Camerons' own brands include the renowned Strongarm, the major family product. The brewery is expanding its tied estate and has 50 tenanted and 30 managed outlets, including 16 of the specialist Head of Steam bars based in or close to railway stations. The bars stretch from Newcastle to Birmingham and include three in Leeds. As well as Camerons' beers, Head of Steam offers brews from local breweries and those further afield plus imported craft beers.

Heineken has a 24 per cent stake in Camerons, which helps safeguard such cask ales as Tetley Imperial, Mild and Dark Mild, and John Smith's Magnet – beers that otherwise would likely have disappeared.

Camerons has one of the finest brewhouses in the country. Built in the 1970s, the elegant stainless steel vessels with tall chimneys plus floors made from imported Italian marble combine to make a brewhouse that has more in common with a Munich lager brewery than anything found in Britain. It can produce lager as well as ale – a necessary requisite as Camerons makes all the Kingfisher lager found in Asian restaurants and supermarkets throughout the country.

Humble beginnings

The Lion Brewery today is a long way removed from the humble brewing operation created by a farmer called William Waldon in 1835. Waldon and his family set up home in the village of New Stranton on the coast with a small fishing village called Hartlepool just to the north. Hartlepool had once been a thriving port with military ships stationed there in the 13th and 14th centuries to defend king and country against foreign invasion from Europe. The area went into decline but revived in the 19th century with the arrival of the railway. A new dock opened in 1835 and two railway companies were created to carry coal from the Durham mines. There were already two breweries in New Stranton, but William Waldon thought the fast-growing population of the area could afford one more.

He was remarkably prescient. The area thrived with new docks, harbour and railway lines and in 1852 Waldon bought 857 square yards (717m²) of land and built a new brewery he called the Lion. He didn't oversee production for long, suddenly dying two years later. The brewery was run by his widow Jane who passed it to her son, also named William, when he became of legal age. He busily built the brewing side of the business and added several pubs to the estate. Jane Waldon died in 1860 and her son followed in 1872. William had engaged the services of a clerk and apprentice brewer called John William Cameron who was given a 21-year lease by the Waldon family to run the brewery and its 14 inns and beerhouses. The JW Cameron dynasty had arrived and when the lease came up for renewal in 1893 the trustees of the Waldons sold the land, brewery and pubs to Cameron for £34,442 and six shillings.

A business to be proud of

Cameron set out to build a new brewery, making use of all the innovative technologies of the time. He bought land that was three times the size of the old brewery and he engaged the skills of the famed brewery architect William Bradford to design the new plant. (Bradford was also involved in designing several other breweries featured in this book, including Harvey's and Hook Norton.)

A brochure published in 1893 gives a graphic depiction of the new brewery: 'The plant is of 70 quarter capacity. The mash house, copper room, hop back room, coolers and tun rooms are spacious, well-lighted structures with ventilated roofs. There are two 35-quarters mash tuns, fitted with copper covers and Steel's mashers and internal rakes. There is one copper, 170 barrels capacity, and spacious hop stores. There are two vertical Mortons refrigerators and a large iron cooler … Messrs Cameron and Co produce pale, mild and bitter ales and stouts, all noted for their flavour and excellent tonic properties.' The description vividly shows the advances made in brewing in the 19th century, with cooling equipment as important to an ale brewery as it was to continental lager brewers. In common with many breweries at the time, Camerons was not

The Lion Brewery, c.1900

shy in promoting the healthy quality of products made from malted grain, hops and pure water.

Cameron turned his business into a limited company in 1894. The first board meeting was held in London at the offices of John Reeves Ellerman, who went on to found the Ellerman Lines shipping company, which was to play a fateful role in the history of the Lion Brewery in the late 20th century. As well as his shipping interests, Ellerman specialised in buying up small but viable businesses and he may well have encouraged Cameron to acquire in short order the Brunswick Brewery and the wine and spirit merchants M&J Rickinson in Hartlepool. In 1897 the Lambton Brewery in Sunderland was bought along with 100 licensed outlets.

The Lion Brewery entered the 20th century with an estate of more than 200 pubs, two warehouses and numerous shops. The local historian Robert Wood later wrote: 'When Colonel Cameron took his seat as chairman of the board of directors, he had every reason to be proud. In the 30 years that had elapsed since he first entered the Lion Brewery, he had made it into a great and thriving business'. Cameron was known as 'Colonel' as a result of rising to the rank of lieutenant colonel in the local volunteer

John William Cameron

176

force. He died in 1896, and as he had no children, he passed the brewery to his brother Watson Cameron, who became managing director, with Sir John Reeves Ellerman, now knighted, holding the role of chairman.

Strongarm to the rescue

The early years of the new century were difficult ones for the brewery. A slump in iron, steel and shipping impacted on beer drinking and these problems were compounded by government restrictions on beer strength and rising duties during the First World War. Watson Cameron died in 1920, and his son, John Watson Cameron, took over two years later when he reached the age of 21. He had hoped to go to Cambridge University after attending an exclusive preparatory school and then Lancing College in Sussex, but his father told him in no uncertain terms: 'If I die then you must forget about Cambridge and come straight into the business.' He accepted his father's order but the fact he was Watson Cameron's son didn't entitle him to an easy ride. He was sent to the shop floor where his day started at 4am and for the next eight years he

was schooled in all aspects of beer making, including mashing, fermenting and filling casks. The directors told him: 'If you don't get on, you are out!' and the brewery foreman was instructed to be strict with him.

John survived his rites of passage and in 1930 was finally allowed to join the board. Five years later he was promoted to managing director and in 1943 he added the chairmanship to his roles.

He guided the Lion Brewery through the difficult times of the 1930s that followed the recession of the previous decade. When peace returned following the Second World War, Camerons forged ahead and met a growing demand for bottled beer in the 1950s by opening a new bottling hall in 1955. The packaged beers included Bitter Ale, Double Lion Export, Barley Wine, Nut Brown Ale and Old Stranton Strong Ale.

In a bid to halt the decline in sales of cask beer, the brewery launched a new beer in 1955 that was to become its icon. Strongarm was advertised as 'the strongest ale on sale in Teesside at one shilling and seven pence a pint'. Pumpclips and labels showed a muscular man, stripped to the waist, forging steel links with a hammer and anvil. The beer was an immediate success and by the end of 1955 its sales were not only buoyant but had revived all Camerons' cask ales.

In 1959 Camerons bought the West Auckland Brewery with 78 pubs and Russell & Wrangham of Malton in Yorkshire. The Lion Brewery entered the 1960s with 750 licensed outlets and a rising demand for ale and lager. The old brewery was creaking at the seams and plans for a new plant were drawn up. It came on stream in all its modern glory in the 1970s, and with John Watson Cameron and his son John Martin Cameron in control, the company seemed well set for the future. In 1972 the Camerons launched their first major lager brand, Icegold, with 14 storage tanks added to the plant. This was followed by new kegging lines one year later and a continued increase in sales of cask Strongarm. But this success was overshadowed by rumours of a takeover for the company.

BIRTH OF A LEGEND

It's claimed that the name of Strongarm was the result of a director at the Lion Brewery looking out of his window one day and seeing the name of a factory across the road called Armstrong. The director reworked the word and a brewing legend was born.

Today the four per cent beer is called Strongarm Ruby Red Ale. The original recipe is still used and is made up of pale malt, 20 per cent crystal malt, brewing sugar and Fuggles, Goldings and Progress English hops, with Fuggles and Goldings added late in the copper boil for additional aroma.

The beer is unusual in having such a large proportion of crystal malt in its recipe. Most brewers use only two to four per cent, as the malt adds a pronounced toffee or barley sugar character to the finished beer. Crystal is used primarily for what brewers call 'mouthfeel' – a rich malt note on the palate that balances hop bitterness.

Crystal malt is not kilned or gently heated like conventional malt. It undergoes a stewing process similar to the way in which toffee is made. When it's blended with pale malt in the mash tun, its starch has already been converted into fermentable sugar. Despite the high level of crystal used in Strongarm, the beer is not sweet but is a fine balance of toasted malt and spicy hops with a delectable butterscotch note.

Pass-the-parcel

Sir John Ellerman, son of John Reeves Ellerman, died in 1973. He owned 26 per cent of Camerons' shares – worth £3 million – and they passed to Ellerman Lines on his death. Ellerman Lines said it would not bid for the brewery, but added, ominously, it would 'take a more active part in the company's management'. Its word was not its bond and in 1975 Ellerman paid £10 million for the remaining shares and became the new owner of the brewery and its substantial pub estate. The deal was in keeping with similar takeovers of breweries with large tied estates throughout the country by companies primarily interested in buying lucrative property.

At first the new ownership didn't seem a cause for concern. Martin Cameron stayed on as managing director and John Watson Cameron became president. In 1989 Martin Cameron was replaced by Jim Mackenzie and under his management close to £2 million pounds was invested in new plant, enabling the brewery to produce Hansa Lager. The beer was brewed in collaboration with one of Germany's leading breweries, Dortmunder Actien Brauerei, and was advertised in Britain on TV and hoardings with the risible slogan of 'lager – ve haf zie Hansa'.

Again, brewing success was overshadowed by events in the business world that were beyond the control of the Lion Brewery. A slump in world shipping in the early 1980s led to the collapse of Ellerman Lines, which owned the Tolly Cobbold brewery in Ipswich as well as Camerons. In 1983 the whole Ellerman group, including the breweries and pubs, were bought for £45 million by Sir David and Sir Frederick Barclay, better known as the Barclay Brothers. They are billionaires who live reclusive lives in the tax haven of the Channel Islands and are best known today as owners of the Telegraph group of newspapers. One year later, Scottish & Newcastle Breweries (S&N) attempted to buy Camerons but this was met with stiff resistance by the trade unions representing brewery workers, Hartlepool Council and CAMRA.

The council asked the Office of Fair Trading to refer the bid to the Monopolies Commission as S&N was one of Britain's biggest brewers. As a result, S&N withdrew its bid.

David Barclay, Camerons' chairman, announced that he and his brother had decided not to sell the company. 'We have taken a positive view of the brewing industry and we feel we can improve the Cameron business substantially.' So much for being positive: four years later the Barclays sold both Camerons and Tolly Cobbold to the property company Brent Walker for £240 million. The sale included 1,200 pubs, a tempting amount of bricks and mortar.

The game of pass-the-parcel at Camerons was not yet over. In 1992 the brewery and its remaining 51 pubs were bought for £18.7 million by Wolverhampton & Dudley Breweries (W&D), turning it into the biggest regional brewer in the country. The new managing director, Derek Andrew, said he planned to invest in both brewery and pubs but ran into early problems. Contracts to brew Hansa and to supply own-label brands to the Co-op and Spar came to an end, and with volumes in decline, 220 redundancies were announced.

But with Strongarm on sale in selected W&D pubs and new contracts to brew Heineken, Kronenbourg and Harp signed, production started to pick up. The joy, however, was short-lived. In 1999 W&D made a takeover bid for Marston's, the Burton upon Trent brewer. Marston's responded with a reverse bid for W&D, but the Wolverhampton company won the day, finally acquiring Marston's for £292 million. To offset the cost of the takeover, W&D disposed of some its assets – including Camerons.

Back in family hands

Stability and sanity returned to Hartlepool in 2002 when the Lion Brewery was bought by a family with genuine brewing roots in the region. David Soley was a local businessman who heard that the national brewer Whitbread planned to close the Castle Eden Brewery based in the small village of the same name, close to Peterlee. The brewery had been founded in 1826 by the Nimmo family and was best known for an ale that rivalled Strongarm in affection in the region – Nimmo's XXXX. David Soley bought the brewery for £4 million but soon realised that it was too dilapidated to save.

PUNCH DRUNK WITH PROPERTY

Brent Walker, owner of Camerons and Tolly Cobbold in the late 80s, was run by George Walker, who grew up in the East End of London and worked briefly for a local gangster before becoming a professional boxer. He gave up the ring following a bad accident and moved into property with his brother Billy, who had a more successful boxing career and was known as the Blond Bombshell or, when he lost a fight, the Horizontal Heavyweight. The brothers bought large amounts of property in London, with the 'Brent' in Brent Walker coming from their control of the Brent Cross shopping centre.

Tolly Cobbold

When George and Billy fell out, George forged ahead on his own. He announced he planned to close Tolly Cobbold and turn the site into a marina, with the Tolly beers produced by Camerons.

The deal fell through due to a vigorous campaign to save Tolly by Ipswich Council and local CAMRA branches.

The whole Brent Walker sorry saga came to an end in 1991. George Walker had bought the William Hill betting group for £685 million, but he finally over-reached himself and his business world collapsed in 1991 with debts of £1.4 billion. Brent Walker Inns, a subsidiary chain of pubs, was renamed Pubmaster and had its head office at Camerons until it became part of the giant national pub company, Punch. Tolly Cobbold closed in 2002.

He opened talks with Wolverhampton & Dudley and finally bought Camerons in 2002. David and his son Chris, now managing director, own the rights to beers brewed at Castle Eden, namely Nimmo's XXXX and Trophy Special, which are occasionally still brewed.

The Soleys first major investment in 2003 was a 10-barrel microbrewery that cost £500,000. It was overseen by head brewer Martin Dutoy and called the Lion's Den. It produces bottled and guest draught beers and can also undertake contract brewing and bottling. Beers that meet with consumer approval can be moved to the main brewery where the minimum run is 160 barrels. The small brewing plant was followed in 2004 by the Brewery Visitor Centre in the former Stranton pub adjacent to the brewery. The centre is packed with fascinating memorabilia of the Lion Brewery while a tap room offers a range of brewery beers.

In 2007 the Soleys sold their free trade and wholesale business to Molson Coors and the sale enabled them to invest £4 million in expanding the brewery's capacity. As a result, an 11-year brewing contract was signed with Scottish & Newcastle, now Heineken UK. Further contract brewing is carried out for Carlsberg among others. The Camerons side of the operation has not been neglected. Strongarm has been complemented by new cask beers and the arrival of the Head of Steam bars has seen the tied estate grow to 80 outlets.

Chris Deakin is the new head brewer following the retirement of Martin Dutoy. Chris has a formidable CV, having worked for Bass for 18 years, then Molson Coors, AB InBev and Heineken before arriving in Hartlepool. He produces 50 beers a year, both regulars and seasonals, and says his cask ales, with Strongarm leading the pack, are in growth. As well as the 10-barrel micro plant, he now has a 70-litre kit where members of the Tooth & Claw brewing team are given free rein to develop innovative new brews. The better ones are moved to the 10-barrel plant and are packed in can and keg. Tooth & Claw beers can be found in the Head of Steam bars and in many pubs and bottle shops across the north-east.

The magnificent modern brewhouse at Camerons

Two beers have been created for the heavy rock group Motörhead. The beers, exported in keg, bottle and can to 26 countries, are Road Crew and Overkill, with a stout planned for 2020.

Cask is very much in focus, with an Anchor range of ales brewed in collaboration with the London-based American artist Travis Moore. He specialises in drawing with Sharpie pens on a variety of surfaces including paper, canvas and glass. The beers include a pale ale called Sanctuary (4%), Old Sea Dog, a north-east brown ale (4.3%), Boathouse (4.4%), a premium blonde beer, and an East Coast pale ale, Bowline (4.3%). A donation of 5 pence from the sales of Sanctuary goes to the Royal National Lifeboat Institution.

Managing director Chris Soley says the success

Chris Soley

of the Anchor Range and the continued popularity of Strongarm show that Camerons has not given up on cask ale. 'But it's a challenge,' he says. 'Small Brewers Relief is a double-edged sword. It stimulated the market but there's now so much competition from small brewers that prices have been driven into the ground. Wholesalers have catalogues of hundreds of cask beers. It's wonderful for consumers but it's tough for brewers who don't qualify for SBR. Consumers expect cask to be the cheapest beer on the bar, but it has a short shelf life and needs more care. We've got to maintain pubs and communities out of beer sales and perhaps there's a case for brewers of our size to pay less duty.'

Despite tough market conditions, Camerons has survived and revived. 'Ellerman treated the brewery as a cash cow,' Chris Soley says, 'and Camerons got a bad reputation for beer when Brent Walker owned it.' The chairman of Wolverhampton & Dudley, David Thompson, was appalled by the cheap ingredients Brent Walker had used and demanded a return to top-quality malt and hops. Even though Camerons became surplus to requirements for W&D, the group did 'turn the tide at the Lion Brewery with new investment,' Chris acknowledges.

The Soleys' faith in the brewery can be seen in a subtle rebranding that has turned the heraldic red lion symbol round. The lion now looks not to the left but to the right – not to the past but the future.

Camerons, Lion Brewery, Stranton, Hartlepool, Co Durham TS24 7QS · 01429 852000
www.cameronsbrewery.com
Brewery tours available:
book with the visitor centre

Regular cask beers:
Sanctuary (3.8%)
Strongarm Ruby Red Ale (4%)
Old Sea Dog (4.3%)
Boathouse (4.4%)
Road Crew (4.5%)

Adnams

1872 · SOUTHWOLD · SUFFOLK

JUST about every journalist and travel writer who has visited Southwold has regaled readers with the story that George Adnams, who bought the brewery with his brother Ernest in 1872, went off to Africa where he was promptly eaten by a crocodile. It's a grisly tale but it's manna from heaven for a journo looking for a good 'intro' to a colour piece. Sadly, it seems it's not true.

As this book was nearing completion, I heard that Robert Porter, who has spent several years researching the Adnams' family, declared he could find no evidence to back up the crocodile story. It now seems that George did indeed go to Africa where he fought in the Boer War and then settled in the Transvaal. He died there in 1922 aged 73, drowning in a lake close to his home. He was recorded as working as a chimney sweep and he left the princely sum of thirty pounds, nine shillings and one penny.

George might have fared better if he had stayed in Southwold. With his brother Ernest Adnams, he arrived in Southwold from Essex in 1872 and bought the Sole Bay Brewery behind the town's leading hotel, the Swan. George was a restless character who dissolved the partnership just two years later and departed to Africa. Fortunately, his brother Ernest remained in Suffolk to develop the brewery and build sales of beer.

At Adnams they will tell you that half their potential sales are made up of the North Sea, but the geography hasn't hindered their progress. In the late 19th century Southwold had a narrow-gauge railway that not only brought holidaymakers to the town but also enabled the brewery to send casks to Halesworth where the main line transported the beer further afield.

Southwold may have lost its train service, but the brewery isn't isolated in a small seaside town. It enjoys national sales and such recent beers as Ghost Ship and Mosaic have chalked up impressive volumes. This success is set against a background of a company that has developed a quite different approach to the modern beer world than other family brewers. Far from relying on its tied trade, Adnams is reducing the number of pubs it owns and has become a major player in the free trade with cask, keg and bottled beers, supported by a vigorous export policy.

With the future of the planet in mind, the current chairman Jonathan Adnams has turned the brewery green with initiatives that save on energy, reduce carbon dioxide emissions, and recycle water and raw materials such as spent grain and hops (see box p.187).

Adnams' brewery in the late 1800s

Centuries of Southwold brews

Adnams claims its location has the longest unbroken tradition of brewing in Britain, stretching back more than 670 years, with most of it taking place in and around the Swan Hotel. In December 1345, before the Swan was built, Johanna de Corby and 17 other 'ale wives' were charged with breaking the Assize of Bread & Ale, a royal law that laid down strict rules for the prices that could be charged for beer and bread. Johanna was fined three pennies for her misdemeanour but was undeterred and appeared regularly before the local court for the next 20 years for selling ale in unmarked measures at too high a price or of poor quality. Her husband Robert, a baker, was also in constant trouble for selling underweight bread.

Thankfully, more reputable people took over from the de Corbys. Southwold in the 15th century started to use hops in brewing long before bigger towns in England. This was due to Southwold's proximity to the Low Countries with mariners from the Suffolk coastal town enjoying the hopped beers produced by Dutch and Flemish brewers. By 1489, when Southwold became a chartered town or legal municipality, hops were being imported from Holland. A century later Bullein, in his *Governance of Health*, said that he knew of many places in Suffolk where 'they brew their beers with the hops that groweth upon their own grounds.'

The Swan started life as a medieval tavern but soon grew into the most important inn in the town. The local bailiffs held their annual feast there on St Nicholas Day and the town chamberlain reported on the health of the citizens or settled his accounts over a flagon of beer. The inn, along with the rest of the town, was destroyed by the Great Fire of Southwold in 1659. It was rebuilt by John Rous in a timely fashion in order to provide refreshment for bell ringers and other local people who celebrated the restoration of the monarchy in 1660. It was around this time that the brewhouse was moved, as a fire precaution, away from the inn to its present site at the rear of Swan yard.

The reputation of the beers from the brewery grew in the 18th century when it was owned by the Thompson family. In his *Suffolk Traveller*, published in 1735, John Kirby mentioned 'Southwold's excellent springs of good water, which may be one reason why their Beer is so much esteemed.' In the 19th century the Swan and the brewery were bought for £350 by a local maltster, William Crisp. The brewery flourished under his ownership and he went on to start a malting company, now based at Great Ryburgh in neighbouring Norfolk, which is a major supplier of grain to the brewing industry, including the prized Maris Otter variety. When Crisp died in 1844 the brewery passed through a few owners before the Adnams brothers arrived in 1872. When George left for Africa, Ernest formed a partnership with his brewer, Thomas Sargeant, and in 1890 they turned the brewery into a limited company, Adnams & Co Ltd.

They brewed a variety of mild ales all branded with Xs, from single X to XXXX, with single X having a modest strength of 3 per cent alcohol. This was a time when drinkers were engaged in heavy labour on land and sea and needed sweeter mild ales to not only refresh them but also restore lost energy. In 1880 Adnams and Sargeant added a barley wine, Tally Ho, which continues to be brewed today and is a potent link, in every way, with the early days of the Adnams' dynasty. Tally Ho is now 7 per cent alcohol but may have been considerably stronger in the late 19th century and aged in wood.

Ernest Adnams (lower right). Tally Ho was first brewed 1880.

The Adnams and Loftus partnership

Adnams and Sargeant appeared to prosper. They rebuilt the brewery, bought pubs and constructed and enlarged hotels. But they overreached themselves and ran up substantial debts. They were rescued by the arrival of the Loftus family in 1902, who established a partnership with the Adnams that has lasted to this day.

Pierse Loftus came from a family with Irish origins. He'd worked as a brewer in Copenhagen and South Africa and he brought both technical skills and much-needed business acumen to Adnams. Within a year of his joining the company, Adnams bought the small Fisher brewery in Eye and this was followed by Rope & Sons of Orford in 1922. Two years later the Southwold brewery bought Flintham Hall & Co of Aldeburgh.

The brewery survived the difficult times of the inter-war and post-war years, in no small measure due to the loyalty of the workforce, many of whom

THE GHOST AT THE BEER FEAST

Adnams' biggest-selling beer, Ghost Ship, commemorates the rich history of Southwold and the many naval battles that have taken place there. The most famous was the Battle of Sole Bay in 1672 when the English fleet was based in the town under the command of the Duke of York. The Dutch fleet caught the English by surprise, and it took four hours for the authorities, aided by a drummer boy, to rouse the English sailors from the local taverns to return to their ships.

The Dutch were eventually driven back to Holland but many ships on both sides were lost.

It's claimed that remains of the ships can be seen on the seabed and Ghost Ship marks their contribution to Southwold's naval history. In 1972 another Adnams' ale, Broadside, was launched to mark the tercentenary of the battle.

Ghost Ship was designed by head brewer Fergus Fitzgerald. Despite its name, it's a beer with some colour in its cheeks, with rye crystal and caramalt added to pale malt. The main hop used is American Citra with American Chinook and Motueka from New Zealand added as late hops during the boil in the copper. Unusually, further Citra hops are added in the fermenter.

It's a highly complex beer with an aroma of citrus fruit, spicy hops and lightly toasted malt. Tart fruit, tangy hop resins and biscuit malt fill the mouth while the finish is long, dry and bitter but with fruit notes from the Citra hops.

Drays outside the brewery in the 1950s

dedicated their entire lives to the business. Typical of this dedication was the head brewer Percy Coveney – described as 'a small, combative and thirsty man' – who was head brewer from 1928 until 1953. His under brewer, Greg Wright, retired in 1965 at the age of 77.

As the older Adnams and Loftuses retired or died, a new younger generation from both families took over and guided the brewery through the challenging times of the 1950s and 60s, with the rise of national brewers and keg beer. Simon Loftus, grandson of Pierse Loftus, played the key role for many years, first developing a wine department that turned Adnams in to one of the leading wine merchants in the country, and then as chairman building beer sales nationally before he handed over to Jonathan Adnams.

The arrival of CAMRA in the early 1970s turned the spotlight on Adnams. Beer lovers would weep at the mere mention of the ales from Southwold that were hard to find outside their heartland. Many made the arduous pilgrimage to sup deep of Southwold Bitter and Broadside in the remote town famous not only for its brewery but also its multi-coloured beach huts and inshore lighthouse. The beers were available on handpump or straight from the cask in such fine pubs as the Sole Bay Inn beneath the lighthouse and the Harbour Inn by the river. The fame of Adnams' beer was not lost on the new aggressive national brewers and several of them attempted to buy the brewery but were thwarted by the determination of the families to maintain their independence.

Looking to the future

The brewery has won many awards, including CAMRA's Champion Beer of Britain for Adnams Extra in 1993, but it has not rested on its laurels. The 21st century has seen a major overhaul of the brewery to enable it to produce keg beer and lager as well as cask. A distillery has been added where gin, whisky and vodka are made.

Chairman Jonathan Adnams started working at the brewery in the 1970s as an apprentice brewery engineer. At the time, Adnams delivered beer to Cambridge twice a week but that was as far as sales went until a distributor got the beers into London. Adnams' 72 pubs accounted for 60 per cent of beer sales.

Jonathan became managing director in 1997 and chairman in 2006 and he's played a key role in the redevelopment of the brewery since 2001. He says: 'Back in 1999 we believed that cask beer would sustain us, and the first phase of the renewal programme was the installation of 17 top fermentation vessels designed for Adnams' yeast and cask beer. By 2005, as we specified the detail of our new brewhouse, we

Jonathan Adnams

could see accelerating changes in the beer market. I felt with the new brewhouse we had to forego traditional views and opt for maximum flexibility to help meet a changing future.'

Work on the new brewhouse started in 2007 replacing a mash tun and copper kettle that were threatening to burst at the seams. The plant is a German Huppmann kit and is fully automated.

PUTTING SOMETHING BACK

Adnams has been a pacesetter in the brewing industry for aiding the environment. A new warehouse in Reydon, just outside Southwold, was designed to be mainly below ground so as not to disrupt the view of the countryside. The building has a 'living roof' of natural vegetation that captures rainwater, which is used to clean the building, flush toilets and wash delivery vehicles.

In the brewhouse, steam is captured by a heat recovery system and recycled. Water use has been massively reduced, with water from the distillery pumped to the brewhouse, with grain moving in the opposite direction. The gas bill for the complex has been reduced by 30 per cent. Refrigeration has been replaced with more eco-friendly plant. Used grain is supplied to local farmers while spent hops are a popular pig feed.

It's based on the continental system of mash mixer, lauter (filtration) vessel, and a combined boiling kettle and whirlpool. Four brews a day can be handled, with each batch producing between 90 and 300 barrels. The brewhouse feeds 17 fermenting squares and 11 conical fermenters.

Up to seven tons of malt are used for each brew and a total of 60 to 90 tons a week of Concerto and Propena spring malts go through the system. Hop pellets range from traditional English Fuggles and Goldings to American and Australian varieties. Head brewer Fergus Fitzgerald goes to the harvest in the Yakima Valley of Washington State every autumn to choose the best hops for his modern beers. The only survivor from the old brewhouse is the 80-year-old yeast culture. The local water is extremely hard and is ideal for producing ales.

Jonathan Adnams says: 'There's been a perfect storm in the cask beer world. The rapid growth in micro brewers has flooded the market with new cask beer brands – some of it not very good quality – at a time when fewer people are going to the pub. Pubs with too many cask beers can suffer from a slow rate of sale to the detriment of the beer being sold. When they're paying £3.50 to £4 for a pint, beer drinkers have every right to expect a perfect pint and they're quick to change their drinking habits if they have a bad experience.

'By 2009 I could see that the growth in micro brewers together with the large differential in beer duty taxation was putting Adnams at a distinct disadvantage in cask beer. My reaction was to develop a new market of craft spirit distillation and the Copper House Distillery was born in 2010. We enjoyed great success with gin and the plant was expanded in 2016 with two additional stills.'

In 2013 Jonathan and Fergus Fitzgerald wrote a paper to the Adnams board proposing the addition of plant that could produce beer and lager to meet the growing demand for craft keg beer. In 2016–17 the brewery installed conical fermenters and conditioning tanks, new filtration plant and an automated kegging line.

The most recent addition to the brewhouse in 2018 is equipment that removes alcohol from beer. This enables Fergus Fitzgerald and his team to produce a low alcohol version of Ghost Ship at 0.5 per cent. This has been such a remarkable success that the equipment had to be extended in 2019 as the low alcohol beer now accounts for 12 per cent of annual production.

Southwold Bitter and Broadside remain mainly cask beers, but Ghost Ship and Mosaic are available in both cask and keg. Other keg beers include Ease Up IPA and Dry Hop Lager. Jonathan agrees the infamous keg beers of the 1960s and 70s stripped flavour out of the beer but Fergus says his versions are neither sterile filtered nor pasteurised and have a lower level of CO_2 than many keg beers.

As well as the mainstream beers, Adnams produces a wide range of occasional and seasonal beers, as many as 40 a year. They include a barrel-ageing programme with beers matured for a year in whisky barrels and a Belgian tripel aged for six months.

Fergus Fitzgerald, head brewer

Modern fementation vessels

Total production is running at 115,000 barrels a year, of which cask now accounts for 40 per cent – and falling. Jonathan Adnams says he sees no reason to think that cask will not go on declining.

He runs just 36 pubs now, though he's at pains to stress that any pub that's sold must go to people who will retain it as licensed premises so that villages don't lose the heartbeat of their communities. But Adnams' business is now all about the free trade. Packaged and craft beer continue to grow while cask declines. There's also a vigorous export policy, with beer sold in most European countries, Australia, Russia, Scandinavia, South America, the US and Singapore.

The brewery has come a long way since the late 19th century. Lovers of cask ale may regret its change of direction in recent years, but its survival and range of fine beers are cause for cheer.

Adnams Sole Bay Brewery, Southwold, Suffolk IP18 6JW · 01502 727200
www.adnams.co.uk · Tours available

Regular cask beers:
Lighthouse (3.4%)
Southwold Bitter (3.7%)
Mosaic (4.1%)
Ghost Ship (4.5%)
Broadside (4.7%)

Batemans

1874 · WAINFLEET · LINCOLNSHIRE

IF Batemans ever needs a theme tune it should surely adopt the Jerome Kern ditty from the 1930s 'Pick Yourself Up', which is all about dusting yourself off and starting all over again. It perfectly captures the myriad ups and downs of a brewery where the family members, on their knees and apparently out for the count, have fought back to success and acclaim.

In the 1980s a split in the family threatened its very survival, but George Bateman, his wife Pat and their children battled for three exhausting years to find the cash to buy out their relatives. They succeeded and today Batemans is not only flourishing but is also one of the best-loved breweries in the country. It's run by Stuart and Jaclyn, George's children and the fourth generation to manage the company.

It is now a slim-downed operation. Stuart and his board took the decision in 2017 to cut production ruthlessly from 30,000 barrels a year to just 6,000. It wasn't a move designed just to gain Progressive Beer Duty but to survive in brewing. 'If we hadn't made the move, we wouldn't be here today,' Stuart Bateman says emphatically. Batemans is still the major brewery in Lincolnshire but today the county has more than 20 small artisan producers, while the giant national brewers dominate the free trade. Batemans is a classic case of a 'squeezed middle' brewery, undercut by competitors big and small.

It's always been a hands-on brewery, but now there are fewer hands. Some directors have gone as can be seen in Stuart's umbrella job title of managing director, sales director, retail director and brewing director. As well as Jaclyn, who oversees marketing, Stuart's wife Rachael is an area sales manager and their children Harri, Edward and Eliza work at the brewery during university holidays. This is a family brewery *sui generis*.

The first Salem brews

The brewery's origins were inauspicious. The first George Bateman was just 29 years old in 1874 and had been cheated out of his 42-acre farm at Friskney by unscrupulous lawyers. He needed a living and bought the inventory of a brewery in Wainfleet for £505 10 shillings – around £30,000 in today's money. That sum bought him not only the brewing kit, but a cow shed, cucumber frame, currant trees and rhubarb beds. Smart young artisan brewers today would take the cucumbers, currants and rhubarb to make fashionable fruit and vegetable beers, but George stuck with malt and hops.

He was supported by his wife Susannah who had made ale on their farm while she was also baking bread. The Batemans were helped by Edwin Crowe, the former owner of the brewery who stayed for a while and passed

George Bateman

191

on his experience of both small-scale commercial brewing and retailing. Brewing was rudimentary. Before thermometers came into use in rural areas, Edwin would test the temperature of a brew by sticking his elbow into the mash tun. If he could keep it in for some time, the mash was too cold; if he had to take his elbow straight out, it was too hot.

Sales of beer at first were mainly to farmers who bought supplies for their families and workers. They would pay their bills twice a year and payment was not always in cash but could include meat and potatoes. George's business grew when the railway reached Wainfleet and he was able to send beer to such major towns as Boston, Grantham, Lincoln and Scunthorpe.

His first brewery was close to the railway but by 1880 he had made sufficient money to move 200 yards to a large Georgian building called Salem House. Salem became notorious as the town in Massachusetts where alleged witches were put on trial in the late 17th century: a current Batemans' beer called Salem Porter features a flying witch on a broomstick. But the name has its origins in Lincolnshire when Wainfleet was a major port and a bridge over the river in the town was called Salem Bridge: salem is derived from 'sail home'. Puritans from old England may have taken the name with them to the New World.

George and Susannah built their new plant in the coach house at Salem House. As well as brewing beer, they bottled gin, rum and whisky and Susannah went

back to making bread that was sold to supplement their income. On Fair Day, which was held twice a year, local farmers would come to settle their bills and would then join the Batemans in their kitchen for a feast, a tradition that continued until the 1930s.

George was boosted further by an unfortunate calamity in Wainfleet when local water pits mysteriously dried up, depriving two rival breweries of vital brewing 'liquor'. George's plant backed on to the River Steeping and he had a plentiful supply of fresh water to hand. He brewed dark and amber beers before pale malts became widely available and offered mild, table beer and nut-brown ale to his customers.

Never giving up

In his time, George bought just three pubs, but this side of the business started to blossom when his son Harry came on board in 1894. When other breweries staggered under the burden of increased taxes, reduced beer strength and pub opening hours in the First World War, Harry won a special licence to supply beer to workers in such key industries as munitions, steel and engineering in Lincoln and Scunthorpe. He also brewed for the army and navy canteen boards, later renamed the NAAFI.

Salem House

Harry Bateman

Mrs Burnett, who joined the brewery as a secretary in 1916, told George and Pat Bateman many years later, and long after she had retired, that she recalled seeing giant 54-gallon oak hogsheads being filled then rolled down to the station. They would be transported to Scunthorpe for pubs and working men's clubs.

Following the war, Harry took full control of the brewery, buying his father out for £4,299 one shilling and eight pence. His father had bought him a pub to celebrate his 21st birthday and in the 1920s Harry decided to go on a spending spree and buy more outlets.

He recalled later: 'Despite money being difficult, which seems to be the story of our lives, I acquired a group of pubs that everybody else thought was worthless. An auctioneer friend of mine from Boston decided I had gone completely mad and said I should give up brewing and join him, especially as I had a young family to support. One of the finest principles my parents had instilled in me was never to give up, so I told a friend during especially hard times, "If the ship's going down, I'm going down with her".'

The ship stayed afloat and in 1927, when Harry's son George was born, Harry celebrated by buying the Vine Hotel in Skegness. Skegness, five miles from Wainfleet, was emerging as a major seaside resort and in 1935 the family built a brand-new hotel there, the County. Harry's three children, Helen, George and John, helped lay the foundation stone on a plot that was next door to a former skittle alley run by a friend of Harry's called Billy Butlin. Butlin later became celebrated as the owner of holiday camps throughout the country and Harry supplied the camp's bars in Skegness with beer.

The beer he made was changing. Batemans continued to brew dark beers such as mild and brown ale, but consumer preference was turning to lighter ales

and Harry added bitter and India Pale Ale. IPA rapidly became his leading brand. In the 1930s he expanded the brewery but not before he had had to battle through the economic depression of that decade. At one time sales had slumped to such a degree that he was forced to lay off his entire workforce.

'It was a very sad day,' he recalled. 'I was so upset at seeing them wandering around Wainfleet with nothing to do that I invited them back and was determined to find them work at the brewery – somehow.' To accommodate them, he bought buildings across the lane from Salem House and installed a bottling plant, a shrewd move as bottled beer was becoming more popular. The buildings included a windmill that had been used in earlier times to grind corn for bread and horse feed. The sails were in a state of disrepair and the cost of replacing them was prohibitive, so Harry decided to remove them. As a result, the ivy-covered, arm-less windmill was not only a landmark in the town and but also went on to become the logo for Batemans when the entire brewing operation was moved there.

Mr George's Good Honest Ales

The Second World War, in common with the Great War, brought some advantages for the brewery. Butlin's holiday camp in Skegness was requisitioned and became a naval station called HMS Royal Arthur. Batemans continued to supply beer but in greater quantities as the sailors had prodigious thirsts.

By 1948 the brewery had an impressive pub estate of 68 outlets, which was destined to grow further when Harry's son George joined the company in 1950 as executive director. George had trained as a brewer with Greens of Luton and he used that experience to tackle old-fashioned methods at Wainfleet that were injurious to beer quality.

'Mr George'

'Mr George', as he became known fondly to the staff, recalled in later years: 'As far back as 1953, fermentation took place in the same casks that were used to ship beer to the trade. The casks were stacked on pine troughs in a way that allowed the fermenting beer to flow out of the bung hole and down the belly of the cask. The casks were then topped up again every two hours, using beer from the troughs. The casks were stored in a downstairs area where, despite an annual coat of whitewash, the temperature could reach 80 degrees F [25 degrees C] in the summer.

'This wasn't good for the quality of the beer and we needed a more sophisticated temperature control system. So, in 1953 we invested a lot of money in stainless steel fermenters with internal temperature control mechanisms. We did everything we could to reduce the chance of yeast infection. I arranged for a number of fruit trees outside the brewery to be cut down as fruit is a potential carrier of wild yeasts. The trees cut down included – to my father's horror – a fine old pear tree by the brewery wall.'

George, who branded brewery and pubs with the slogan 'Good Honest Ales', which was introduced by his father and is still in use today, continued to build the tied estate. He recognised that tied pubs were the best route to market for family brewers as bigger groups were beginning to emerge and threatened to dominate the free trade with the new fashion for keg beers. In 1957 he bought 29 pubs, including a number from Steward & Patteson, a Norwich brewery with extensive holdings throughout East Anglia.

To fund the purchases, George borrowed £50,000 from Guinness. He had to spend eight years changing the licences for many of the pubs that still had restrictions dating back to the First World War. Many had beer-only licences and it was necessary to change these to full licences at a time when wine was growing in popularity. 'Perpendicular drinking' was banned in the quaint belief that people became drunk faster if they consumed standing up. As a result, some of the pubs George bought had no seats or bar counters. His task was to make the pubs comfortable and welcoming to women and families, rather than just men's drinking dens, and this required endless court hearings to win full licences.

The brewery faced a serious dilemma in the 1970s. As a result of a series of mergers and takeovers, new national brewers had been created and they were hell-bent on flooding the market with keg beers. Keg was considerably more profitable than cask ale as a result of enjoying long shelf life. The new beers became popular, not as a result of their quality but from saturation advertising, including commercial television. The decline in sales of Batemans' cask beers was so drastic that George Bateman was forced to produce his own keg beer, using bottle-washing tanks as a rudimentary pasteurising unit. He had to install quarter-pint pumps in his pubs as the demand for cask beer was so low.

'The prospects looked grim,' he recalled, 'and then a knight in shining armour rode in. The Campaign for Real Ale began to reawaken people's enthusiasm for beer with more flavour and varied character. So once again the foaming head on a Batemans' ale was in

demand – so much so that we began to venture beyond our home county.'

When a CAMRA-run pub in Cambridge, the Salisbury Arms, announced it was selling Batemans XB, George proudly turned up with his wife, Pat, and daughter, Jaclyn, but was dismayed to find it wasn't his beer when he tasted it. When the manager insisted it was, George demanded to see the cellar and found the pipe from the beer engine on the bar had been connected to a cask of Sam Smith's. 'They didn't make the same mistake twice,' he said.

After many trials and tribulations, the future looked secure, based on a beer range that included light mild, dark mild and XB, with the strong premium XXXB introduced in 1978. In 1984 Jaclyn, who had trained as a nurse, joined the brewery, followed by her brother Stuart who had been on a three-year brewing and business course with Mansfield Brewery in Nottinghamshire, after studying business at St Paul's in Cheltenham. Stuart had been blooded many years earlier. At the age of six, he was taken by his father to spend a day helping Peter Sharpe, the brewery's maintenance engineer. 'Does he swear?' Peter asked. 'Of course not,' George replied. 'He ******* well will by the end of the day!' Peter promised.

Victory at a price

George and his family had no idea of the maelstrom that was approaching. In 1985 his brother John and sister Helen suddenly announced they wanted to sell the brewery. John planned to retire to Guernsey in the Channel Islands on the proceeds. The problem for George was he owned 40 per cent of the shares, while John and Helen controlled the majority 60 per cent. In order to save the brewery, George would have to raise the money to buy them out. Once the news leaked out, the Batemans saga became a major story, with George in great demand for press interviews. When he spoke at CAMRA's annual conference on the need to save the brewery, more than 1,000 members gave him a long and emotional standing ovation.

Two exhausting years followed, with George repeatedly visiting the City of London attempting to raise the funds. Back home, the family was heartened by local support. 'One day, a local farmer knocked on my door and said he had £3,000 to invest, if it would help,' George recalled. 'Two daughters of one our tenants asked if they could put a bottle on the bar to raise money for the brewery.'

The tide turned for George and his family in a dramatic fashion in August 1986 when XXXB won

BREWERS UNITE TO CELEBRATE XXXB

The importance of XXXB to Batemans' success cannot be underestimated. As well as Champion Beer of Britain, it has also won prizes from CAMRA in the same competition for Champion Best Bitter and Champion Premium Bitter.

To celebrate the beer's 40th anniversary, Stuart Bateman organised a special event in January 2018 that returned the beer to its original recipe and strength – the strength had slipped over the years from 4.8% to 4.5%. Three previous head brewers returned

to Wainfleet – Dennis Hartley, Ken Dixon and Martin Cullimore – who joined the current head brewer Scott Lawrence. Ken Dixon had first brewed the beer in 1978.

Stuart had run a quiz about Batemans' beers on Facebook and the winners, Michael and Hannah Borrill from Lincoln, joined Scott to brew the first batch of the revived beer. It was made with pale Flagon malt along with crystal, pale chocolate and wheat malts. The whole hops were Bobek, Challenger and Goldings. At the end of a long, exhausting day, the beer had gone from mash tun to copper and then to fermenters in preparation for being racked into casks a week later.

the great accolade of Champion Beer of Britain at CAMRA's Great British Beer Festival. The brewery and its battle for survival were now even bigger national news. A solicitor who heard a radio interview with George and Pat introduced George to the board of the Midland Bank, and after protracted negotiations, the bank agreed to advance the money that enabled George to pay off his relations. As he said, 'Serious parties followed,' and a special beer, Victory Ale, was brewed to underscore the successful outcome.

The tide may have turned but it was not yet plain sailing. The bank had to be repaid the enormous sum of £3.6 million and the only route was to sell pubs. Batemans had an estate of 120 pubs and the gloomiest prospect was to cut this down to just 13, with a big cut in production at the brewery. A merchant bank handled the negotiations, with potential buyers putting in sealed bids for the pubs.

Again, fortune favoured the brave. The property boom of the time came to the brewery's rescue and Batemans' pubs suddenly became a far more attractive proposition. One rural pub that sold just 45 barrels of beer a year and had a reserve price of £35,000 was bought for £168,000. It turned out that far fewer pubs needed to be sold but more cash was needed to repay the brewery's debts.

Stuart and Jaclyn threw themselves into a frenzy of activity to grow sales of their beer. Jaclyn set up a network of wholesalers and export agents that led to the beers becoming available nationally on draught and abroad in bottle.

Stuart overhauled the free trade business. The brewery had had long-term agreements with Whitbread for the supply of Heineken and Ansells' beers from Birmingham, but when the big brewing groups started to relentlessly increase the price of their beers year after year, Batemans found its income from the deals falling. In 1998 Stuart reached an agreement with Carlsberg Tetley to buy Batemans' free trade business. The payment of £3.6 million enabled the brewery finally to repay its bank loans and at long

Jaclyn and Stuart

last Batemans could breathe again and look forward to a period free from debt. More pubs were bought and today Batemans has 50 outlets in Lincolnshire, East Anglia, the Midlands and the North – the latter including pubs in Beverley and York.

After the jubilation of winning the battle to survive, sadness followed in its wake. George and Pat both died, in no small measure worn down by the long struggles. When George's funeral cortege passed through the town in 2007, Wainfleet closed for the day. Shops were shuttered and curtains were drawn as people paid their respects to a local hero.

George's last and enduring contribution to his company was to install a new brewhouse in 2002. In the same year, Stuart designed a visitor centre and museum that attracts large numbers every year. An on-site pub is called Mr George's Windmill Bar while other rooms trace the history of the brewery, with artefacts dating back to 1899, along with a collection of bottles and vintage brewing posters. The centre was officially opened by members of the 617 Dambusters Squadron, who had trained in Lincolnshire for their famous raids on German dams in the Ruhr during the Second World War.

A fresh strategy

Stuart took a long, hard look at his tenanted pubs and decided it was time for a complete overhaul of the relationship between brewery and tenant. He abolished the antiquated 'wet rent' system and rent reviews. In their place, he brought in free trade pricing and a code of practice, the first by any British brewer.

'The traditional tenanted rent model meant that publicans were penalised for doing well – with rent going up and sometimes through the roof as business got better. On top of that, they had to pay more for their beer than free trade pub owners. So, I put together a new team and transformed the publican-brewery relationship.' As a result of the code of practice, Batemans won the prestigious Publican award two years running.

Trading, on the other hand, became more difficult as a result of what Stuart calls 'the perfect storm' of Progressive Beer Duty. Not only was the brewery squeezed by small brewers who were able to sell beer at much lower prices, but some key wholesalers stopped handling cask beer. The Beer Seller, for example, had taken 6,000 barrels a year from Batemans but that dried up when the company was bought by Bulmers, which in turn became part of Heineken UK. Batemans also ended its relationship with Liquid Assets, Matthew Clark and Tavern Wholesale. It meant that important routes to market and substantial volumes of beer were lost.

The strategy changed at Wainfleet. The brewery pulled back from national sales and supermarkets and concentrated on its tied estate, now standing at 50 pubs. Free trade sales started again and are now bigger than at the time of the Carlsberg deal.

Producing just 6,000 barrels a year makes Batemans lean and hungry. The flexible brewing plant means that as well as the core brands, monthly specials can be produced, of which the winter Rosey Nosey is the best known and in great demand at Christmas time. A golden ale has joined the portfolio and has become a major brand – it's known simply as Gold outside Lincolnshire but is called Yella Belly in the county, commemorating a local army regiment whose soldiers wore distinctive yellow waistcoats.

Stuart Bateman looks to the future with optimism. He says his sons Harri and Edward are 'desperate to run the brewery when they have sufficient experience. The older generation need to hand on the baton.'

Not that he is planning to retire just yet. He's still fizzing with enthusiasm and bold ideas. In the summer of 2019, he brought a 150-year-old mash tun out of retirement and with head brewer Scott Lawrence he will brew special batches of XXXB that will be aged in whisky and wine casks.

'We're good at cask beer – that's our heritage,' he says. 'A keg plant would cost about £150,000 and we're not going there. We need to shout about the delights of cask.'

Head brewer, Scott Lawrence

George Bateman & Son, Salem Bridge Brewery, Mill Lane, Wainfleet, Lincolnshire PE24 4JE
01754 880317 · www.bateman.co.uk
Brewery tours available; visitor centre.

Regular cask beers:
XB (3.7%)
Gold/Yella Belly Gold (3.9%)
Salem Porter (4.8%)
XXXB (4.8%)

Wadworth

1875 · DEVIZES · WILTSHIRE

WADWORTH may be a venerable Victorian brewery, but youth and enthusiasm are driving it today. New beers have been added in recent years, developed by Rob Jacobson, a credited Master Brewer aged just 32 years. The dynamic managing director, Chris Welham, has packed a wealth of experience into a career with Greenall Whitley and the Spirit pub company. The chairman, Charles Bartholomew, has worked at the brewery for 50 years but his son Toby is standing in the wings and will take over when Charles decides to call it a day.

Tradition also plays an important role in the imposing red-brick complex of brewery, offices, visitor centre, warehouse and stables that dominates Devizes. When a new brewhouse was installed by Steinecker between 2008 and 2009, Charles Bartholomew insisted that the brewing vessels should be clad in wood. 'It was the first time the Germans had been asked to do that!' he chuckles.

Charles Bartholomew, chairman

Wadworth is a familiar name on the streets of Devizes and surrounding towns and villages as beer continues to be delivered by horse-drawn drays pulled by two giant shire horses, Jac and Sam, each standing 18 hands high. They enjoy a fine and healthy life feeding on hopped hay and molasses.

The beer travels further than Jac and Sam can take it. Can and keg versions are exported to the US, France and Italy. The leading and most famous ale, 6X, is sold throughout England and Wales, while bespoke beers are supplied to the Royal Navy's new aircraft carriers. Five pence from the sale of each pint of Swordfish and an IPA called Tommy Ale goes to army and navy charities.

Packaged beers account for only a small part of the brewery's output of 33,000 barrels a year: 80 per cent of production is in cask form and half of that is 6X, the ale that has made Wadworth famous throughout the country. In its time, Wadworth has brewed mild, porter and stout but it has always been a major producer of pale ale and IPA.

'Back in the 1950s we brewed mild but a lot of pale ale, too,' Charles Bartholomew says. 'We didn't go down the keg route and sales of our cask ales took off in the 1970s when CAMRA arrived. We had what people wanted and we became popular in university bars in Oxford, Bristol and Southampton.'

Chris Welham has conducted research among 1,000 drinkers and suppliers, and the results show that consumers over 35 years of age prefer darker ales while those under 35 plump for golden, hoppy beers. 'But both age groups still love traditional cask beer,' he says. 'There's a lot more breweries and competition today and drinkers want choice but they also like the comfort of recognised brands.'

A brewing adventure

The youthful spirit found at Wadworth is part of the DNA of the company. The founder, Henry Alfred Wadworth, was just 22 years old when he bought the brewery in 1875. He came from farming stock and had an adventurous spirit. On the August bank holiday in 1875 he made a hot air balloon voyage from Wilton Park in Wiltshire to Poole in Dorset. The balloon rose to 6,000 feet (1,829m) and Henry landed at Poole just before he was in danger of being blown out to sea. He said the trip had been 'most enjoyable'. He was also the first man to cycle from London to Bath, using a bicycle with iron tyres specially imported from France. The 100-mile, bone-shaking journey was completed in 2½ days and Henry wrote in his diary that he was 'pleased with the sensation'.

Opening a brewery was a straightforward business when compared to these examples of derring-do. When he bought the Northgate Brewery in 1875, from three brothers called Sainsbury, he had learned the brewing skills as a pupil with Chandlers & Co in London and then as the manager of a small brewery

Henry Wadworth

in Devizes. The market town had many beerhouses in the 19th century, but Henry Wadworth built a viable trade with a large number of outlets in the area. Within 10 years his business had outgrown the original brewery and he designed and built a substantial new plant close to the original. It was typical of its time, a tower brewery with a steam beam engine that lifted ingredients to the top storey, with the brewing process then flowing by gravity from floor to floor.

Wadworth and Bartholomew

In 1887 Henry Wadworth formed a business partnership with his brother-in-law and lifelong friend John Smith Bartholomew, who invested £6,000 in the company for a quarter share of the business. As well as supplying local customers, the two partners looked for outlets further afield and just before the outbreak of the First World War they had the good fortune to become one of the first suppliers of beer to the Army Canteen Board, later renamed the NAAFI – the Navy, Army and Air Force Institute. The sale of substantial amounts of beer to the board helped Wadworth survive the war years with less hardship than other regional and family brewers.

John Smith Bartholomew died in 1924 and was followed as managing director by his son, who was also named John. Henry Wadworth died five years later aged 78. Given his youthful exploits, it was not

STICKS AND STONES

One golden ale that caused a legal tussle is called Game of Stones, a 3.8 per cent pale keg beer that's a bridge between ale and lager. The producers of the television series *Game of Thrones* sued for breach of copyright, but the judge threw the case out, saying the name

of the beer had nothing to do with the TV drama. Wadworth argued that the beer is named after the Avebury stone circle, a Neolithic site dating from between 2850 BC and 2200 BC, close to Devizes. The ring, together with nearby Stonehenge, forms a UNESCO World Heritage Site.

SMALL TOWN, BIG HISTORY

Devizes is a small market town with, remarkably, more than 500 listed buildings. Its name comes from the Latin *ad devizas* and the Norman French *les devizes*, meaning the boundary: a Norman castle built in the 11th century marked the boundary or division between three Saxon parishes.

The castle was besieged in the 12th century during a civil war fought between King Stephen of England and the Empress Matilda. It was besieged again during the English Civil War when the town was first held by Royalist forces and then by Cromwell's troops. Following the end of the war, Cromwell ordered the castle to be demolished.

From the 16th century, Devizes became an important centre for wool and corn, with the largest corn market in the West Country. Brewing developed in the 18th century, leading to the Northgate Brewery becoming a dominant business a century later.

Devizes is close to both Stonehenge and Avebury and the 29 locks on the Caen Hill flight of the Kennet and Avon Canal.

perhaps surprising that his death was caused by falling from a horse. There was no male heir on Henry's side of the family and ownership passed to, and remains in the hands of, the Bartholomews.

John Bartholomew busily expanded the brewery during the inter-war years and bought the Godwins brewery with pubs in the Swindon area. The year 1923 was a significant one for Wadworth as it saw the launch of 6X, which was to become its biggest-selling and best-known beer. It was first brewed with a strength of 6 per cent but that was reduced during the Second World War as a result of restrictions on the supply of raw materials and the strength of beer. Malt, sugar and hops were all rationed, but as in the First World War, Wadworth was able to maintain a good trade by supplying beer to the armed forces.

In the post-war world Wadworth, as Charles Bartholomew says, remained true to cask ale and didn't follow the trend to keg beer, though it did launch its own lager, Norstein, in 1972. In 1952, when John Bartholomew died, he was succeeded by his son Major John Cairns Bartholomew, who stayed in post until 1996 before handing over to his son, Charles. During the major's long reign, further expansion took place, with more pubs bought and additional sales made to the free trade and clubs.

Blending the best of the old and new

The modern and traditional faces of Wadworth can be seen at close hand on one of the popular tours of the brewery. The site attracts 16,000 visitors a year to see inside the brewery, admire the shire horses and enjoy food and beer in an impressive, beautifully designed visitor centre.

The Devizes brewhouse with Steinecker vessels clad in wood

Brewer Andy Weaver shows visitors two mash tuns: one 80 years old, the second dating from the time the brewery was built in 1885. There's a coolship at the top of the brewery, a large open pan where the hopped wort – the sugary liquid boiled with hops – was cooled prior to fermentation. The pan is no longer used as the wort is wide open to infection from wild yeasts. The current brewer's yeast culture is at least 80 years old and the local water is hard, ideal for brewing pale beers.

The steam engine, installed in 1900, which once delivered malt and hops to the top of the brewery, is still in situ but has not been used since 1932. Two mash tuns can handle brews that range from 300 barrels to 70 barrels. And there's an original 80-barrel copper that was coal fired. As well as the modern Steinecker brewhouse, a 2½ barrel pilot plant has been instal-led where the brewing team can develop new beers. Fermentation takes place in 12 traditional square vessels and conicals and lasts for seven days – the 'two sabbaths' beloved of brewers.

The core beers all have tried and trusted recipes using, in the main, British ingredients. 6X is brewed with pale, crystal and black malts and hopped with

Fuggles and Goldings. Henry's IPA, named in honour of the founder, is the same recipe but without the black malt. The much-loved winter beer, Old Timer, has the same recipe as 6X.

Two recent additions to the range have a more modern twist. Horizon is a golden ale brewed with pale and cara gold malts with some flaked barley and an impressive five hops in the copper: as well as English Fuggles, there are Styrian Goldings from Slovenia and Cascade, Centennial and Mosaic from the United States. Swordfish is a rich-tasting brew. As well as pale, crystal and black malts and Fuggles and Goldings hops, Muscovado sugar and Pussers Rum are added, with 21 bottles of rum for every 100 barrels of beer.

ARTISTS IN BEER

Wadworth employs both an artist and two sign writers to design new pub signs and repair existing ones. Artist David Young paints new signs and cleans up older ones affected by the elements while Wayne Ritchings and Paul Martin add the brewery name to delivery vehicles, including the horse-drawn drays, and sign write amenity boards for pubs.

Chris Welham

Chris Welham says Horizon shows the way in which Wadworth is reaching out to a younger audience of drinkers with the beer available at the usual cask temperature of 10 to 12 degrees C and in a colder format.

Since 2016, chairman Charles Bartholomew has continued to invest substantial sums in both the Northgate site and his pubs. The estate now numbers 175 outlets, including 56 managed pubs and 119 tenancies, and covers Wiltshire, Gloucestershire, Oxfordshire, Somerset, Avon, Hereford and Worcester, Hampshire and Surrey. There's even one London pub by Putney Bridge station. The emphasis, Charles says, is increasingly on good food along with beer and wine – Wadworth has its own wine and spirits company.

Charles says around 50 pubs have been sold in the past five years. They were mainly in rural locations and 'there was increasingly less in it for the tenants or the brewery,' he says with regret.

That's a sad fact of modern life, but Wadworth is in for the long haul with its policy of blending the best of the old and new world, stressed by Jac and Sam clip-clopping through Devizes with another batch of tasty ales for local pubs.

In December 2019 Chris Welham and Charles Bartholomew announced they were looking for a site to build a new brewery. They said the present brewery needs so much investment to make it fit for purpose that it would make better sense to build a new plant. They hope the brewery will stay in Devizes. It will take between two and three years for the new brewery to be built and in the meantime the existing site will stay in operation and the visitor centre will remain open.

Wadworth, Northgate Brewery, Devizes, Wiltshire SN10 1JW · 01380 723361
www.wadworth.co.uk

Regular cask beers:
Henry's IPA (3.6%)
Horizon (4%)
6X (4.1%)
Swordfish (5%)

WELLS ALES

ARE WONDERFUL

BY CHARLES WELLS OF BEDFORD OF COURSE

Charles Wells

CHARLES WELLS epitomises the changing face of family brewing in Britain. It has been inextricably linked to Bedford since the late 19th century, but in 2017 the family took the critical decision to sell the Eagle brewery to Marston's for £55 million. It has used part of that sum to invest in a new brewery on a modern industrial estate in the town where it will concentrate on supplying its 175 pubs in Britain and a further 20 in France.

The new site is called Brewpoint and is close to the A6 that will transport beer quickly to Wells' pubs in Bedfordshire and neighbouring counties. Paul and Peter Wells, the fourth and fifth generation of the family to run the brewery, say they looked at other potential sites in such places as Milton Keynes but decided they had to remain in Bedford.

Brewpoint, which came on stream in 2020, can produce 18,000 barrels a year but has the space to expand up to 35,000 barrels. It replaces the Eagle plant with a capacity of 750,000 barrels a year. It had become too big for Wells' needs – 'it was just washing its face,' chairman Paul Wells says. 'Cask beer was in decline and the brewery was just breaking even while the return from our pubs was strong. We had to make a decision about where to invest for the future.'

The decision was to concentrate on the pub estate. It includes the 10 successful venues in the Pizza, Pots & Pints concept that specialise in offering simple but quality meals alongside a range of ales and lagers. Wells' most recent acquisition is in Oxford, with a strong appeal to 'town and gown', while the 20 pubs in France have brought the English pub to a new and intrigued audience that is confronted by not only ale but such rare culinary delights as 'bangairs et mash'. The French pubs are found in Paris, Lyon, Reims, Lille, Montpellier, La Rochelle, Toulouse and Bordeaux.

The sale of the old brewery to Marston's included Wells' two main brands, Eagle IPA and Bombardier. While both beers continue to be supplied to Wells' pubs, Paul Wells says the problems he encountered with Bombardier highlight the fate of middle-ranking

Charles Wells, founder

Office workers outside the brewery entrance, c. 1902

brands that are up against the heavily promoted beers of the giant global and national brewers.

'Thanks to the rise of microbrewers, we were the "squeezed middle" between giant brewers and a couple of thousand new brewers,' he says. 'It explains why some family brewers have been forced to change strategy if they don't have strong brands.' Bombardier was advertised for several years on television using leading comedians Rik Mayall and Bob Mortimer. But Paul says when he ran focus groups with pubgoers they admitted that while they loved the ads, with so much new choice, they rarely drank the beer. 'Nowadays we are finding our new Wandering Brewer project is going down very well, providing much more choice,' he adds.

Romantic origins

Love was the driving force that turned Charles Wells into a brewer: love for a woman, not beer. Charles was a sailor, born in Bedford in 1842. He joined the Merchant Navy and rapidly rose through the ranks to become a chief officer by 1868 and finally a captain.

Charles Wells as a young midshipman around 1852

Coopers and maltsters pose with tools of their trade at Horne Lane, c. 1893

While he was on leave in the early 1870s, he met and fell in love with Josephine Grimbly from Banbury in Oxfordshire. When he proposed to her, he encountered the strict Victorian code of the time: Josephine's father said he would agree to the marriage if Charles gave up the sea and found a career that kept him at home. As a result Charles worked for a while in his father's furniture shop in the town, but when the local Horne Lane brewery was up for sale he saw the opportunity to join an industry that was growing fast in pace with the rising population of Bedford.

Horne Lane was a substantial brewery with modern equipment, including coolers and refrigerators. It produced 3,500 barrels a year and, most importantly, owned an impressive estate of 35 pubs in Bedfordshire and Northamptonshire. Charles had financial support from his father and a local investor and was able to buy the site for £16,700. The business flourished. The main beers were mild ale and porter, and within four years of Charles's ownership production had grown close to 6,000 barrels a year. In 1881 he bought nine additional pubs and then borrowed £3,500 from a local bank to rebuild the brewery. A new tun room, where beer was matured before going to trade, was installed and a maltings was added at a cost of £3,000. The loan was quickly paid off as production rose to an impressive 10,000 barrels a year.

The closing years of the 19th century witnessed a furious pace of change and growth at the brewery. Twenty-eight pubs were added to the estate in 1895 and at the same time Charles started to produce substantial amounts of bottled beer as the glass-blowing industry developed. At the turn of the century, Wells & Co, as the company was called, produced 27,000 barrels a year and supplied a tied estate of 100 pubs. Charles invested in his pubs in order to meet the changing needs of a more sophisticated clientele who desired creature comforts as well as pints of beer. A stone inscribed 'CW' was placed prominently in every pub as it was rebuilt or refurbished.

NEW CENTURY, NEW BEERS

A new century saw new beers being brewed. The age of porter was largely over and the beers brewed included XX mild, PA or pale ale, IPA, XXX strong ale and SS extra stout. Bottled beers, almost certainly bottle conditioned at that time, included pale ale, IPA and extra stout. In the 1920s the brewery won awards at the prestigious Brewer's Exhibition for its Sparkling Family Ale and Family Stout. The term 'family' was widely used in the brewing industry at the time and it encouraged the consumption of beer with meals at home when little wine was drunk by middle and working-class families.

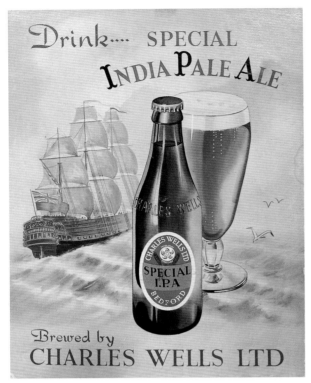

In 1910 Wells & Co became a private limited company, valued at £150,000 and with an estate of 141 pubs. Charles was nearing retirement age and his sons Ernest, Hayward, Harry and Richard became directors with equal shares. Charles insisted they all lived in Bedford, and as a true Victorian patriarch, he vetoed Richard's wish to move just two miles out of town when he married.

Charles Wells died in 1914. He had been in poor health for several years, with his sons effectively running the brewery day to day. The family, with Josephine still alive, hoped for a quiet funeral but the papers reported a sizeable turnout of local people. The *Bedfordshire Times* reported: 'Shortly before the hour appointed the bells of town churches commenced to toll and a large company of townspeople, tenants and workpeople had assembled when the mourners arrived.' The paper added that Charles Wells would be 'much lamented by the brewery staff, some of whom were old servants. It was a good trait of their employer that he never troubled about their political and religious views.' He had been a familiar figure in the area, visiting his pubs by pony and trap and later in a Lanchester when the age of the car arrived.

Success despite difficult times

Despite the restrictions imposed during the First World War, Wells maintained production at 20,000 barrels. Strong beers such as pale ale and extra stout were not brewed until the conflict ended and the main wartime beer was a weak mild in which malt was blended with cheaper cereals, colouring and sugar.

In 1917 Richard Wells, who ran the brewery while Ernest and Hayward were on military service, bought the Jarvis Phoenix Brewery in Bedford, which came with 66 pubs. This was followed with the acquisition of the Newport Pagnell brewery in 1919 that added a further 49 pubs to the estate. In the same year, Wells bought 27 freehold and three leased pubs when the Priory Brewery in St Neots was put up for auction.

Wells entered the 1920s in a strong position. It was producing 36,000 barrels a year and had an impressive estate of 290 pubs. The post-war boom soon ended and beer sales declined. The main brands produced were XXX Mild, IPA and SIPA or Special India Pale Ale. Bottled beers were increasingly popular and the main ones were Family Ale, Family Stout and Double Stout. Mild was such a popular style that a brewers' price war broke out to maximise sales. Wells reduced

The Wells family on war duty – Pat Wells, seated, on the fuselage

AMERICA'S WARTIME INVASION

The site at Havelock Street included a building where Glenn Miller and the US Airforce Band rehearsed and recorded programmes for American troops based in Britain and Europe. Miller, who famously disappeared while on a flight to France in 1944, has a bronze bust in Bedford's Corn Exchange.

His orchestra was based in Bedford during the war and the building that they recorded in was known as the Shrine. Bing Crosby and Dinah Shore were among several singing stars who also recorded there. The building was demolished in 2002 to make way for the new Eagle Centre, which houses offices and a visitor hub.

the price of its mild to 5d (2.5p) but it was undercut by Fuller's of London and Paine's of St Neots, who both charged just 4d a pint.

The economic depression of the 1930s had a major impact on the brewery. Production fell to 28,000 barrels, substantially down on the levels of the early 1920s. However, the directors made improvements to the plant, installing four new fermenting vessels and a pasteurisation unit for bottled beer. A new malting was commissioned just before the Second World War broke out. Production by then had soared to 34,000 barrels, with 365 pubs based in Bedfordshire, Buckinghamshire, Cambridgeshire, Hertfordshire, Huntingdonshire and Northamptonshire.

While the brewery survived the war intact, with bombing concentrated further south in the London area, the Wells family suffered the loss of three sons of Sir Richard and Lady Wells. The sons were killed in action, as was Charles Ian Wells, the son of Ernest. The brewery had the good fortune to supply beer to the NAAFI – the Navy, Army and Air Force Institute – and wartime production increased to 40,000 barrels a year. But severe restrictions on raw materials meant that only two draught beers, XX Mild and SIPA, and two bottled beers, pale ale and stout, were produced.

When peace returned, Charles Wells had to face a surge in demand for bottled beer, with such national brands as Double Diamond and Guinness taking trade away from regional and family brewers. Wells responded by improving and enlarging its bottling line and promoting the beers with show cards with a registered Starfish trademark.

New beers and mergers all around

An era ended in 1956 when Sir Richard Wells, the last surviving son of the founder, died. He had a remarkable career with the brewery, becoming a director in 1910 and chairman in 1952. His sons David and Oliver took over as joint managing directors. They responded to the demand for bottled beers with Old Bedford Ale for the winter months while Strong Ale in bottles was relaunched as Fargo Strong Ale. When the name was changed to Wells Fargo it led to a dispute with the American bank of the same name. The dispute was amicably settled but the beer was never sold in the United States.

The Swinging Sixties saw yet another mood swing among beer drinkers. Their interest turned from bottled beer to the new, heavily promoted keg beers such as Flowers and Watneys Red Barrel. Wells responded by selling Flowers keg in some of its pubs. The 1960s were also a time of major mergers and takeovers in the industry, and in a bid to prevent the new national brewers encroaching on Bedfordshire, Wells & Winch in Biggleswade approached Charles

Wells with the suggestion that the two breweries should merge. Despite the name, Wells & Winch was not connected to the Charles Wells family and the merger was politely turned down. Wells & Winch was then taken over Greene King of Bury St Edmunds and the Biggleswade plant later became a production unit for Harp lager.

Further concentration took place when JW Green in Luton was taken over by the national brewer Whitbread, which closed the Luton plant in 1969. Green was far and away the biggest brewer in Hertfordshire and Bedfordshire and had earlier merged with Flowers of Stratford-upon-Avon.

Wells could now claim proudly that it was the only independent brewery in Bedfordshire, and in 1962 the company launched its own keg beer called Noggin. It became a leading and important brand for the brewery and its fortunes were boosted when it won gold and silver medals in the International Brewers'

Exhibition. Strong brands were vital as mergers and takeovers continued unabated. To the north of Bedford, Phipps NBC brewery in Northampton was bought by the giant national company Watney Mann, a takeover that handed it 1,200 pubs in the region which it could flood with its Red Barrel keg.

With the industry resembling a battleground, Wells moved to strengthen its position. In 1963 it bought the Abington Brewery in Northampton, adding 23 pubs to the Wells estate. In 1964 Wells brewed a record 43,000 barrels and seemed safe from marauders.

The Eagle was born

The 1970s began with further expansion at the brewery. A new mash tun and two stainless steel fermenters were installed and plans were drawn up for a new fermenting room and keg beer tank room. Despite these innovations, it was clear that the Horne Lane site was creaking at the seams and was struggling to meet the demand for its beers, especially as the tide turned again in the 1970s with the arrival of CAMRA. Keg beer went into rapid decline and real ale was on drinkers' lips.

Charles Wells' hand was forced in 1973 when Bedford town council told the brewery it wanted the Horne Lane site to build a riverside walk for locals and visitors. An 11-acre site was earmarked on land owned

Oliver Wells standing on the 'raft' that was built as the base for the new brewery at Havelock Street

The imposing façade of the Horne Lane brewery alongside the River Ouse, demolished in 1976

by Eastern Gas next to Bedford Town football ground. The deal caused a furore when the local newspaper reported that the council had offered Wells £1,250,000 for Horne Lane, double the price previously paid for development land in the town. The deal with the council was agreed and the sum proved to be a comparatively small one when Wells encountered serious problems with the new land at Havelock Street. Years of gas production had contaminated the subsoil with extracts from coke and coal. The subsoil was also unstable and plans for piled foundations had to be abandoned. The ground had to be dug out to a depth of one and a half metres and filled with concrete. A new head brewer, Roy Morewood, said the new brewery was built on a concrete raft. The new Eagle Brewery cost £3,600,000, more than one million pounds over budget: the name eagle reflected the town's historic symbol.

The Eagle Brewery opened in 1976. Beer was brewed at both Horne Lane and Havelock Street until Roy Morewood and the directors, led by John and Oliver Wells, were satisfied the beers from the new site matched those from the old. It was a difficult transition as Horne Lane had been a traditional tower brewery, while the Eagle plant was one of the most modern in Britain, capable of producing 100,000 barrels a year. Morewood had argued successfully for a flexible brewery that could produce lager as well as ale, using enclosed conical fermenting vessels. Significantly, the first new beer brewed at the Eagle site was Kellerbrau, a lager brewed in the traditional European fashion with imported lager yeast. The lager beer joined the main portfolio made up of XX

Mild, IPA, Noggin, Gold Eagle Bitter, Silver Eagle Light Bitter and Ace lager on draught, with Light, Brown, Welcome Brown, Double Star, Fargo, Ace and Old Bedford Ale in bottle. Within a couple of years Fargo was made available on draught.

Roy Morewood took particular care with his cask ales. He found that the new system of fermentation created too much excess yeast when racked into casks. He devised a method whereby the beer was centrifuged to remove the yeast and was then reseeded with fresh yeast to ensure a good secondary fermentation in cask. The system caused concern with CAMRA, with some of its members questioning whether a beer with reseeded yeast could be considered to be 'real ale'. But the problem was quickly settled on the basis that the beer tasted good and met with drinkers' satisfaction.

More than 80,000 barrels were brewed in the first year at Havelock Street. This figure was soon extended due to major developments in both lager and ale. Soon after the opening of the new site, Wells was approached by the major national brewer Whitbread with the suggestion that Wells should brew Red

Stripe, the leading beer in the Caribbean. The owners of Red Stripe, Desnoes & Geddes, had held talks with Whitbread, but they said the proposed volume of 15,000 barrels a year was too small for them, but they thought Wells might be interested. Wells took the beer on and Whitbread must have cursed a lost opportunity when production of Red Stripe eventually peaked at 130,000 barrels.

On a different front, Wells launched a new premium cask beer in 1980 called Bombardier. It was named in honour of Bombardier Billy Wells, a famous prewar professional boxer, who had no connection with the family. This link was later replaced by the image of a military figure, which continued with the television advertisements that featured Rik Mayall and Bob Mortimer as soldiers with the rank of bombardier. The beer became one of the most popular premium cask ales in the country, with sales in the free as well as the tied trade. A stronger version became the linchpin of the brewery's export initiative as the company looked for sales in both the United States and Italy. Italy proved fertile ground, with young Italians leaving wine to their parents and enjoying strong English ale.

The brewery continued to expand. When Bedford's football club went into receivership, Wells moved on to the ground with new warehousing while additional brewing, fermenting and conditioning capacity was installed. New pubs were added to the estate, which grew in 1988 to 306 outlets. This increased again to 354 in the early 1990s following the government's Beer Orders which forced the national brewers to divest

The brewhouse at Havelock Street

positive note, Wells was able to sign contracts to brew first Kirin lager from Japan, one of the world's top brands, and then Corona Extra from Mexico.

In 1998 the directors, facing the problem of declining sales, took the decision to withdraw from the production of own-label beers for supermarkets. National brewers supplied supermarkets with beers that were sold as 'loss leaders' at deep discounts with the result that Wells could make only minimal profits from this sector. The brewery was further affected by the government's Beer Orders which had introduced a guest policy that allowed tied pubs to sell beers from other breweries. The national brewers set out to dominate the new guest beer sector by offering tempting beers at generous discounts. Small rural pubs were badly affected and Wells had to restructure by selling 50 tenanted pubs, reducing the estate to 254.

Wells faced further problems in the new century. In 2010 it lost the contracts to brew both Red Stripe and Corona along with Cobra lager: the owners of Cobra had gone into administration. Although these losses were offset by an agreement to market a leading Spanish lager, Estrella Damm, the new generation of the family, led by Paul, Peter and Tom Wells, felt the company had to restructure itself to face future challenges.

Wells & Young's

In 2006 Wells shook the industry with an audacious merger that created a new company, Wells & Young's. Young's brewery in Wandsworth dated from 1831 and achieved fame in the 1960s and 70s as one of the few family brewers that refused to go down the keg route and stayed loyal to cask beer. The brewery, close to the South Circular Road, was effectively in the middle of a large traffic jam and the local council announced it planned to redevelop the area. Young's directors had the choice of building a new brewery or having their beers brewed elsewhere. A suitable site proved impossible to find and Paul Wells suggested to his opposite number at Young's, Stephen Goodyear, a third course: to create a new company, with Young's

themselves of several thousand pubs. This enabled Wells to buy 43 pubs from Bass and Whitbread and gave the company a much-needed presence in London.

Expansion continued unabated in the 1990s. A second brewhouse was commissioned enabling 14 brews a day to be produced and creating a capacity of 750,000 barrels a year. But problems followed. The open borders policy of the European Union led to 'booze cruises', with hordes of people from Britain travelling to Calais to pick up large quantities of French beer that cost half the price of British beers as a result of far lower rates of duty in France. The result for Wells and other family and regional brewers was a sharp decline in sales in the tied trade and in supermarkets. Wells sold 21 pubs but there was further pressure on sales and profits when national brewers, new pub companies or 'pubcos' and supermarkets started to buy and sell beer at deep discounts that smaller brewers couldn't contemplate. On a more beers brewed at Bedford. As a result, Wells & Young's was formed in 2006 and Young's former head brewer, Ken Don, spent several months matching his beers at the Eagle Brewery. Young's tied estate, similar in size to that of Wells, brought a boost to production at Bedford, with 500,000 barrels brewed in 2008. Fortunes at the new company were also improved in 2007 when it bought the famous Courage beers from Scottish & Newcastle (S&N). They included an old Cockney favourite, Courage Best, and the premium ale Directors Bitter. When S&N became part of Heineken, the Dutch owners were happy to sell the Scottish McEwan's range to Wells & Young's, giving them a foothold in the Scottish market and bringing the revered McEwan's Export to England.

After five years of successful partnership, Wells and Young's decided to go their separate ways. It was an amicable parting. Stephen Goodyear said Young's wanted to invest in its pubs while Wells wanted to invest in brands. It took two years before the name of Wells & Young's disappeared as Wells had to redesign its trademarks, brand names, and point-of-sale and promotional material, but by 2015 the name of Charles Wells returned to the Eagle Brewery.

The Wandering Brewer

The name of Charles Wells didn't survive for long. In 2017 there came the fateful decision to sell the brewery and leading brands to Marston's. Today Wells & Co – the company has reverted to the original 19th century name – faces a new future with a scaled down, modern plant that cost £7.5 million. Paul Wells says his pubs will be offered beers from the new brewery along with Bombardier and Eagle IPA, now owned by Marston's. Beers planned at Brewpoint include Charlie's Dry Hopped Lager, keg Charlie's Triple Hopped IPA and cask Late Hopped IPA, with the John Bull brands produced for the French pubs.

ALORS! BIÈRE ANGLAISE

The opportunity for Wells to break into the French market came in the 1990s with an approach from the drinks firm Allied Domecq which owned the John Bull Pub Company, the John Bull brands and a portfolio of franchised pubs in both eastern and western Europe. In 1998, Allied invited Wells to buy 28 pubs in eastern Europe and two in France. The following year Wells bought the John Bull pubs and beer brands for just £1. The pubs in eastern Europe are now run on a franchise basis and Wells has concentrated on building its estate in France, which by 2020 numbered 20. The pubs have no uniform design and avoid kitsch and clichéd 'Olde English' styling, but they are clearly and definably English, with such names as George & Dragon, King Arthur, Shakespeare, Charles Dickens and Sherlock Holmes. At first some of the pubs had handpumped cask ale but Paul Wells admits this was a step too far and the French failed to appreciate beer served at a comparatively warm temperature and without a big foaming head. Meals include fish and chips, bangers and mash, cheese ploughman's, curries, jacket potatoes and Sunday roasts.

The architect's impression of the new Brewpoint building

Wells will also continue with a scheme known as the Wandering Brewer. While Brewpoint was being built, head brewer Ian Jones produced a range of beers for the Wells pubs in collaboration with other independent breweries, including Castle Rock, Purity, Nethergate, Thornbridge, Tring and Windsor & Eton. The beers have proved popular and the scheme will continue even when Brewpoint has opened. Paul Wells is not at all gloomy about cask beer: he thinks it will revive and he expects 30 per cent of production at Brewpoint will be cask.

'We plan specialist beers for our pubs,' he says. 'The Great British Pub is the future and we have to applaud it in all its infinite variety. Whether the pub is in Bedford or Bordeaux, drinkers want the same: good beer and good food.'

With the sixth generation of the Wells family primed to follow Paul, Peter and Tom, the eagle will continue to soar in Bedford.

Wells & Co, Brewpoint, Fairhill, Bedford MK41 7FY
www.wellsandco.com

Regular cask beer:
Charlie Wells Triple Hopped IPA (5.2%)
Other beers to be confirmed

THE
GREAT BEER BATTLE
OF MASHAM

THEAKSTON · BLACK SHEEP

THE THEAKSTON family in the Yorkshire Dales has been involved in a saga, the stuff of which pulp novels and TV soaps are made. It's the long and dramatic tale of how a famous family of brewers fell out with such acrimony in the 1980s that the two sides exchanged writs, complained of conspiracy, and ended up in the High Court surrounded by bewigged lawyers and a leading judge. The outcome was that the town of Masham – pronounced Massum – boasts two independent breweries run by members of the same family. A century earlier, a similar situation happened with the Smith family in Tadcaster. They're fighting folk up north.

As in Tadcaster, as in Masham: the two breweries stand a short distance apart, pumping the rich aromas of malt and hops into the crisp air. The Masham dispute ended with Paul Theakston leaving the family brewery where he'd worked from the age of 19, becoming managing director at 23. He licked his wounds and then launched Black Sheep in maltings once owned by Theakston.

The Theakston family has been in Masham since the 16th century when Robert Theakston was a church warden. Over two centuries later, another Robert Theakston started brewing in 1827 and two of his sons, Thomas and Robert, built the current brewery in 1875. After the First World War they bought and closed Lightfoot's brewery in the town.

The first of many crises took place in 1968 when Thomas Theakston, who was in charge of both pubs and accounts, declared that because the price of a pint of beer had passed the two shillings barrier he could see no future in brewing. He pressured the family to sell the brewery when his cousin, and Paul's father, Frank, was dying of leukaemia. Before he died, Frank declared 'a brewery like ours is not an old shoe to be cast off. 18 to 20 people depend on us for their jobs.'

Paul and his cousins Michael and Dick Theakston joined forces to save the brewery. They gave Thomas a life pension and in return he sold them his shares. In early 1969, Michael became chairman and Paul was named managing director, with Dick also on the board.

'We had small horizons,' Paul recalls. 'We had a turnover of £200,000 a year, 22 tied pubs and almost no free trade. We brewed three beers, Mild, Best Bitter and Old Peculier, with a brew length of 40 barrels. We sold beer mainly in Masham, Ripon, Northallerton and Wensleydale and we needed to get bigger to survive. The arrival of CAMRA put the focus on cask beer and that helped us to expand our cask sales in the free trade.'

The opportunity to increase brewing capacity came in 1974 when the government announced it was selling the Carlisle Brewery that had been nationalised during the First World War. Theakston paid £117,500 for the plant. They were brewing 250 barrels a week in Masham and here was a brewery 80 miles from home with 2,000 barrels-a-week capacity. They moved Best Bitter there, and because Carlisle came with a bottling line, they started selling beer to supermarkets. By 1980 they were brewing close to 70,000 barrels a year, but financially it had been tough. Most of the tied houses were sold to fund growth, with additional help coming from new shareholders brought in from outside the family.

But financial pressure on the business continued and decisions that were taken for the future of the company split the family in two. One of the non-family directors proposed selling shares to a local businessman who would gain a controlling interest in the company. Michael Theakston supported this move, but Paul strongly opposed it and was able to block it through the company's articles of association. Paul turned to Matthew Brown, a large regional brewery in Blackburn, for support while Michael went to the Scottish whisky distiller William Grant for backing.

Michael Theakston's side took out an injunction, preventing the transfer of shares Paul had bought from being registered. The following February, the family ended up in the High Court, with Paul's side accused of conspiracy. The first morning in court, the conspiracy claim was withdrawn for lack of evidence, and after a further two days Lord Justice Harman judged that nothing improper had taken place and found for Paul and his supporters, who sold their shares to Matthew Brown. Four months later Theakston became part of the Blackburn company. Paul was reinstated as managing director and Matthew Brown invested in the business and bought a few pubs. But what Paul saw as a good deal was seen in a different light by other family members.

Simon Theakston, now executive director of the family brewery, describes the row as 'a deeply upsetting episode for us all'. Although he was on the losing side in the court case, Simon nevertheless decided to remain with the company he had joined three years earlier in 1981. Simon describes himself as a humble marketing manager at the time but says he was 'heartbroken when the brewery was taken over by another brewer'.

Then, in 1985, Scottish & Newcastle (S&N) arrived on the scene. S&N was turning itself from a big regional brewer into a national player through the acquisition of other regional brewers. It bid for Matthew Brown, failed, then bid again 18 months later and succeeded in October 1987.

Paul was offered a job but was told it wouldn't be in Masham. He was determined to stay in his home town, so in May 1988 he recalls, 'I took a package from S&N and folded my tent and left.'

In buying Matthew Brown, S&N had picked up more than 400 pubs in the north-west of England and with Theakston it had a brewery with nationally recognised, quality brands. At first S&N put its considerable muscle behind the beers, which went national between 1987 and 1995.

But the glory days soon ended. Simon Theakston says that when S&N bought the Courage group in 1995, and with it such brands as Foster's, Kronenbourg and John Smith's, it concentrated on John Smith's as its main ale. Theakston's volumes declined and in 2001 the brothers, Simon, Nick, Tim and Edward, with the support of Collin Wood, a former S&N executive, started to negotiate buying back the Masham site and the brands. It took two years to resolve but in 2003 Theakston was once again an independent family brewery. On the day of the purchase, Simon phoned his cousin Paul and told him the news 'and he was genuinely pleased the brewery was back in family hands.'

Theakston

1827 · MASHAM · NORTH YORKSHIRE

'WE wanted to carry on the family tradition,' Simon says emphatically. The family has invested heavily in the brewery, adding new fermenters and expanding capacity to 60,000 barrels a year.

The first development was to increase the strength of Best Bitter back from 3.6 per cent to 3.8 but without a price increase. 'It was saying thank you to our customers for their loyalty,' Simon says. S&N had sold them land next to the White Bear and they were able to expand the site and turn it into their showcase pub, restaurant and hotel. It's the only tied house Theakston owns.

Jonathan Manby, cooper

Four new fermenting vessels have been installed in a converted maltings to cope with demand, but most of the equipment in the Grade II-listed brewery is old but robust. Ten original fermenters were made of slate but have been converted to stainless steel. Head brewer Mark Slater says the change didn't affect the flavour of the beer, even though slate is thought to be an important contributor to the character of Yorkshire beer.

The brewery was built on the tower principle, with a malt mill at the top that is between 50 and 60 years old. The mill feeds a mash tun one floor down that is celebrating its centenary while the boiling copper – 'a real *copper* copper,' Mark stresses – also chalks up 100 years. The hopped wort drops down a floor to an enormous hop back that holds 80 barrels of beer. It has an open top, but Mark says the depth of the vessel and the temperature of the wort mean it's not open to infection from wild yeasts.

Fermentation is fast, lasting just three days. Mark, a vastly experienced brewer who has worked at the Mortlake plant in London and St Peter's in Suffolk, says the yeast 'gobbles up the sugars'. Finally, the fermented beer is pumped to the racking plant where casks and kegs are filled.

Simon and his brothers have added a five-barrel pilot brewery, which is an exact replica of the main brewery in Lilliputian form. It means that new beers trialled in the small plant that meet with consumer favour can easily be transferred to the main brewery.

Best Bitter accounts for 50 per cent of the brewery's output. It's brewed with pale and crystal malts, wheat malt and maize, with Challenger and Fuggles hops. The second biggest brand is the legendary Old Peculier, which has been brewed since the early days of the brewery and was given the name of Old Peculier in the 1890s. It's brewed with pale malt and 'a lot of crystal malt,' Mark Slater says, 'and invert sugar, which we need for the strength.' The hop recipe is complex, with Bramling Cross, Challenger, Fuggles and Progress; the beer is dry hopped with Fuggles. Many pubs, including the King's Head in Masham, prefer to serve the beer from the wood: whisky casks are used and are maintained and rebuilt by Theakston's resident cooper Jonathan Manby. From the wood, the beer has a smoky, oak and dark fruit aroma with rich malt and spicy hops. There's a hint of molasses and liquorice on the palate with continuing oak and peppery hops,

while the finish is intensely fruity and spicy with notes of vanilla from the wood.

The other regular beers are Lightfoot, which Mark calls a type of wheat beer, using 30 per cent wheat, XB 'a bigger version of Best Bitter', and Black Bull with greater hop character than the other beers. The regular range is complemented by monthly seasonals, including Shot in the Dark, which coincides with the crime writing festival. A small range of premium beers are being developed and they include Pale Ale and Barista Stout brewed with New World hops.

Theakston's is a convivial brewery. A fine visitor centre is called the Black Bull in Paradise, the Black Bull being the brewery's first pub in the 19th century. The full range of beers can be sampled there and visitors can also view the cooper's shop where master cooper Jonathan Manby reveals the time-honoured skills of fashioning wooden casks. The demand for

CRIME AND NOURISHMENT

Old Peculier belongs to an ancient family of Yorkshire strong beers, including Stingo. The name and peculiar spelling go back to Norman times when Masham was a centre of the wool industry and was known as the 'golden prebend of York'. As a powerful town, it gained a degree of independence from the bishops based in York who were wary of making the long journey to the Dales with the ever-present risk of being attacked by robbers. Masham was granted permission to establish its own 'peculier' ecclesiastical court. The court of 'four and twenty men' still sits to choose church wardens, as they did Robert Theakston in the 16th century.

Today Old Peculier is not only a popular brand in Britain but is widely exported. 'The Chinese love Old Peculier!' Simon Theakston

says. It has become a cult beer in the United States thanks to an unexpected appearance in an episode of the crime series *NCIS*. This showed a woman commander serving beer from an oak cask and telling her colleagues 'This is Theakston Christmas ale all the way from England where they have been brewing beer like this since Charles Dickens' time.' When viewers learnt the beer featured was Old Peculier, there was a national demand for it and there's

now an Old Peculier Appreciation Society in San Francisco.

The American love of the beer helped publicise Theakston's Old Peculier Crime Writers' Festival that has been held in Harrogate for more than 15 years. Harrogate was chosen as it was the town where Agatha Christie was found when she mysteriously disappeared for 11 days in 1926. The festival allows lovers of crime novels to meet and discuss the subject with leading writers. Regular participants include Ian Rankin and Val McDermid; the late Colin Dexter, creator of Inspector Morse, also attended. Now the event attracts writers from the US including Lee Child and John Grisham. Grisham says the main reason he is willing to make the journey is because Old Peculier is his favourite beer.

The Theakston brothers,
Edward, Simon, Nick and Tim

Theakston's beers from the wood led to the brewery appointing an apprentice cooper, Ewan Findlay, in 2019.

Simon Theakston and his brothers are looking with confidence to the future and to celebrating the brewery's 200th anniversary in 2027. They are exporting to 19 countries, mainly in bottle: overseas markets include Australia and New Zealand, China, Italy, Hong Kong and Russia, with plans to add Vietnam to the list.

The only cloud on the horizon is Small Brewers Relief. 'Small brewers have a 25 per cent advantage over us,' Simon says. 'We don't want special favours, just to operate on the same duty basis as everyone else in the industry. We want the government to review the scheme, which is no longer fit for purpose. The family brewers raise the awareness of cask beer – it helps build communities and without us cask would wither on the vine.'

He's keenly aware of the community role of the pub and chairs The Pub is the Hub, the organisation founded by Prince Charles to safeguard community locals. The brewery is also active locally: it invests in local rivers to encourage wild salmon to return and sponsors the Nidderdale Cricket League.

Furthermore old animosities appear to be receding. 'Paul Theakston is my cousin and colleague. We buried the hatchet many years ago,' Simon says with warmth in his voice.

Theakston, The Brewery, Masham,
North Yorkshire HG4 4YD · 01765 680000
www.theakstons.co.uk · Tours available

Theakston's regular cask beers:
Best Bitter (3.8%)
Black Bull Bitter (3.9%)
Lightfoot (4.1%)
XB (4.5%)
Old Peculier (5.6%)

Black Sheep

WHEN Paul Theakston started to plan his own brewery – 'it was a case of the cobbler sticking to his last' – he found there were many hurdles in the way. He needed financial backing and he also had to find suitable premises. A site came in the shape of the former Lightfoot maltings. It was owned by a local milling company I'Ansons and it was willing to sell to Paul, but access to the buildings was through the White Bear pub now owned by S&N.

'We had to change the access. It took I'Ansons two years to negotiate a deal with S&N to build a new entrance and I sat at home chewing my nails,' Paul says. 'But in spring 1991 we finally exchanged contracts and I set out on the rocky road of recreation.'

He was determined to brew beers with a proper Yorkshire taste. He raised £750,000 from the government's Business Expansion Scheme and attracted 700 shareholders who backed his vision of a brewery with

strong Yorkshire roots. When Robinsons in Stockport closed its subsidiary brewery, Hartley's in Cumbria, Paul was able to buy the mash tun, copper, hop back and malt mill at scrap prices.

The key to the character of the beer, Paul knew, could come from using Yorkshire squares. These are two-storey vessels in which fermenting beer rises from the bottom chamber to the top one where some of the yeast is retained (see also p.28).

Paul wanted traditional squares made of slate, not steel, and they came in the shape of the vessels on offer at Hardy & Hanson's brewery in Nottingham that had been bought by Greene King and was due to close.

'The squares make the difference. I didn't want a clone of Theakston's Best. We used Maris Otter malt and Fuggles and Goldings hops and we got the H&H yeast strain that had been in use since at least the 1920s,' he says. 'We're now the guardians of that yeast. It's highly flocculent [i.e., the yeast cells clump together] and needs constant rousing. Rousing introduces oxygen and you get a classic Yorkshire bitter with a smooth mouthfeel.'

Paul had a brewery and he had a vision. 'We set up the plant with the express intention of creating a country brewery producing traditional cask beer with simple, traditional materials – proper cask beer born and bred in Yorkshire.'

He lacked one vital thing: a name for the brewery. He couldn't use Lightfoot as that was owned by S&N via Theakston. The proverbial lightbulb flared

Paul Theakston in the early days

thanks to Paul's wife, Sue, who told him that when he produced his beers he would 'become the black sheep of the family.' It was a fitting name, given Masham's history in the wool trade with the surrounding hills dotted with black-faced sheep.

A design agency produced a logo featuring a sheep and in 1992 Paul launched Black Sheep Best Bitter and Special: the beers were blessed by the local vicar, much to the chagrin of S&N next door.

Paul relied on the free trade to take his beer and there was a clamour for them throughout Yorkshire and beyond. The very first brew of Special went to Marks & Spencer in bottle at a time when there were no premium ales in supermarkets.

Growth was rapid and today Black Sheep produces around 60,000 barrels a year with wholesalers distributing the beers nationally. The three main pub groups – Ei, Mitchells & Butlers and Punch – take the beers and Black Sheep is the second biggest cask beer in the Punch group.

Caught on the hop

Recent years, though, have been tough. Paul admits he was 'caught on the hop' by changing consumer demands and the burgeoning microbrewing sector, aided by Small Brewers Relief. 'Micros now account for 30 per cent of the cask sector,' Paul says. 'Older brewers are being squeezed. If you have to pay the full rates of duty, the margins are very thin.'

Paul's sons, Rob, the managing director, and Jo, the sales director, have stabilised the brewery and are returning the business to profit. They are growing supermarket sales and export, have expanded the range of beers and have introduced a lager, 54° Degrees – Masham's geographical position – using German malt, imported hops and four to five weeks'

Jo Theakston

Rob and Paul Theakston

maturation. They have a five-barrel micro plant where they devise new beers and there's a rolling programme of seasonal ales.

The big departure is that Black Sheep is planning a small estate of pubs in order to get some protection from cost-cutting micros. They will complement the superb visitor centre that offers brewery tours, a large bar and bistro meals planned by Sue Theakston. Andy Slee, ex-Punch Taverns, has joined as company chairman and will use his experience to buy the right pubs in the right places.

The marketing strategy may be changing but Paul Theakston's vision back in the early 1990s remains untouched: brewing proper traditional beer made by proud Yorkshire folk. Paul can afford to take the long view of that turbulent history. He is now a non-

executive director and has handed over the day-to-day running of Black Sheep to Rob and Jo.

He keeps a close eye on developments, however, and his agreement was sought when Black Sheep bought the York Brewery in 2018. It wasn't a takeover as York had gone into administration and closed. Black Sheep now runs York's four pubs in York and Leeds. The beers are currently brewed in Masham but will move back to York when a suitable site is found.

But let there be no doubt that Paul's and Black Sheep's roots remain firmly in Masham, the family home.

Black Sheep Brewery, Wellgarth, Masham, North Yorkshire HG4 4EN · 01765 689227
www.blacksheepbrewery.co.uk · Tours available

Black Sheep regular cask beers:
Best Bitter (3.8%)
Pale Ale (4%)
Special Ale (4.4%)
Riggwelter (5.9%)

York Brewery regular cask beers:
Guzzler (3.6%)
Hansom Blonde (3.9%)
Yorkshire Terrier (4.2%)
Otherside IPA (4.5%)
Centurion's Ghost (5.4%)

WHITE KNIGHTS OF THE BLACK COUNTRY

BATHAMS · HOLDEN'S

BEER runs like a river through the Black Country. In the 19th and early 20th centuries vast numbers of people worked up prodigious thirsts in coal mines, coking plants, steels mills, iron foundries and glass works, with many others making nails and metal links in their homes. Anchors and chains for the ill-fated Titanic ocean liner were forged in the region. The workers' thirsts were catered for by a legion of breweries, many of them small, including brewpubs and simple beerhouses.

The region, which includes the towns and boroughs of Wolverhampton, West Bromwich, Dudley, Sandwell and Walsall, was one of the most industrialised areas in Britain during the 19th century. It was dubbed the Black Country as a result of pollution from factory chimneys which was so dense that people said it turned day into night.

Pubs were open at all hours to cope with the demand from workers whose shifts were in factories, mines and mills that operated 24 hours a day. The most popular beer style was mild ale, which was less aggressively hopped than pale ale and bitter and had some residual sweetness that helped restore manual workers' lost energy.

Sadly, demand for mild has declined alarmingly, almost to the point of extinction. It can be saved only if beer lovers do not just cherish this historically important style but visit the pubs of Bathams and Holden's and consume it. As well as the two breweries described in this section, it's also worth visiting two brewpubs which offer a fascinating glimpse of the small establishments that once dotted the region. They are the Olde Swan in Netherton – better known as Ma Pardoe's after the stern matriarch who ran the pub for decades – and Sarah Hughes at Sedgley, named after another woman who both brewed and sold beer. The Olde Swan brews both light and dark mild while Sarah Hughes' Dark Ruby Mild, at 6 per cent, proves the style doesn't have to be low in alcohol.

No visit to the region is complete without visiting the Black Country Living Museum in Dudley, which traces the history of the region with a collection of industrial machinery and its own pub that is a fine example of a beerhouse from the 19th century.

Bathams

1877 · BRIERLEY HILL · WEST MIDLANDS

THE course of brewing history in the West Midlands changed dramatically in the 1950s when Bathams Brewery bought a pub, the Swan Inn, in the village of Chaddesley Corbett in Worcestershire. The rural location was in sharp contrast to other Bathams' pubs in the sprawling Black Country. For decades, workers in mines and forges had downed vast quantities of mild ale but the good folk of Worcestershire expected a more refined beer, the type of pale ales that had come to prominence in Burton upon Trent.

Bathams responded to the demand and added Best Bitter to its Mild. The beer became popular and it gained nationwide prominence when it won the top prize in the bitter category of CAMRA's Champion Beer of Britain competition in 1991. The rise of the beer has been unstoppable. As heavy industry has declined and all but disappeared from the region, mild has gone into almost terminal decline. Bathams' Best Bitter now accounts for 97.5 per cent of the brewery's annual output and Tim Batham says he's producing just four barrels a week of Mild.

'Mild is dying because the people who drink it are dying,' he says bluntly. 'I'll go on making it as long as people drink it.' The beer is available in firkins – nine-gallon casks – while Best Bitter is supplied to some pubs in 54-gallon hogsheads. Bathams is one of the last breweries in Britain to still use hogsheads.

Tim and his brother Matthew are the fifth generation of the family to run the Black Country brewery. It stands next door to the Vine pub famous for its

Doris May Batham, grandmother of Matthew and Tim, on the step of the Vine, c.1920s

Shakespeare quotation emblazoned on the exterior: Blessing of your heart, you brew good ale.* Bathams owns 12 pubs and the brothers celebrated in 2019 when they made it a round dozen by buying the Bird in Hand in Old Swinford from Wolverhampton & Dudley Breweries (W&D). The brothers' great grand-father had run the pub from 1926 to 1939, but it was sold to W&D in 1940 in order to pay death duties. It's now pleasingly back in the family's hands.

*Pub quiz question: which play does the quotation come from?
Answer: *The Two Gentlemen of Verona.*

The origins of Dan Crusty

The founder of the dynasty, Daniel Batham, was born in the Quarry Bank area in 1806 and worked as a nailer. Nail making was an important small industry in the region and was carried out by families in their own homes. It was said that a good worker could produce 250 nails an hour. Daniel and his wife had nine children, including Daniel II who was to found the family's brewery. In fact, the first Bathams beer was produced by Daniel's wife Charlotte while he worked as a miner. Charlotte found she was good at making ale and produced well-regarded strong, sweet, dark mild ale at her house.

In 1881 Daniel lost his mining job and he and Charlotte helped run the White Horse pub in Cradley Heath, where beer was brewed on the premises. It was the custom at the time for pubs and inns to employ travelling brewers, who would spend a day or two at pubs and produce sufficient beer until their next visit. Daniel helped in the beerhouse, producing dark mild ale served in pewter pots. As drinkers couldn't see the beer they were drinking, the clarity of the brew was not important.

Daniel Batham II

As trade at the White Horse grew, Daniel was joined by two of his sons to help him brew and serve. Shift work in the area meant there was custom at all hours and miners would call in for a pint on their way to work and when their shift ended. At the end of the 19th century Cradley had 20 taverns and inns and 42 beerhouses, which meant there was a licensed house for every 74 people. Despite the intense competition, Daniel senior sold his beer not only at the White Horse but throughout the region, in Walsall, Stourbridge, Dudley and West Bromwich. He held the licence at the pub from 1882 to 1922, a remarkable tenure of 40 years.

Daniel was nicknamed Dan Crusty, which suggests he may have been either bad tempered or tight with money – or both. Without doubt, he was a successful brewer and licensee. He was not content to own a single pub. He bought the King William in Netherton, but he cemented his reputation when he added the Vine in Brierley Hill to his estate in 1905.

The Bull and Bladder

The Vine on Delph Lane was known – and is still known today – by its nickname of the Bull and Bladder. The premises had started out as a butcher's shop with a slaughterhouse attached. Bathams' logo today shows a happy, smiling bull, unaware of the fate that awaited it. When butchering ceased, the buildings became the Vine brewpub, which was put up for sale in 1905. The property was on the market for six months. Not only was the business run down and dilapidated, but the buildings were in danger of collapse due to subsidence caused by the local mining industry. Another pub and brewery in the area, the Duke William Inn, had completely collapsed due to shallow mining. The Batham family took over and spent several years rebuilding and shoring up the premises. The new Vine Hotel, as it was then called, was ready for action in 1912.

The pub became a model of a good community local. The Vine Pipe Club, made of up men who smoked pipes, met there as did pigeon fanciers and the local branch of the Royal Antediluvian Order of Buffaloes. The Buffs, as they are known for short, are a working men's version of the Freemasons, helping members who fall on hard times and raising money for charities. It is controlled, in common with the Masons, by a Grand Lodge, but most local branches meet in the convivial atmosphere of the pub. Daniel Batham was a fully paid-up member.

When Daniel's wife died in 1920, he tended to stay at home and he left the running of the Vine to his sons Arthur, Daniel and Caleb. The 1920s was a period of consolidation. The White Horse at Cradley was sold but the brothers embarked on a course of buying or leasing other pubs. At a time of economic depression, especially badly felt in the Black Country, the free trade was an unreliable source of income as many owners went bankrupt or were slow to pay for beer.

The family entered the 1930s with an estate of around 10 pubs, but their business was shaken by a dispute between Daniel and his brother Caleb. Caleb ran the Brickmakers Arms in Lye and had run up a mountain of debt. The family had no option but to buy out Caleb and this was achieved by selling or leasing several of their pubs to William Butler's Springfield Brewery in Wolverhampton. Despite this upheaval, Caleb continued to work for the family business and lived in Delph Lane, close to the Vine.

Bathams' hogsheads in the cellar

BEER ROCKS THE BOAT

In 1950 Bathams hit the headlines when it supplied beer to the Oxford crew training for the annual boat race with Cambridge. A member of the Oxford University Boat Club had sampled Delph Strong Ale while visiting friends in Stourbridge. There were different attitudes at the time to fitness and drinking, and as a result of the Stourbridge sampling, every week for five weeks a nine-gallon firkin of Strong Ale was sent by train to the crew's hotel in Richmond, Surrey, where they trained on the Thames.

The crew was allowed one pint a day each except for the cox, JEH Hinchcliffe, who weighed 8 stone 9 pounds and was considered heavy and struggling with his weight. The Cambridge crew preferred an unnamed local ale that must have been weaker than Delph Strong Ale as they were permitted half a pint for lunch and two pints with their dinner.

Sadly, Bathams' ale did not help Oxford. During the race, a clash of blades resulted in the crew losing their rhythm and they failed to recover, losing to Cambridge by three and a half lengths. There were suggestions that the Oxford rowers had perhaps supped too deeply of Bathams' beer!

In 1936 the business was formerly restructured as a partnership between Daniel and his son Arthur Joseph, and was known as Daniel Batham & Son Ltd at the Delph Brewery. The following year, the company leased the Swan Inn in Brierley Hill and the inventory gives a fascinating glimpse of a pub at that time: 'Bar, tap room, including 6 cast iron spittoons, 1 enamel, smoke room including 3 enamelled spittoons for quality spitting, club room and 2 bedrooms.' Fortunately, there was no description of 'quality spitting' and how it differed from spitting in cast iron spittoons.

With a new world war looming, the family suffered the loss of Daniel junior, who died in June 1939, aged 72. Fittingly, he was living at the Vine at the time of his death. His eldest son, Arthur Joseph, was now in charge of the company and he brought much-needed professionalism to the brewing side of the business. He had been wounded in the trenches during the First World War but had recovered sufficiently to train as a brewer at Spreckley Brothers in Worcester, where the head brewer Ross McKenzie had a fine reputation throughout the industry for training pupils for work.

Fortunes boosted

1951 marked a milestone in Bathams' history, with Best Bitter launched to coincide with the acquisition of the Swan Inn in Chaddesley Corbett. In the same year, Daniel Bertram Arthur Batham, known as Arthur, joined the family company after studying science at Edinburgh University and then taking a post-graduate course at Birmingham Brewing School. He arrived at the Vine at a difficult time for all small brewers, with sales of draught beer in decline and the market dominated by big bottled brands such as Guinness and Double Diamond. Considering ways to cut costs, there was talk in 1953 of Bathams merging with its near neighbour Holden's at Woodsetton. The proposals included closing the Delph Brewery and concentrating production at Holden's. Losing the Vine was too much for the family and the merger never took place. The two families remain on good terms, exchanging their beers in both breweries' pubs and enthusiastically supporting the same football team, West Bromwich Albion – the Baggies.

Bathams' fortunes were boosted in 1954 when it won a diploma for its Delph Strong Ale at the Brewers' Exhibition in London. Despite the rise of keg beer in the 1960s and the domination of the market by new national brewers, Bathams survived these hard years and was then given a major fillip with the arrival of CAMRA in 1971. Cask beer was back on drinkers' agendas and Bathams came to national attention in 1972 when a major report on beer and prices

Matt and Tim Batham with their mother, Jean, at the King Arthur pub, named after their father, Arthur, whose portrait is on the wall

Matthew graduated in hotel catering management and now runs the company's pubs while Tim controls the brewing side.

Bathams produces 8,000 barrels a year and uses the finest raw materials: Flagon barley malt supplied by Crisp of Norfolk and Fuggles and Goldings hops, with East Kent Goldings used to 'dry hop' the finished beers. The original brewing kit is still in use, though additional fermenters have been added in recent years to keep pace with demand: the fermenting vessels are a mix of rounds and squares. The yeast culture first came from Julia Hanson's Brewery in Dudley, which closed in 1993.

As well as pale and amber malts, Tim and his brewing team use a range of specialist brewing sugars including candy sugar and glucose. 'The sugars encourage a fast fermentation,' he explains. 'And they're more expensive than malt!'

The ingredients may be expensive, but the finished beers are remarkable value: £2.45 for a pint of Mild, £2.95 for Best Bitter and £3.70 for the winter XXX (at the time of writing in early 2020).

Tim has three daughters, Ruth, Claire and Alice, and they will carry on the family tradition in due course. Claire managed Bathams' Plough & Harrow pub for three years and is now understudy to Matt. Alice is a qualified brewer. She previously worked at Brewster's Brewery in Grantham and in 2019 she won the prestigious award of Young Brewer of the Year.

The family's long-term control of the business is guaranteed. Whether Bathams' Mild will survive is down to beer lovers rediscovering this Black Country legend and boosting its fortunes.

Daniel Batham & Son, Delph Brewery,
Delph Road, Brierley Hill, West Midlands DYS 2TN
01384 77229 · www.bathams.com
Regular cask beers:
Mild (3.5%)
Best Bitter (4.3%)
XXX (winter, 6.3%)

by the *Daily Mirror* singled out the Delph Brewery for special praise for the good value of its ales.

Daniel Arthur Batham died in 2010, aged 76, with a lifetime of service to the family and its brewery. His two sons, Tim and Matthew, took over the company. Tim had a three-year pupillage, or apprenticeship, with Wolverhampton & Dudley Breweries (W&D) and then worked for W&D before taking over at the Delph. His dedication to the family brewery is shown by the fact that when he married in 1981 he spent the first night of his honeymoon with his wife Linda at a local hotel but then went to the brewery early the next morning to put the mash in before flying off to Corfu.

Holden's

1915 · WOODSETTON · WEST MIDLANDS

THE date of 1915 masks the extent of Holden's role in Black Country brewing as the family was involved in running pubs – including some that brewed on the premises – from the late Victorian era. The brewery next to the Park Inn at Woodsetton is as much a local icon as Bathams' Vine, and with the fourth and fifth generations firmly in control, it's set for an upgrade.

Jonothan Holden says the plant will be expanded, extended and generally updated over the next two to three years. The work is necessary not only to keep up with demand for the beers but also because 'the mash tun is cracked and the copper leaks,' he says. 'But we will keep the Steel's Masher' – that's the cylinder with an Archimedes screw that mixes grain and brewing 'liquor' (water) before they flow into the mash tun.

When work is finished, the new brewery will have a capacity of 50 barrels per brew and it will enable Jonothan and his team to increase the current production of 10,000 barrels a year. The main beer is Golden Glow, introduced by Jonothan in 2001 as 'the beer with the glow'. He saw that drinkers were changing their allegiances. 'They were aware of different styles and were going for more bitter and hoppy beers,' he says. In common with the situation at Bathams, his Black Country Mild now accounts for only a small proportion of his output and is brewed once every three weeks. Sales of mild are better in bottle than on draught. Black Country Bitter and Special make up the regular portfolio, backed by monthly seasonal ales, including Old Ale and Toffee Porter.

Beer in his boots

The story of Holden's begins with a pub with the prophetic name of Trust in Providence. Edwin Holden was the youngest of seven sons. He worked in the family's boot-making factory and refreshed himself in the pub where he met and courted Lucy, the landlord's daughter. Edwin thought he would prefer to run a pub than make boots, and he and Lucy took the tenancy of

Edwin Alfred Holden, founder

the Britannia Inn in Netherton and remained there for six years before moving on to several other pubs in the area. Their son Edwin, known as Teddy to avoid confusion, was born in 1907, and he and his parents took over the Summer House in Woodsetton. From there, they moved to the Park Inn, also in Woodsetton, where commercial brewing started in 1915 and made the Holden's name in the Black Country. Edwin and Lucy paid £750 for the freehold of the Park Inn and they launched strong dark mild ale in a small brewhouse alongside the pub.

Edwin died suddenly, aged just 45, in 1920 and Lucy took over the licence of the Park Inn. She clearly prospered for in 1928 she bought the freehold of the Painters Arms in Coseley for the sizeable sum of £2,375. The pub was a present for Teddy who was studying brewing at Birmingham University's Brewing School. Lucy was a tough woman: she lost her sight but continued to run the Park Inn until she died in 1930.

Lucy Holden outside the Park Inn, c.1920

Ted Holden

Teddy took over the reins at Woodsetton, where he was in charge of brewing, and continued to run the Painters Arms as well. He survived the turbulent 1930s better than most brewers as the coal and metal industries worked full-bore in preparation for the inevitable outbreak of the Second World War. During the war he had the good fortune to supply beer to a local Royal Air Force base. In 1944 he bought the New Inn at Coseley for a knock-down price of £2,500 as the pub was described as 'slightly bomb damaged': the Black Country had been high on the Germans' list of targets because of its vital importance to Britain's wartime economy.

Bottling a success

A number of pubs were bought during the post-war years and the growing domination of bottled beers encouraged Teddy to launch a subsidiary called Edwin Holden's Bottling Company that not only packaged the brewery's own brands but offered facilities for other brewers in the region. Bottling has remained an important part of Holden's business and today 90 per cent of the output is for other companies.

The brewery was rebuilt and extended in the 1960s, with production increased to 80 or 90 barrels a week. It survived the takeover frenzy and rise of keg beer as a result of the family's determination to stay true to the traditional beers loved by locals. To underscore this tradition the main beers were rebranded Black Country Mild and Black Country Bitter in the 1970s. Teddy died in 1974 and the pubs and brewery were taken over by his son Edwin, who

RAIL ALE

Jonothan Holden worked with his father Edwin on one of the brewery's major pub developments at Codsall train station. They took over some disused railway buildings in 1997 and after 18 months of planning and restoration the site reopened as the Station. It has been restored to its Victorian splendour with spacious lounges, open fires and a fine range of cask beers, with three guest ales alongside Holden's range. Food includes Black Country staples such as fish and chips and Bostin Burgers: bostin is local dialect for something good. The pub is packed with fascinating railway memorabilia. The Station has won the local branch of CAMRA's Pub of the Year award and in 2017 was named pub of the year by the local Wolverhampton newspaper, the *Express & Star*.

Beer o'clock in the 1970s

had done a pupillage, or apprenticeship, at McMullen in Hertford. Considerable time and effort were placed on improving pubs to meet the demands of modern consumers. The work was recognised when the Great Western pub in Wolverhampton was named CAMRA's national Pub of the Year in 1988. Jonothan Holden joined his father in 1991 following a pupillage with Morrell's of Oxford.

Edwin Holden, a popular and respected member of the brewing industry, died suddenly at the early age

of 57 in 2002. Jonothan shouldered the responsibility of running the estate of 19 pubs as well as the brewery. The pubs are within a 25-mile radius of Woodsetton and are based in Shropshire and Staffordshire as well as the Black Country.

In common with his good friend Tim Batham, Jonothan buys his brewing malt from Crisp in Norfolk and he puts his faith in the time-honoured Maris Otter variety: 'I'm the biggest customer for Maris Otter left in Britain,' he says. He uses Fuggles hops from Hereford and Worcester with the American Warrior variety in a seasonal IPA. In the local tradition, he makes generous use of such darker malts as amber, black, chocolate and crystal along with three specialist brewing sugars.

As well as the regular beers, Holden's seasonal range includes Summer Buzz (4.2%), made with the addition of local honey, Original Stout (5%), using an old recipe and fermented longer for strength, and Hopster (5.3%), brewed with lager malt and citrus-led American hops. Forty per cent of production goes to

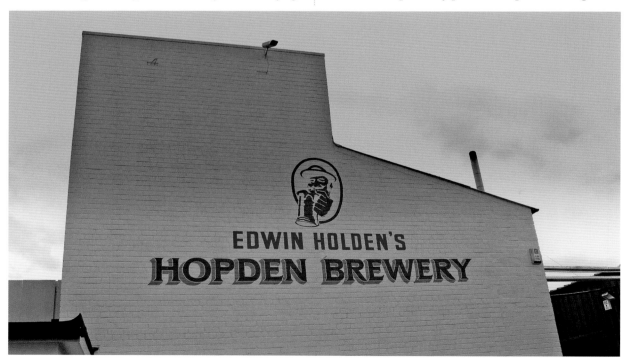

the free trade. Both the mash tun and copper are 50 years old but they will be replaced during the planned renovation. The fermenters are a mixture of round and square vessels.

Jonothan has two daughters, Alice and Charlotte, and a son George, and he hopes they will take over the running of the company in due course. With a mixture of hope and expectation, one of the fermenters is named Alice. No pressure there, then.

Holden's Brewery, George Street, Woodsetton, West Midlands DY1 4LW · 01902 880051
www.holdensbrewery.co.uk
The pub and brewery have a large shop for visitors where branded clothing and packaged beer can be bought. Brewery tours are available but may be curtailed while the site is expanded.

Regular cask beers:
Black Country Mild (3.7%)
Black Country Bitter (3.9%)
Golden Glow (4.4%)
Special (5.1%)

WELSH DRAGONS AND FLAGONS

FELINFOEL · BRAINS

WALES has a distinctive brewing history. Commercial brewing arrived late on the scene and well into the 19th century most beer was produced by publicans on their premises. When 'common brewing' developed and such companies as Brains, Buckley's and Hancock's bestrode south and mid Wales, they were hampered in their activities by the hostile actions of the church and the temperance movement, both supported by powerful local politicians.

Domestically produced beer, however, stretches much further back into local history. As early as the seventh century AD there are records of a beer called Welsh ale and this style continued to be made for many centuries, spiced with cinnamon, cloves and ginger, and sweetened with honey. So popular was the beer that it spread beyond the Welsh border and was also made in England. Over time, Welsh ale developed into two styles known as bragot and cwrwf. The latter name became better known in more recent times as cwrw and this term is still used in Welsh-speaking areas to describe ale. It became the everyday drink of the people while bragot, additionally flavoured with honey, cinnamon, cloves, ginger and sweet gale, was more expensive and consumed by the aristocracy.

Late into the 19th century home-brewed beer produced either by publicans or in private houses dominated the rural areas of Wales. In 1872, in the licensing area of south-west Wales centred on Carmarthen, two-thirds of the pubs – 731 out of 1,158 – still brewed their own beer.

Driven by steel and coal, the new industrial areas of Wales, around Cardiff in particular, grew quickly in the 19th century and witnessed the rapid development of commercial brewing alongside. But as the experience of Brains shows (later in this section), commercial brewers were constrained by the activities of the influential temperance movement, backed by the non-conformist church. The 1881 Welsh Sunday Closing Act shut pubs and led inexorably to the spread of illegal drinking dens.

The restrictions were supported by politicians, notably 'the Welsh Wizard' David Lloyd George. He argued the case for total prohibition of the sale of alcohol. He was rebuffed but went some way to achieving success when he became Minister for Munitions in the First World War. In an infamous speech in 1915 made in Bangor, in north Wales, he declared that 'Drink is doing more damage to the war effort than all the German submarines put together'. As a result of his campaigning, the wartime government – as the main Introduction records – brought in sweeping measures to restrict brewing, weaken the strength of beer and curb pub opening times.

The legislation affected the whole of the UK, but was felt most severely in Wales, where brewers had already lost the Sabbath as a day when beer could be sold. The result of the combined activities of the anti-alcohol lobby was to drive down the strength of Welsh beer. Mild ale was the predominant style in the country in the 19th and 20th centuries but even bitter and pale ale were kept low in strength to avoid attack by the enemies of beer. Brains' SA is known by the nickname of Skull Attack, but for a premium bitter it has a comparatively modest strength of 4.2 per cent.

In one respect, Welsh brewing followed a similar course to England's. After the Second World War big brewers, notably Bass and Whitbread, moved into the regions of Wales, buying, merging and closing smaller brewers. The decline of heavy industry led to the demise of a once mighty force, the Clubs United co-operative brewery, founded by miners and other workers' clubs. And as the big national English brewers went into meltdown in the 1990s, the giant of South Wales brewing, Hancock's, handed over its iconic Cardiff site to Brains.

Brewing has changed out of all recognition in recent years as the beer revolution has made its impact felt in Wales. There are now around 90 small

artisan breweries in the country, bringing improved choice and wider styles of beer to consumers. Glamorgan alone has 34 breweries and the ranks of the artisan producers reach as far as Anglesey. Some of the new breweries, such as Tiny Rebel, have built sales far beyond Wales.

Despite all this activity, Brains and Felinfoel remain the champions of Welsh beer and reach out to a whole new audience of beer lovers.

Felinfoel

YOU can't move for dragons in Wales. Brains has its new Dragon Brewery and in Llanelli the Felinfoel Brewery is best known for its award-winning beer Double Dragon. The brewery takes its name from a village on the outskirts of Llanelli, and as well as winning awards it has a place in history as the first British brewery to sell beer in cans.

It has the double distinction of being based in a Grade II-listed building and is now the oldest brewery in Wales. The imposing buildings house a traditional plant based on the tower system, with the brewing processes flowing from floor to floor. There's a cast-iron mash tun with brass plates while the copper is 40 years old as are 12 open square fermenting vessels. The raw materials for the main beers are as traditional as the brewery: English pale malt with Challenger and Whitbread Goldings Variety hops.

Felinfoel – pronounced 'Vellinvoil' – is run by the fifth generation of the Lewis family, with Philip Lewis as managing director and Beryn Lewis in the chair.

Beryn's son Jeremy has been primed to take over in due course.

'We're an ale brewery,' Philip Lewis stresses. 'We stick to what we do best.' He admits the brewery now produces more keg than cask for its 65 pubs and hotels though he's quick to add that cask output is growing again. 'It's bottomed out. Quality is the key. If cask is poor in a pub then we take it out and replace it with keg. We'll put cask back on once we're satisfied it will be served in good condition.'

Iron, tin and beer

The story of the brewery is linked to Llanelli's historic role as a major producer of iron and tinplate. The founder of the brewery, David John, owned two factories in the area. The date of 1878 refers to the opening of the present site but in the 1830s John bought the King's Head opposite his home on a busy turnpike where the pub also acted as a coaching inn. In common with many inns and pubs at the time, the King's Head had its own small brewery and John's ales were sufficiently regarded for him to build the current site on the other side of the road in the grounds of his house. It became a focal point in the area and farmers would come to the brewery for 'the sog' – the spent grain from the mash tun to feed to their animals. As a result the road became known as Farmers Row.

The brewery served both the church and the second religion of Llanelli – rugby. A local clergyman

would baptise people with water from the River Lliedi that runs through the brewery, while rugby enthusiasts would go to the Union Inn close by where they would debate the outcome of matches over many flagons of ale. But David John didn't confine sales of his beer to local inns and pubs and he gradually built his trade across the old counties of Carmarthen, Cardigan and Pembroke, buying pubs along the way. When David John retired he passed the brewery to his sons David and Martin, while a third son, Llewellyn, looked after the family's tinplate factory.

When David John's daughter Mary Anne married John Lewis, the manager of the Wern Ironworks, a second family became involved in the running of the brewery. The marriage proved to be rocky. John Lewis was a compulsive gambler who was prepared to risk all on the throw of the dice or the turn of a card. He was reputed to have lost a tinworks as a result of a bet and would probably have gambled away the brewery save for the fact that his wife controlled the shares. Tragically, in the 1920s he shot himself in his office at the brewery.

Mary Anne took over and ran the brewery with great determination. She was a matriarch who brooked no argument. She carried a big stick when she visited the brewery and if she was unhappy with the performance of one her employees she would hit him with the stick. Her weapon is on show at the brewery as an example of different times and attitudes to employee relations.

Canning a success

The difficulties of the 1920s and 30s – recession and unemployment – were eased for Felinfoel when it made the dramatic move into canning its beers. Canning had been experimented with in the United States when Prohibition ended in 1933. The first results were unsatisfactory, but by 1935 some 37 American breweries were producing canned beer. It proved popular with consumers who could store cans in the refrigerators that were becoming widespread in the country. British brewers were sceptical that canned beer would be acceptable to British drinkers, but in a remote part of Wales the hard-pressed tinplate industry was determined to prove them wrong. In 1935 the *Western Mail* newspaper reported that Buckley's Brewery in Llanelli was considering experimenting with canned beer. Felinfoel was determined to beat them to the punch and while it

was smaller than Buckley's it had the advantage of family interests in the local tinplate industry. As a result, the St David's Tinplate Works supplied sheets to Metal Box in London, which turned them into cans and sent them back to Felinfoel to fill with beer.

On 3 December 1935, the *Llanelli and County Guardian* reported under a triple headline: 'Canned Beer Arrives: Epoch-Making Process at Felinfoel Brewery: New Hope for Tinplate Industry'. The paper's report said the first can of beer was produced 'without a hitch' in the presence of the chairman, Martin John, and brewer Sidney John. The conical cans were filled on adapted bottling machines and sealed with a standard bottle top, known as a crown cork. The 10 oz cans of pale ale were the equivalent of half-pint bottles. The newspaper reported: 'One of the most impressive features of the process was its simplicity and speed. Girls, who in the past have handled many thousands of bottles, adapted themselves to new conditions with apparent ease and, once started, the cans were filled and corked with unbroken regularity.'

Head brewer Sidney John believed Felinfoel had improved on the canned beers produced in the US. 'The Americans brewed beer to suit the can while we have found a can to hold the perfect beer,' he said. 'Their beer is pasteurised and the result is that natural ingredients are being destroyed. That is not and will not be case with our beer. The difficulties of the London Metal Box Company have been to find a lining to preserve beer in its best state. After considerable research work, they have succeeded in doing so – the Americans have not.' Success was achieved by Metal Box giving the inside of the cans a coating of lacquer followed by a final lining of wax.

Other brewers rushed to follow Felinfoel's lead. Jeffreys of Edinburgh canned its lager with other Scottish brewers, including McEwan and Tennent's, joining them. In London and the south, major ale brewers such as Barclay Perkins, Simonds and Hammerton's launched canned versions of their

The brewery celebrates George VI's coronation, 1937

beers. Such was the interest in the project that Felinfoel workers became film stars for a short time. The local newspaper reported in July 1936: 'The growth of Llanelli's new industry – canned beer – brought forth recognition in the town on Monday when a newsreel cameraman, representative of one of the biggest film companies in the world, presented himself at the Felinfoel Brewery and obtained the permission of the management to shoot a film of the processes. And so for a day the long-established brewery took on the temporary garb of a film studio as mysterious gadgets were erected in the various departments. High-powered lights and glistening screens were thrown here, there and everywhere, and for a few brief hours the female workers fulfilled their life's ambition – to figure on the modern film screen.'

Felinfoel took on extra workers to cope with the demand for canned beer and a batch was even sent on a world tour to see if it would survive in the tropics. By the end of 1936 two million cans had been produced with some 27 British breweries selling more than 40 brands in cans. They included Lassell &

Sharman in North Wales that canned its Famous Strong Ale, while Felinfoel celebrated the coronation of George VI in May 1937 with a special ale in cans.

Despite the activity and publicity, canned beer accounted for a tiny proportion of total beer sales and many consumers were put off by the appearance of containers that looked like Brasso metal-polish cans. The canning of beer ended abruptly when the Second World War broke out. Tinplate was needed for the war effort and only Felinfoel was allowed to continue making canned beer, most of which went to the NAAFI for members of the armed forces fighting overseas.

The sale of Felinfoel's cans around the world opened up new markets for the company and after the Second World War the brewery built a good export trade with such beers as St David's Porter, Cream Stout, Heritage Ale and Hercules Strong Ale. There was brisk trade with California, which accounted for some 650 barrels a year, but these beers were all in bottles. New technology enabled Felinfoel to produce flat-topped cans that prevented them looking like metal polish, but bigger brewers came to dominate the canned sector.

A bitter struggle

The brewery had more pressing problems than pursuing canned sales. The privations of war, with restrictions on output, had not allowed the management to maintain the brewery or its 80 pubs. Fred Cheesewright, who was head brewer from 1951 to 1982, said the brewery was on the point of collapse when he arrived. 'Felinfoel had a terrible name,' he recalled. 'In one year, the brewery lost 30 per cent of its trade. Some pubs were selling as little as 18 gallons a week. We were close to bankruptcy.'

As the business was slowly turned round, with much-needed investment in the brewing kit and the pubs, a bitter struggle for control of the company erupted. The brewery was jointly run by the John and Lewis families but the Lewises were in the driving seat in more ways than one. After the war they had moved the offices to Knightsbridge in London where they also ran a car company.

A major problem arose in 1965 when the neighbouring Buckley's brewery made a bid of £500,000 for Felinfoel. Prior to the bid going public, Buckley's had privately approached the John family and were able to claim that 48.7 per cent of shareholders supported the takeover. A month later this figure had increased to 49.5 per cent and Buckley's was almost over the line.

Buckley's told the press its sole motivation was to maintain brewing in Llanelli. But Cyril Marks, Felinfoel's manager, responded: 'We have no intention whatsoever of being taken over by anybody, local or national. It could mean the closure of the brewery and our employees losing their jobs.'

Eleven shares were owned by a Lady Davies. Buckley's offered her £2,750 and if she had accepted the takeover would have succeeded. But she rejected

A SUP AFTER SILENCE

In July 2017 the BBC's main newsreader, Huw Edwards, created his own headlines when he remained silent for a painful two minutes at the start of the *Ten O'Clock News*. Due to a technical hitch in the studios, the credits didn't roll and Edwards wasn't given the signal to begin reading. Eventually, what was dubbed the Two Minutes Past Ten News got underway. Later, Edwards tweeted with the image of a can of Double Dragon: 'I think I'm going to enjoy this little beauty after that Ten. Iechyd da [good health].'

Huw Edwards was born in Bridgend to a Welsh-speaking family. His mother taught in a school in Llanelli.

246

the offer and gave her shares to the Lewis family. While it had only a tiny majority, the Lewis family remained in control, though it had to agree to Buckley's having a seat on the board. As a sign of faith in the business, when the chairman, Trevor Lewis, died in 1974, the London office was closed and control came back to Llanelli. Trevor Lewis's son John started to make long-overdue improvements to the brewery, installing new fermenters and replacing an open, coal-fired copper which was bursting at the seams, with a modern enclosed vessel.

'We no longer have to work in a fog!' head brewer Fred Cheesewright said with much relief. In 1974 his long work at the brewery was recognised when Double Dragon won the prestigious Challenge Cup for best cask beer at the Brewers' Exhibition in London, and Felinfoel Bitter also won first prize in its class. In 1978, to celebrate the centenary of the brewery, Fred Cheesewright made one of the strongest beers ever brewed in Wales. Centenary Ale had a gravity of 1100 degrees or 11 per cent ABV in modern terms, as strong as wine. Close to 50,000 half-pint bottles were produced.

Against all the odds, Felinfoel has survived and thrived. It exports beer to China while closer to home Double Dragon is the official beer at Llanelli rugby ground. The brewery produces 5,000 barrels a year but no longer makes mild: 'It was big in clubs when the steel works were going,' Philip Lewis says. But those days are long gone. Unlike some of his colleagues in other family breweries, he has a benign attitude to Small Brewers Relief, for which he qualifies. 'It helps the grassroots and gives drinkers more choice,' he says. 'We do collaborations with other breweries and the scheme has led to brewpubs opening in tourist areas.'

The brewery has had to endure for many years the cruel and undeserved nickname of 'Feeling Foul'. But a visit to the plant, with its majestic central tower, along with the management's firm belief in traditional brewing methods and the superb beers will make you feel good rather than bad.

Felinfoel Brewery, Farmers Row, Felinfoel, Llanelli SA14 8LB · 01554 773357
www.felinfoel-brewery.com

Regular cask beers:
Felinfoel IPA (3.6%)
Celtic Pride (3.9%)
Stout (4.1%)
Double Dragon (4.2%)

Brains

THE beery dragon still breathes fire in Cardiff. When Brains took the decision to build a new brewery, the chairman John Rhys said it had to be in the Welsh capital. As the great grandson of the founder, Samuel Arthur Brain, he knew he had to stay true to Cardiff. Since the 19th century the brewery has built deep roots in the community, with historic pubs and the famous brewery chimney that stands proud over the city centre with the name BRAINS emblazoned on its side.

While Brains' home for more than 100 years was the Old Brewery in St Mary Street – now the Brewery Quarter – the famous chimney still stands on the site of the Cardiff Brewery, owned by Brains from 1999 to 2019. In 2019 production moved to the new Dragon Brewery in Pacific Road, Cardiff Bay. The family had been looking for a new site for some time and the switch took three years to complete. Head brewer Bill Dobson spent a year producing beer at both sites until he was satisfied the Dragon Brewery's output perfectly matched the beers from the old site just yards from Cardiff Central Station.

The malt, hops, yeast and water are identical on both sites. The brewing water is soft, with salts added to make it suitable for ale production. The kit at the Dragon Brewery was built in Britain, Germany and China and is designed along modern European lines, with a mash converter, lauter or filtration vessel and a brewing kettle and whirlpool. The brewing cycle lasts three hours and eight brews can be produced every 24 hours. The brewhouse feeds 24 conical fermenting vessels ranging in size from 25 hectolitres to 250. The old site had traditional mash tuns, coppers and fermenters and could produce more than 200,000 barrels a year. As well as its own beers, Brains had contracts to brew for several major breweries, but the family knew it was time to look for a new site, given the age of the Cardiff Brewery, which was on a prime development site in the city centre and was not a suitable location to build a state-of-the-art new plant.

Samuel Arthur Brain, founder

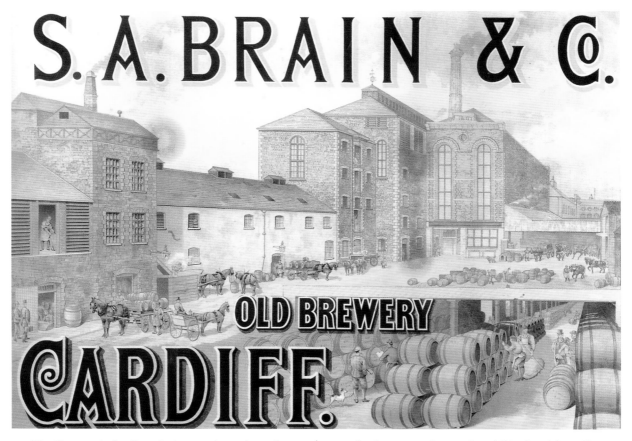

The Dragon is far from being a micro plant. It can produce 45,000 barrels a year and it still has contracts with Molson Coors to produce M&B Brew XI, Hancock's HB and Worthington's Bitter, as well as producing Mackeson for AB InBev.

Cardiff's oldest commercial brewery

The Old Brewery, Brains' original plant in Cardiff, might seem to have an odd name for their first site. But it marks the fact that when it opened in the 1820s it was the only commercial or 'common' brewery in a small town where most publicans brewed on their premises. The brewery expanded in pace with the city. As South Wales boomed under a colossal tide of coal and steel, the population of Cardiff grew from 1,870 in 1801 to 41,000 by 1861. The figure then doubled in the next 20 years to 82,700 as major docks

were built to transfer steel and 'black gold' to all parts of Britain and abroad. There were parched throats to refresh and brewing grew apace.

The Old Brewery changed hands several times prior to the formation of Brains. In the 1850s it was owned by Frederick Prosser who advertised himself as a beer and porter brewer, with ales and stouts in bottle. When Prosser died, John Thomas, who ran another brewery in the town, bought the old site and passed it to his sons. They traded as the Thomas Brothers and adroitly built a small chain of pubs to supply with beer. The Brains entered the picture when the Thomas brothers' sister, Frances Elizabeth, married Samuel Arthur Brain in 1872.

Brains is so deeply imbedded in the history and culture of Cardiff that it comes as a shock to learn that SA Brain was not Welsh. He came from a prosperous family in Gloucestershire that had made its money from mining and engineering, and consequently took a keen interest in the Welsh mining industry. The Brains were also involved in banking and Samuel Arthur went into partnership with his uncle, Joseph Benjamin Brain, the chairman of the Bristol and West of England Bank, to buy the Old Brewery in 1882. SA Brain & Company was formed.

Brewing up a storm with the church

It was not an ideal time to buy a brewery as the powerful temperance movement had succeeded a year earlier in forcing through parliament the Welsh Sunday Closing Act. According to a local legend, when John Thomas at the Old Brewery heard the news, he threw down his pen in anger, declared 'Anarchy!' and decided to quit the brewing business. The temperance movement had been supported by the nonconformist churches which also had no time for the 'demon drink'. Their success in closing all Welsh pubs on the Sabbath was a classic case of unintended consequences.

In common with Prohibition in the United States in the 1920s, the closure of Welsh pubs led to illicit drinking in what were called shebeens, where drinking was carried on from early until late on Sundays. When a Royal Commission looked into the effects of the closure act in 1889, SA Brain gave evidence and reported that, 'It is not unusual for the well-conducted licensed victualler to stand at his door on Saturday nights, after he has closed his premises at 11 o'clock, and see brewers' drays and agents' carts delivering 70 or 80 small casks into private houses within 100 yards of his premises.' Brain argued the case for allowing Cardiff pubs to re-open on Sundays as the act 'has simply deluged the town with illicit drinking'. His words were of no avail as the law remained unchanged. It was a bitter blow for Brains as the family had invested substantially in a new brewhouse, built on additional land alongside the brewery, and had added to its tied estate.

Brains' problems were eased by the spectacular growth of Cardiff, whose population doubled yet again between 1881 and 1901, from 82,700 to 164,300. Samuel Arthur didn't lack trade – he had to rush to keep up with it and the new brewhouse, which had cost £50,000, was soon working full-bore. The old brewhouse was brought back to complement the new one and production increased more than ten times, from 100 to 1,100 barrels a week. The celebrated writer Alfred Barnard, author of *Noted Breweries of Great Britain and Ireland*, visited Brains and was struck by its 'elegant structure built on the tower principle…the iron joists which support the massive floors are as broad as a man's body. The mash tun is one of the handsomest we have ever seen, being a fine construction of cast iron encased in varnished pine and bound with massive brass hoops.' Barnard was equally entranced by the new fermentation department that contained six 150-barrel tuns 'constructed of the finest white cedar', fitted with attemperators or cooling devices and 'a parachute of new design for carrying off the yeast'.

The turn of the century saw a scramble for pubs in Cardiff and South Wales. Brains faced intense competition from 18 other Cardiff brewers, while major Burton brewers, including Allsopp, Ind Coope and Worthington, had agents busily selling their prized pale ales. Tied pubs were vital for Brains and by 1900 it had 80, around a third of all the licensed premises in the town. Many were in the areas surrounding the docks, including Tiger Bay.

A former regular of one of the Brains' pubs in the docks area recalled the drinking habits of those days. 'Everyone drank Dark or Dark and Bitter mixed. There was no lager in those days. Seamen were used to coming in and trying the local brew. Men used to come in off the dock, covered in coal dust, for a pint and a warm up.' One of the best-known pubs was the Mount Stuart opposite the dock gates. In the palatial back bar, ship owners, sea captains and cargo agents sealed their deals behind an ornamental bar screen that cut them off from the front bar which was packed with dockers, coal workers and sailors. When the bar shut for the afternoon, it was claimed the barmaids could sweep up enough coal dust to keep the pub fires burning.

THROUGH A GLASS DARKLY

Brains' mild ale was officially called Red Dragon but was known – and is still known – to drinkers simply as Dark. Eventually the company gave in and the beer became branded as Dark. Until the 1980s it was by far the brewery's best-selling beer. A ledger shows that in one week in September 1940, when 1,579 barrels were produced, RD (Dark) accounted for 1,155 barrels. The next most popular beer was IPA with 213 barrels, followed by LB (Light Bitter) with just 138 barrels. Some Cardiff pubs, such as the Railway Inn in Fairwater, sold only Dark on draught until as late as the 1980s.

People started drinking it at an early age. David Jones of Splott recalls he had his first taste of Dark in 1927, aged just seven. 'My grandmother used to send me out when I was young to get a jug filled up with ale. She would then mull it with a hot poker and give me a sip. But the sips just got bigger and bigger!'

Brains' Dark, unlike many mild ales that are sweet on the palate, is refreshingly dry. It's brewed with pale and chocolate malts and is hopped with Fuggles and Goldings varieties.

New generation, torrid times

Samuel Arthur Brain died in 1903. His career spanned politics as well as brewing as he was a popular member of Cardiff County Council and became mayor in 1899. His uncle and co-founder of the family brewery, Joseph Benjamin Brain, took over as chairman for four years and then handed the business to his two sons, JH Brain and WH Brain, who were both professional cricketers. They arrived at the brewery at a difficult time. In common with all Welsh breweries, Brains faced a torrid time during the First World War. The Minister of Munitions, David Lloyd George, was a Welshman and a teetotaller. All British breweries suffered at his hands with restricted pub opening hours, massive increases in duty and limits on ingredients and the strength of beer. But Welsh brewers were at the sharp end of Lloyd George's assault on the industry, which became worse when he was appointed prime minister in 1916. He had attempted since the 1880s to force total prohibition on Wales but was defeated in the House of Commons. He got his revenge with wartime legislation that allowed pubs to open for just 5½ hours a day, with one hour less on Saturday. 'Treating' – buying rounds of beer – was banned as an attempt to reduce the convivial atmosphere of the local.

Brains fought back against the power of the prime minister. In one newspaper notice in the *Evening Express* in 1916, the company declared: 'We believe there is to be an effort made by a few busybodies with time on their hands, who take advantage of the absence of the brave fellows who are fighting so nobly for us and for them, to promote the cause (if it be a cause) of prohibition.' A second notice went even further: 'We suggest that men and women should decide for themselves whether they will drink ale or not, and not allow this peculiar section of the community to decide what other people shall do. For anyone to say, "I don't want a glass of ale, therefore YOU shall not have one" is nothing less than priggish insolence.'

The restrictions on drinking became a major political issue. In 1917 the government's food controller wanted to limit production of beer even more severely, but the politicians were forced to bow to growing public anger. The Home Secretary, Sir George Cave, told the House of Commons that the shortage of beer was interfering with the output of munitions. 'There is discontent, loss of time, loss of work and in some cases even strikes are threatened and indeed caused by the shortage of beer.' Further restrictions were refused and the production of beer was allowed to increase. Brains' brave stance had come to the rescue of the entire brewing industry.

Before the war started, Brains had taken the decision to build a new brewery in order to cope with

Brains' brewery during the Second World War

the rising demand for their beers. In the late 1890s it had opened a bottling store in the Roath district and a bigger site was bought there. The New Brewery, with an imposing red tower, was finished in 1914 but the plant didn't come on stream until the war ended and restrictions on ingredients and production were lifted. The new site was described as 'austere' and lacked the harmonies of the Old Brewery that Barnard had so much admired. One notable feature of the new plant was the production of two-pint flagons as well as pint bottles. The flagons contained all Brains' beers of the time – Dark, Bitter, Strong Ale and Stout – and they were in great demand as Sunday 'sustainers' when the pubs were shut.

CAMRA to the rescue

Brains survived the trials and tribulations of the 1930s, 40s and 50s – depression, a second world war and post-war rationing – and then faced new threats to its independence in the 1960s. The Swinging Sixties saw many independent brewers in Wales disappear as national giants set out to dominate the recovering beer market with their heavily promoted keg beers. Rhymney Brewery, which had dominated the coal mining region, fell to Whitbread, which also bought

IT'S BRAINS YOU WANT

The brewery was fortunate to have hidden talents among the workforce, which saved the company a fortune in fees to marketing companies. Mrs E George, who had worked as a barmaid at the Canton Hotel after the First World War before joining the brewery, claimed she coined the saying 'It's Brains You Want', which went on to become an enduring slogan for the brewery. Albert Jones, a painter and sign writer, devised the enlarged AI in Brains' name in 1900. As a result, BRAINS became a permanent feature of Cardiff life.

Evan Evans Bevan of Neath. The result was a new and powerful group called Whitbread Wales. Brains' main rival in Cardiff, Hancock's, had gone on the takeover trail and had swallowed no fewer than 17 breweries and ended up with an impressive total of 500 pubs. It had close trading relations with Bass and in 1968 the Burton giant took over Hancock's and created Welsh Brewers. Brains' chairman, Michael Brain, declared the company would remain independent, with the shares controlled by the family. But the future was daunting: Brains had seven per cent of the South Wales market while Bass/Welsh Brewers had 40 per cent and Whitbread Wales 15 per cent.

Bass and Whitbread concentrated on flooding the Welsh market with such keg brands as Worthington E and Tankard. Brains' own keg brands, Gold Dragon and Tudor Light, failed to impress drinkers and the brewery seemed destined to lose market share to its bigger competitors. Then CAMRA came riding to its aid. When a new chairman, Bill Rhys, took over in 1971 he found himself facing not takeover and oblivion but a rising demand for his cask ales. Additional space was made available at the New Brewery, but the biggest change came at the Old Brewery, where £2.8 million was invested in new fermenting vessels, mash tuns and coppers. The expansion was finished by 1979 and Brains had increased capacity by 50 per cent, equivalent to an additional 18 million pints a year. With an ironic twist of history, the New Brewery closed in 1993: it had failed to outlast the original site.

With additional capacity available, Brains went outside its South Wales heartland and began to build sales and buy pubs in England. When a shop opened in the Old Brewery on St Mary's Street, orders flooded in from around the world for T-shirts and tankards that bore the legend 'It's Brains You Want'. In 1990 Brains reached an agreement with Whitbread for the national group to sell Dark and Bitter in its pubs and the brewery's profile was raised higher when Dark was named Champion Mild in 1991 in CAMRA's Champion Beer of Britain competition.

'SKULL ATTACK' WINS THE BEER WAR

Consumers' preferences changed in the late 20th century. In the 1980s the legendary Dark was overtaken by Brains Bitter, which was soon selling three times as much as mild. But a new flagship beer soon ruled the roost. Brains had attempted since the post-war years to launch a successful premium ale but with only limited success. Sales of IPA were not strong and it was replaced by Extra, again with limited success.

Brains tried again with a beer called SA Best Bitter, launched in 1958 to coincide with the British Empire & Commonwealth Games in Cardiff. This time the beer was in tune with drinkers. They called it simply SA and while the brewery said the name came from the initials of founder Samuel Arthur Brain, drinkers preferred Skull Attack, even though its strength of 4.2 per cent was relatively modest. It has become the brewery's best-known brand and has spawned a popular paler version called SA Gold.

The move into England didn't go well with some Welsh drinkers, especially supporters of Plaid Cymru, the Welsh Nationalist Party. The *South Wales Echo*'s cartoonist Gren had great fun with a series of lampoons showing disgruntled Cardiff drinkers in Brains' pubs anticipating the loss of their favourite pints. But Brains didn't ignore its roots. In 1991 it invested in a new complex called The Wharf, with bars and restaurants, in the old, run-down docks area. Then in 1997 a decision was taken that consolidated Brains' position in Wales and, it was hoped, would make it secure from takeover by English predators.

To the surprise of the industry, Brains announced it had reached an agreement to buy the Crown Buckley brewery. The merger was a good fit as it allowed Brains to move out of its South Wales heartland and into West Wales, where Crown Buckley was strong in both the tied and free trade.

Buckley's was an old family brewery in Llanelli that had been run by the unlikely figure of the Reverend James Buckley in the early 19th century. It became a major company in its region with 250 pubs, but in the 1980s, with a sizeable proportion of its shares owned by non-family members, Buckley's became increasingly liable to takeover by the national brewers. An unlikely white knight came to the rescue in the shape of the Crown Brewery in Pontyclun which had been formed as a clubs' brewery following the First World War. Several co-operative workers' breweries were created at the time when, as a result of shortages of ingredients, brewers supplied their own tied estates and kept clubs short of beer.

The United Clubs Brewery became a massive business, serving 300 clubs in South Wales by 1969. But by the 1980s, both Buckley's and United had run into financial difficulties. United had broadened its market by moving into England with a marked lack of success, while several Welsh clubs had closed their doors. The brewery had become more like a commercial business than a co-operative and had changed its name to the Crown Brewery. In 1988 a merger created Crown Buckley and the new company revived its fortunes with a new cask ale called the Rev James after Buckley's founder. But the company was saddled with huge debts and following a management buy-out in 1997 the business was sold to Brains.

Strength for the future

Brains' position as the unchallenged brewery in Wales was underscored in 1997 when Bass announced it was to close the Hancock's site behind Central Station. The Buckley's plant in Llanelli had shut

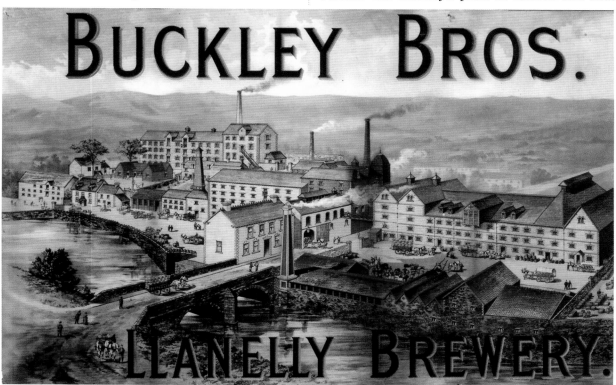

following the merger and Brains' Old Brewery was bursting at the seams while its congested city centre site in St Mary's Street caused major traffic problems. There was sadness among the family when production moved to Hancock's old site – a sadness softened by the name of Brains on the famous brewery chimney – but chairman Christopher Brain said the company had to be in a strong position to hand on to their children. With a new chief executive, Scott Waddington, Christopher Brain set out to forge a new style of drinks business for the 21st century. They were aided by John Rhys, great grandson of SA Brain, who brought his experience as a marketing consultant to reposition the company.

Great emphasis was placed on pubs. The age of dockers and Dark had long gone. Consumers wanted good food as well as beer in comfortable surroundings and major investment was made in updating the pub estate. The original St Mary's Street site was not neglected and was redeveloped as the Old Brewery Quarter with the ancient brewery tap, the Albert, remodelled as the Yard Bar & Kitchen. This modernisation was followed with two new bars at Mermaid Quay on the rebuilt and stylish Cardiff Bay waterfront.

With the Crown Buckley pubs, Brains entered the new century with an estate of 223 outlets.

The brewery now had the capacity to enlarge its beer range. Seasonal beers were produced, and special brews were launched to cement the brewery's links with Welsh rugby, football and cricket. In 2004 Brains became the official sponsor of Welsh rugby and as a result had its name emblazoned on the side's famous red shirts. It was an enormous bonus for the brewery when the national rugby team went on to win the Six Nations and the Grand Slam in 2005, with their games shown on TV worldwide.

The brewery also had a three-year sponsorship deal with Glamorgan cricket, a fitting arrangement as two members of the family, Joseph and William, had been professional players. A beer called Hat Trick commemorated the remarkable achievement of William Brain in 1893 who took the only first-class hat trick to date by a wicket keeper with three stumpings off successive balls. Where football was concerned, the brewery didn't ignore the round ball version and a sponsorship deal was struck with the Football Association of Wales, complete with a new continental-style beer called 45, after its strength of 4.5 per cent.

Brains had such a dominant position in the former Hancock's site, close to the city centre, football, rugby and cricket grounds, that it's difficult to grasp it was only there for little more than two decades. In the new Dragon Brewery, the range of beers has been further extended to satisfy a pub estate that stretches the length and breadth of Wales and reaches to near Bristol and Hereford in England. The brewery remains the official beer of both Welsh rugby and football. It has a joint venture with Gareth Bale at the Elevens Bar & Grill in Cardiff, and it has brewed a seasonal ale with Welsh rugby captain Alun Wynn Jones.

The cask ales remain firmly traditional, using Challenger, Fuggles and Goldings as the main hops, while SA Gold has more esoteric varieties with American Cascade and Styrian Goldings from Slovenia. Brains continues to brew beers for Molson Coors.

John Rhys says people's tastes are changing and many of them want hoppier and paler beers. There were plans to introduce an extended range of 'craft keg' beers in 2020 to add to the success of Barry Island IPA, launched in 2012, along with a new lager.

Dark is now just a minor brand and it comes as something of a shock to learn that Brains' biggest-selling cask beer is now Rev James, the former Buckley's brand. In a sense that's comforting: when breweries are taken over their beers tend to disappear, but the Reverend continues to command his pulpit.

In March 2020 Brains announced it planned to sell 40 of its 160 pubs and would concentrate on its 'core outlets'.

Brains' Dragon Brewery, Pacific Road, Cardiff CF24 5HJ · 029 2040 2060
www.sabrain.com

Regular cask beers:
Dark (3.5%)
Bitter (3.7%)
Rev James Gold (4.1%)
SA (4.2%)
SA Gold (4.2%)
Rev James Rye (4.3%)
Rev James (4.5%)

BREWING IN SCOTLAND

TRAQUAIR HOUSE

Brewing in Scotland can be traced back to the time of the Picts, cave dwellers who fought the Romans and refreshed themselves with a drink called heather ale. This was made by placing the flowers of the heather in a vessel that was then filled with wort made from barley and other grains: the wort filtered through the heather. Heather ale, using the Gaelic name of Fraoch, is brewed today by the Williams Bros in Alloa.

Centuries later, conventional ale was mainly a domestic product, made without hops as they were difficult to grow in Scotland. Commercial brewing began to develop in the 18th century: Tennents was formed in Glasgow in 1740. Scottish brewers at first concentrated on strong beers, often dark in colour, to satisfy drinkers in a cold climate, but in the 19th century they introduced their own interpretations of English IPA, with the preferred name of Export. McEwan's Export became a cult beer and is still brewed today, though the brand is now owned by Marston's in England.

The Scots also developed a taste for lager, the result of many Scots moving abroad to work and discovering lager in Australia, New Zealand and elsewhere. Over time, two lager brands came to the fore in Scotland, McEwan's and Tennents. Tennents is now the undisputed leader of the field, its lager accounting for 60 per cent of all the beer sold in Scotland.

Takeovers, mergers and closures after the Second World War led to two groups – Scottish & Newcastle (S&N) and Tennent Caledonian – that not only dominated Scottish brewing but closed many smaller companies. Today S&N is owned by Heineken, which also owns the renowned former family brewer Caledonian in Edinburgh. Tennents, once part of the Bass group, is now owned by the Irish company C&C.

Despite the stranglehold of the big brewing groups, more than 100 small artisan breweries have sprung up in recent decades to give drinkers greater choice and range, while BrewDog in Ellon, near Aberdeen, has become an international phenomenon. The revival of independent brewing in Scotland is worthy of a book in its own right, but here we concentrate on one genuine family brewery with arguably the most fascinating and tumultuous history of any in Britain.

Traquair House

18th CENTURY/1965 · INNERLEITHEN · BORDERS

YOU tiptoe around Traquair with due reverence for the age and the turbulent history of Scotland's oldest inhabited house which dates from 1107. Great oak doors and wood floors creak while winding stone stairs take you to spacious rooms where the kings of Scotland once dined and slept.

Mary Queen of Scots stayed here with her infant son who became James VI of Scotland and James I of a united Great Britain. Mary was unsuccessful in her attempt to oust Elizabeth I from the throne and paid with her life. Prince Charles Edward Stuart – Bonnie Prince Charlie – called at the house to raise support for his equally unsuccessful campaign to win back the crown.

Traquair is owned by a branch of the Stuart clan, the Maxwell Stuarts, and they closed and barred the main Bear Gates on the estate following the failure of the 1745 rebellion: they will remain locked until a Stuart once again sits on the throne. Such small matters as the longevity of the House of Windsor, the possibility of Scottish independence and the Stuarts' Catholicism suggest it may be some time before this hope is fulfilled.

The Maxwell Stuarts keep themselves busy. They have opened the house – with its magnificent libraries, oil paintings of monarchs and earls, and Mary's artefacts and letters – to the public. Accommodation is provided in luxurious apartments, and weddings, concerts and festivals are regularly staged.

And they brew beer in an 18th-century brewhouse, one of the oldest in Britain, using simple techniques that haven't changed over the ensuing centuries. The brewhouse is in a stone building alongside the Quair, a winding burn that runs through dense woods where deer roam, until it meets the River Tweed, the watery border with England. The brewery was originally based in the kitchen and made beer for the family, their servants and visitors. The equipment had not been used for more than 100 years when Peter

Peter Maxwell Stuart

261

Maxwell Stuart, the 20th Laird of Traquair, decided to resume brewing in 1965.

With the enthusiastic support of Sandy Hunter, the legendary head brewer at Belhaven in Dunbar, Peter got the equipment back into working order: it's managed today by brewer Frank Smith, who has worked at Traquair for 30 years. The brewing kit comprises a wooden mash tun, underback, copper and cooling trays. The underback is a receiving vessel that holds the wort or sweet extract following the mash and prior to the boil in the copper with hops. The hopped wort rests in the open cooling trays while it reaches a temperature suitable for fermentation. It's then pumped to the Tun Room next door where it's mixed with yeast in large oak vessels known as rounds. Primary fermentation takes five days. The beers are then conditioned for between four and six weeks before bottling off site. Traquair's bottling is carried out by Holden's in the West Midlands.

Peter and Sandy researched old documents in the archives and devised a recipe for House Ale which, at 7.2 per cent alcohol, belongs to an old Scottish style known as a Wee Heavy – similar to an English barley wine. Malt comes from Scottish barley, with soft brewing liquor drawn from a spring on site that's fed with water from the surrounding Pentland Hills. The yeast culture came first from Belhaven, then from Scottish & Newcastle's Fountainbridge Brewery in Edinburgh. Scottish & Newcastle and Fountainbridge no longer exist and Traquair now uses dried yeast. Hops are the only non-local ingredient: East Kent Goldings from south-east England. Hops once grew at Traquair but as the climate changed, they died out in the 18th century.

At first, Peter Maxwell Stuart brewed only small batches of beer on an occasional basis. But interest was aroused in the 1970s when Traquair was discovered by the Campaign for Real Ale and sales grew south of the border as well as in Scotland. When the beer writer Michael Jackson mentioned Traquair House Ale in his *World Guide to Beer*, demand started to come from the United States and several other countries.

Peter Maxwell Stuart died in 1990 and his daughter Catherine gave up a career in the theatre to join her mother, Flora, in running the house and brewery. The brewery has thrived with the addition of the 5.2% Bear Ale, sold on draught as well as in bottle, and Jacobite Ale (8%), spiced with coriander and first brewed in 1995 to celebrate the 250th anniversary of the 1745 rebellion. Occasional beers have celebrated the 50th, 100th and 150th brews, and included a 160 Shilling Ale (9.5%) and a beer for Catherine's 21st birthday. Vintage Ales were launched in 2019 (see below).

The brewery produces 1,000 hectolitres a year, which translates into 250,000 bottles. Production is made up predominantly of House Ale and Jacobite: the US now takes more Jacobite than the original beer. The beers are also exported to Brazil, Chile, Finland, France, Italy, Japan and Sweden. In Scotland, Traquair beers are sold by some supermarkets as well as specialist shops.

Catherine would like to build sales south of the border but is constrained by the capacity of the

Catherine Maxwell Stuart

262

The brewers

brewery and a second micro plant has been added next to the tun room to augment production. There's a tart and slightly acidic note to the beers, House Ale in particular. Perhaps the open coolers attract wild yeasts in the manner of Belgian lambic. Catherine denies this and says production in the new micro plant is in enclosed vessels that wild yeasts couldn't permeate. It's more likely that the tart, oaky note comes from fermentation in wood: the Traquair beers have more in common with another Belgian style – 'sour red' – than lambic.

What is beyond dispute is that visitors and residents centuries ago would have enjoyed the ales of the house. Mary Queen of Scots, when she was held prisoner at Tutbury Castle in Staffordshire, was sent supplies of ale by a brewer in nearby Burton upon Trent and she would surely have relished the ales in the more congenial surroundings of Traquair House.

A remarkable vintage

Traquair's first vintage ale, launched in 2019, commemorates a remarkable episode during the attempt by Prince Charles Edward Stuart to regain the British throne. The 8.5 per cent ale is called Lady Nithsdale and it celebrates the successful effort to

save her husband from the scaffold by smuggling him out of the Tower of London in 1716.

William and Winifred Nithsdale lived in the Scottish Borders, close to Traquair House. They were staunch supporters of the Stuart cause and William – Lord Nithsdale – fought alongside the prince. William was arrested at the Battle of Preston in 1715 during the first Jacobite Rising and taken to the Tower where he was sentenced to death for treason.

Winifred Nithsdale and her maid, Cecilia Evans, travelled by horse to London from Scotland, battling snowstorms and blizzards. In the capital they stayed with friends, the Mills family. Winifred was granted a meeting with King George I and pleaded for mercy for her husband. The king not only refused her petition but was also extremely rude to her.

In despair, Winifred went to the Tower where she bribed the guards to allow her to visit William, who was held in the Lieutenant's Lodgings. Winifred returned two days later on the eve of William's execution. Cecilia accompanied her, wearing an extra petticoat and cloak. William put on the spare clothing and left the Tower with Winifred, hiding his face and fooling the guards.

While Mrs Mills went to the Tower to release Cecilia, the Nithsdales made their escape from London. William was taken to France by Jacobite supporters and was joined by Winifred after she had picked up her children in Scotland. George I was furious about the escape. The cloak used to disguise William is on display at Traquair House.

Lady Nithsdale Ale is deep ruby red in colour, with burnt grain, plums, bitter chocolate, molasses, blood oranges and spicy hops on the aroma. The palate is bittersweet with rich, dark fruit, spicy hops, bitter chocolate and roasted malt. There's smooth creamy malt on the finish balanced by spicy hops, tart fruit and chocolate, finally becoming bitter but with continuing rich malt and fruit notes. The beer, available with labels showing both Lady and Lord Nithsdale, is bottle conditioned and will remain in drinkable condition for 10 years.

Traquair House, Innerleithen, Borders EH44 6PW
01896 830323
www.traquair.co.uk/traquair-house-brewery
The house has a shop and visitor centre and tours of the brewery are available.

Regular beers:
Cask/bottle
Bear Ale (5%)

Bottle conditioned
Traquair House Ale (7.2%)
Jacobite Ale (8%)

NEW BREWS ON THE BLOCK

TITANIC

THIS book celebrates family brewers who have been in operation for many years and centuries. Over the past 30 years, and with growing speed since the introduction of Progressive Beer Duty in 2002, several thousand new breweries have come into operation. The growth of the small brewery sector has been based to a large degree on the success of a new style of beer called golden ale. As lager beer sales grew, most family brewers lacked the funds to invest in the complex equipment needed to make the style. They saw sales of bitter declining as younger drinkers switched to big and heavily promoted lager brands. A handful of new small brewers came to the rescue with a fresh concept: golden ale. It was the idea of a clutch of new producers including Butcombe, Exmoor Ales and Kelham Island. They devised a new type of beer that had the colour of lager – often by using lager malt – but with a high level of bitterness. Imported hops were often used offering a ripe fruitiness that appealed to drinkers' palates.

Golden ales soared to success and that success was sealed when Crouch Vale Brewery in Essex won the Supreme Champion Beer of Britain award two years running in 2005 and 2006 at CAMRA's Great British Beer Festival with its Brewers Gold beer. Today, almost all family brewers have a golden ale in their portfolios and the style has helped rejuvenate interest in all beers in the ale family.

There are now some 2,500 breweries operating in Britain and many of the new companies, first called micros and now known as small independent or craft breweries, are family owned. It's beyond the scope of this book to include such a large number of breweries: their story deserves a book in its own right. But to mark the rise of new breweries, their struggle for recognition and their campaign for fair rates of duty, we review one of the earliest of the new independents which is run by a leading figure in the Society of Independent Brewers (SIBA).

265

Titanic

1985 · STOKE-ON-TRENT

WHEN Titanic Brewery opened in 1985 the small team was not expecting opposition and even downright hostility from the companies that deliver basic ingredients to mainstream brewers. 'A hop merchant refused to supply us,' Keith Bott recalls. 'We had to beg for some and finally got two pockets [sacks] a year of Fuggles and Goldings. As the micro sector grew, we bought in American hops. They were packaged in small quantities and were better quality.'

Keith is now joint managing director with his brother Dave. Titanic was founded by John Pazio, with the technical support of Ted Brown, who had trained with Peter Austin at the Ringwood Brewery in Hampshire: Ringwood was the first new micro in 1978 and the late Peter Austin, who set up small breweries in the United States, China, Belgium, France and many other countries, is revered as the Father of Micro Brewing. He also helped found SIBA.

While Dave Bott looks after Titanic's pubs, Keith is head brewer and regularly mashes in early in the morning. Keith had a civil service job lined up on leaving school, but saw an advertisement for a brewer in Stoke-on-Trent and applied, 'much to my mother's distress'. He didn't get the job, but he was keen to earn his living as a beer maker and joined Titanic as assistant brewer in 1985. Three years later Keith and Dave bought out John Pazio and set about building a major producer of beer as well as creating a new concept of running pubs, with some of the outlets operating in concert with Everards of Leicester.

Stoke's industrial past includes mining and steel but it is best known for its pottery. Titanic Brewery is in Burslem, called the Mother Town of the Potteries. A local legend says you can always tell if someone comes from Burslem as they turn over their dinner plates to see who made them.

The brewery is named after the unfortunate John Smith, who came from Stoke and was captain of the ill-fated Titanic cruise ship. With macabre humour, the brewery's beers include Wreckage, Steerage, Lifeboat, Anchor and Iceberg. There's a Captain Smith's Strong Ale while White Star is named after the shipping company that owned the Titanic.

Keith Bott

The joke in Stoke is that Titanic beers go down well. What's not a joke is that the brewery's biggest-selling beer is none of the above: it's Plum Porter. In an age when most small brewers concentrate on hoppy interpretations of pale ale and IPA, 50 per cent of Titanic's production is a dark beer with the addition of fruit. The beer was introduced in 2011 for a CAMRA beer festival and it aroused so much interest that it became a regular part of the portfolio. It has won more than 30 awards in the subsequent years, including a Gold medal in the Champion Beer of Britain awards in 2015 and Silver the following year.

The fruit flavouring is made in Stoke and is added in the fermenting vessels. 'The beer hits the sweet spot,' Keith says. 'It appeals to people who don't normally like beer.' It has such a following that its fans are known as Plummers. The brewery also runs a scheme for supporters who are known as First Class. There are 250 First Class members to date, and they earn

points for every £1 they spend on Titanic beer, with the income going to support the local community. Keith says Stoke people are very supportive of the brewery, which has won a Lifetime Achievement Award from the local paper, the *Sentinel*.

THE LONG ROAD TO DUTY REFORM

Keith Bott was awarded an MBE in 2016 for his services to the brewing industry. As well as running Titanic with his brother, Keith has been a stalwart member of SIBA, originally called the Small Independent Brewers' Association and now the Society of Independent Brewers.

SIBA celebrates its 40th anniversary in 2020 and Keith has been involved since 1994. 'I remember rolling a barrel of beer across Westminster Bridge on 5 November – Bonfire Night – to take to the Houses of Parliament,' he recalls. It was part of a lobby of MPs to ask for a reduction in excise duty for small brewers. They found it difficult and even impossible to compete with bigger brewers who enjoy economies of scale and can sell beer to pubs and the off trade at discounts smaller producers cannot afford.

'We thought the guest beer policy in the early 1990s would open up the market, but it didn't work – the national brewers continued to dominate,' Keith says. The guest beer policy flowed from the government's Beer Orders, which were the result of an investigation of the industry by the Monopolies Commission in 1989 (see p.11). Keith adds that when pub companies replaced the national brewers, things got worse for small producers as the pubcos demanded ruinously deep discounts from suppliers. 'SIBA argued that a cut in duty was the only way to boost small brewers and increase access to a foreclosed market,' he says. 'It would give consumers greater choice.'

The campaign reached fruition in 2002 when the Chancellor of the Exchequer, Gordon Brown, introduced Progressive Beer Duty

that reduced by 50 per cent the duty paid by the smallest brewers, with smaller reductions up to a ceiling of 30,000 hectolitres.

As a result, the micro or artisan sector has boomed and there are now some 2,500 brewers in Britain. Keith accepts that brewers in the 'squeezed middle' need support and he says the ceiling should be raised to 200,000 hectolitres a year. He argues that taxes in general are punitive: he pays £2.5 million a year – that's a quarter of his turnover.

The brewery bought its first pub, the Bulls Head in Burslem, in 1992 and a second one, the Stafford Arms in Stafford, three years later. The latter was sold to fund brewery expansion in the 1990s.

Collaborative retailing

Keith says he and Dave concentrated on the brewing side but by 2005 there were so many new breweries they realised they had to get seriously into retailing. Help came in the shape of Everards Brewery (see box p.100). The Leicester company had no pubs in the Stoke area and the managing director Stephen Gould discussed the Project William idea with the Bott brothers. The scheme, which now includes several other brewers, involves Everards buying and, if necessary, refurbishing a pub and then leasing it to a smaller brewer. The pubs in the scheme can sell beer from

both breweries with the proviso that all the pubs must take Everard's biggest-selling brand, Tiger. Everards can also supply keg beer and lager when required.

Titanic's most successful pub, the Sun in Stafford, a former Bass outlet, is not part of the Project William scheme, and is owned outright by the Botts. Their policy for all the 13 pubs they run is to root them firmly in local communities and offer great beer, and if food is served, to use as many local ingredients as possible. The pubs account for a quarter of the brewery's output, with free trade throughout the country.

The brewery has expanded exponentially to supply the pubs. It brewed just seven barrels a week back in 1985 but production now stands at 12,000–13,000 barrels a year. The brewing kit is based on a 50-barrel brew length with the mash tun and copper feeding 14 fermenters and 15 conditioning tanks. There's no

Dave and Keith Bott

problem in Titanic sourcing hops these days and a wide variety is used, including English Challenger, Fuggles, Goldings and Jester, along with American Cascade and Chinook, Styrian Goldings from Slovenia and Hercules from Germany. Bottled beers are packaged for Titanic by Marston's in Burton upon Trent and these include a strong version of Plum Porter called Grand Reserve, which comes in 750ml bottles.

Titanic's latest venture is a small chain of specialist Bod Bars that serve high-quality tea, coffee and meals as well as beer. There are four bars so far, in Stoke, Stafford, Trentham and Newport in Shropshire. The Stoke outlet is the former Grade II-listed First Class lounge at the railway station. The name comes from the fact that the first bar was in a former Co-op Bank in Bodmin Avenue in Stafford. Food is sourced locally, and the crockery naturally comes from Stoke.

Titanic has played a dynamic role in creating a modern brewing and pub industry that delivers greater choice for drinkers. Keith has two daughters who are yet to decide what they will do, while Dave's two sons already work in the brewing industry. The brothers are confident the family will continue to fly the flag they helped raise back in the late 1980s.

Titanic Brewery, Callender Place, Lingard Street, Burslem, Stoke-on-Trent, Staffs S16 1JL
01782 823447 · www.titanicbrewery.co.uk
Tours by arrangement

Regular cask beers:
Mild (3.5%)
Steerage (3.8%)
Lifeboat (4%)
Anchor Bitter (4.1%)
Iceberg (4.1%)
Cherry Dark (4.4%)
Cappuccino Stout (4.5%)
Chocolate& Vanilla Stout (4.5%)
Stout (4.5%)
White Star (4.5%)
Plum Porter (4.9%)
Captain Smith's Strong Ale (5.2%)

The bottled version of Titanic Stout is bottle conditioned

How beer is brewed

THE GLASS of beer in your hand is the result of the skills of craftsmen and women who take grain and hops from the land, water from wells and springs, and add the magic of yeast to fashion a drink that is complex, refreshing and sociable. Beer too often is cast as the poor relation to wine and yet is requires greater talent and experience to make. Wine, at its simplest, is made by crushing grapes and allowing wild yeasts on the skins to turn the juice into alcohol. If you crush an ear of barley, all you will get is dust on your fingers.

Before brewing can begin, grain – usually barley but also wheat, oats and rye – is taken to a maltings to start the transition to malt that contains the sugars for yeast to feed on. The grain is washed and then gently heated to encourage germination, with roots breaking through the husk of the grain. During germination, proteins are turned into enzymes that are vital to both malting and the first stage of the brewing process. When germination is complete, the grain is heated in a kiln. The heat is low at first to produce pale malt that is the bedrock of all beer, regardless of colour: pale malt contains a high level of enzymes. The heat is increased to make amber, brown, black and chocolate malts that add flavour and colour to finished beer.

When the grain reaches the brewery it's ground in a mill into powder called grist. This is mixed with pure hot water in a vessel known as a mash tun. Water – known as 'liquor' to brewers – is thoroughly purified to remove agricultural chemicals. Many brewers add minerals such as calcium sulphate and Epsom Salts to their liquor to replicate the water of Burton upon Trent made famous by the pale ales and IPAs produced there in the 19th century. The minerals are flavour enhancers that draw out the full character of malt and hops.

The mash tun is, in effect, a giant tea pot with a perforated base. The mash of grain and liquor is left to stand for an hour or two and during this time the enzymes in the grain convert the remaining starch to sugar. When the brewer is satisfied that full conversion has taken place, the perforated base of the tun is opened and the liquid – called 'wort' – filters through the spent

Illustration by Trevor Hatchett©

grain, which is then sprinkled or 'sparged' to wash out any remaining sugars.

Some family brewers have adopted a less traditional system of mashing, which starts in a mash mixer and the wort is then transferred to a separate filtration vessel called a lauter tun. This process is widely used in Europe and allows more brews to be carried out each day.

The wort is pumped to the copper or kettle where it's boiled vigorously with hops. The hop is a remarkable plant: it provides bitterness to beer, to balance the sweet, juicy and biscuit character of the malt. The cone of the hop contains acids, oils and resins that add delicious aromas and flavours to beer. Depending on the variety – and more than 100 are grown worldwide – the hops impart floral, spicy, peppery, resinous and citrus notes to the beer. In order to extract the full flavours of the hops, they are added at stages during the two-hour boil: at the start, halfway through and just before the boil ends. Special brewing sugars may be added during the boil for colour and flavour, and to encourage a strong fermentation.

When the boil is complete, the liquid, now known as 'hopped wort', is filtered through the bed of spent hops into a vessel called the hop back where it cools prior to fermentation. Fermenters may be round or square, open or covered, and made from stainless steel or, where Yorkshire squares are used (see Samuel Smith and Black Sheep), slate. Yeast is thoroughly mixed, or 'pitched', into the hopped wort and now the brewer can stand back and allow nature to run its course. Yeast is a type of fungus that turns sugary liquids into alcohol. There are two main types of brewers' yeast: ale and lager. Ale yeast works quickly at a warm temperature of 12°C/55°F and creates a dense rocky head on top of the wort as it eats the sugars. As well as alcohol and carbon dioxide, it creates compounds with similar aromas to apples, oranges, pineapples, pear drops, liquorice and molasses. After about seven days, the yeast is overcome by the alcohol it's produced and fermentation is complete. The yeast is removed and stored for future use: excess yeast can be turned into a nutritious spread such as Marmite.

The unfinished or 'green' beer will spend several days in conditioning tanks where it matures and purges itself of rough alcohols. Two types of ale emerge from the brewery. Brewery-conditioned beer is filtered, pasteurised and run into sealed containers called kegs. Keg beer is served by gas pressure in pubs. Many modern 'craft keg' beers are often unfiltered and unpasteurised and served by low gas pressure.

Cask-conditioned beer – real ale – is racked or filled into casks without filtration. Additional brewing sugar may be added to encourage a strong secondary fermentation. Casks are stored in a pub cellar while fermentation continues for a day or two. When the beer is ready for sale, it's drawn to the bar by a suction engine operated by a handpump. No applied pressure is used. Real ale – beer naturally produced – is the supreme example of the brewer's art.

FAMILIES RALLY ROUND THE HOP

Family Brewers are among a host of organisations that have backed efforts to revive the fortunes of the British hop industry. Early in the 21st century, the industry was on its knees. The acreage devoted to hop growing had declined dramatically as more and more brewers bought their hops from abroad, meeting a consumer demand for the citrus flavours delivered in particular from American varieties.

The crisis has been tackled by a dynamic new chairman of the British Hop Association, Alison Capper, working in tandem with Dr Peter Darby of Wye Hops in Kent. The number of British hop varieties has grown in just a few years from 16 to 34, with several new varieties offering the tangy and fruity aromas and flavours wanted by drinkers.

Peter Darby, a leading plant breeder and expert on hops, runs the National Hop Collection at Queen's Court near Faversham in Kent: along with Hereford and Worcester, Kent has for centuries been a leading county for hop growing as a result of the loamy soil there. The land was donated by local family brewer Shepherd Neame and Peter Darby has

planted and grown 70 hop varieties, dating back to Mathon, first grown in 1737.

He has also revived a hop called Ernest, named in honour of Professor Ernest Salmon, who was the first plant breeder to bring a scientific approach to hop cultivation in the 20th century at Wye College in Kent. Among Salmon's new varieties was Brewers Gold, now one of the world's most popular hops. In the 1950s he developed a variety that became known as Ernest. It was dismissed at the time by British brewers as being 'catty' and too much like American citrus-driven hops. Ernest's characteristics, however, appeal to modern brewers and drinkers, and in 2020 it was used in Shepherd Neame's first Cask Club beer of the year called Crossfire.

The collection includes such famous English varieties as Challenger, Fuggles and Goldings along with newer hops such as First Gold. England led the world in developing new 'hedgerow hops' which grow to half the height of traditional varieties. As a result they are easier to harvest and are less prone to disease and attack by predators.

It takes five years to develop a new

hop. Peter Darby has to prepare pollen, make crosses from several existing hops, raise seedlings, transfer them to a field, and when they have grown and been harvested, collect samples for analysis. A key part of his work is developing new hops that are more resistant to diseases, such as wilt, mildew and attack by aphids, which can result in a farm losing its entire harvest.

New hops developed by Dr Darby include Boadicea, Endeavour, Jester and Sovereign. There's a touch of dry humour in the name of Endeavour as it was found on his death to be the forename of the fictional detective Chief Inspector Morse, who was known to enjoy a glass or two of beer.

More recently, Peter Darby has developed an English version of the American hop Cascade, which is grown by Ali Capper at Stocks Farm in Worcestershire. As 'terroir' – environment – is as important to hops as it is to grapes, it will be fascinating to see how Cascade adapts to English conditions.

Further information can be found at www.britishhops.org.uk

Bibliography

Anonymous, *Timothy Taylor: 150 Years*, 2008

Theo Barker, *Shepherd Neame: A Story that's Been Brewing for 300 Years*, 1998

David Boag & Nick Wilcox-Brown, *A Taste of Life: Hall & Woodhouse Celebrating 225 Years*, 2002

Christine Brooke & Fergus Sutherland, *Excellence Through Independence: The History of Everards Brewery*, 2008

Brian Glover, *Brains: 125 Years*, 2007

Brian Glover, *Prince of Ales: The History of Brewing in Wales*, published by Alan Sutton, 1993

Christopher Grayling, *Holt's: The Story of Joseph Holt*, 1985/1998

Tim Heald, *Palmers: The Story of a Dorset Brewer*, 2008

Liz Luck, *Cornish Born & Brewed: A Family Tradition, the Story of St Austell Brewery*, 2001/2011

Marie-Louise McKay, *The History of the Lion Brewery* (Camerons), 2012

John Owen, Shepherd Neame's official archivist and historian, several booklets and pamphlets, available from the brewery shop

Dr Lynn F Pearson, *The History of Robinson's Brewery*, 1997

Roger Protz, *A Brewery in Bedford: the Charles Wells Story*, 2005/2015

John Richards, *The History of Batham's, Black Country Brewers*, Real Ale Books, 1993

Francis Sheppard, *Brakspear's Brewery 1779–1979*, 1979

Jehanne Wake, *Thwaites: The Life and Times of Daniel Thwaites Brewery, 1807–2007*, 2007

The above books, except for *The History of Batham's* and *Prince of Ales*, were not commercial publications but were commissioned by the breweries for their internal use. Some, but not all, are available from the individual brewery shops.

About the author

ROGER PROTZ is a campaigner and broadcaster and the author of more than 25 books about beer and brewing. He was the editor of CAMRA's market-leading *Good Beer Guide* for over two decades and has received Lifetime Achievement Awards from the British Guild of Beer Writers and the Society of Independent Brewers.

Roger appears regularly in the media and in 2016 was the subject of a BBC 4 *Food Show* special. He gives frequent talks and beer tastings at events in the UK and has also lectured at the Smithsonian Institute in Washington DC and Beer Expo in Melbourne, Australia.

Roger's updates and comments on the brewing industry can be read on his website, www.protzonbeer.co.uk, and you can follow him on Twitter @RogerProtzBeer.

Acknowledgements

The author would like to thank all the brewers who gave of their time to grant extensive interviews. Special thanks are due to Damian and Hamish Riley-Smith for help with Samuel Smith; Emma Sweet, Peter Scholey and Rupert Thompson for help with WH Brakspear; John Owen for his help with Shepherd Neame; plus, Tim Batham and Jonothan Holden for their co-operative help.

Index